THE PSYCHOLOGY OF CHARACTER

THE PSYCHOLOGY
OF CHARACTER

By

RUDOLPH ALLERS, M.D.

READER IN PSYCHIATRY AT THE UNIVERSITY OF VIENNA

Translated with an Introduction
By E. B. STRAUSS, M.A., M.D.(OXON.), M.R.C.P.(LOND.)

NEW YORK
SHEED & WARD
1943

TRANSLATOR'S INTRODUCTION

THE sciences are always undergoing re-classification. There was a time when all the sciences which today we know as the "natural sciences" were grouped together under the head of "natural philosophy." This term had its advantages, because it gave priority to their functions of seeking after truth in the natural sphere, and thereby provided a link between God and His creation. Applied science is a later development, and has undoubtedly proved of inestimable benefit to mankind. It is only when the philosophical aspects of a science are completely neglected that one can talk about a degradation of the science and a degradation of the scientist. I do not wish to imply that every branch of natural science should be approached from the philosophic angle ; on the contrary, there are many branches of science (which there is no need to specify), that would definitely suffer from the encroachment of meta-physics or a philosophy of values ; but, to my mind, the science of psychology does not belong to this category. I merely maintain that every student of the natural law should be conscious of the fact that he is seeking to uncover one of the aspects of the truth.

Psychology as an autonomous science is of very recent development ; although a science which takes as its province the human psyche cannot be regarded as a new study. It is not my intention in this brief introduction to give a history of psychology ; but a few retrospective remarks are necessary in order to illustrate the uniqueness of Dr. Allers's book, *Das Werden der sittlichen Person*, which I have here translated for the English-reading public.

v

Until recently, psychology concerned itself largely with the phenomena of consciousness. This form of psychology grew up within the framework of existent metaphysical systems, and therefore had no need to develop a philosophy of its own. A natural evolution from this " faculty psychology " was the study of behaviour and the nature of the senses. Behaviourism and experimental psychology in general have got so far away from the psyche—in which their students show no interest, or the existence of which they deny— that these varieties of biological study should, in my opinion, receive a new name, such as " *metaphysiology*." Influenced by the philosophy of von Hartmann and the brilliant research of Freud in the realm of psychopathology, psychology proper explored new fields belonging to the realm of the unconscious. For the first time, and for reasons which there is no need to indicate, psychology found itself a " popular " science. It is precisely this form of psychology, especially in its application to psychiatry, psychotherapy and education, which has aroused the hostility and mistrust of a very large number of Catholics, clergy and laity alike. It is true that this hostility is directed ultimately against the faulty, determinist philosophy which has developed from the more theoretical and speculative teaching of the various schools of the psychology of the unconscious ; nevertheless, instead of trying to sift the wheat from the chaff, many Catholics have tended to close their minds completely to these most valuable advances in applied psychology.

Freud's earlier—and more valuable—work was primarily concerned with the sexual instinct in man, its development and modification under the influence of cultural, ethical and religious restrictions. His later work, which seeks to interpret the whole person, is to my mind based on a false metaphysic. Jung, a brilliant Swiss psychiatrist, and secessionist from the Freudian school, employed a modification of the Freudian theory of the unconscious to construct an almost mystical conception of the psyche, combining both phylogeny and ontogeny. According to his conception, the key to mental disturbance is to be found in *regression*, not only to the behaviour- and reaction-patterns of childhood and infancy, but also to those postulated for earlier stages in the development of the race. We are not concerned here with the psychology either of Freud or Jung. A new star has recently arisen in the firmament of psychology, namely, Alfred Adler. This psychologist investigated the self-regarding sentiments and the social instincts—both in a sense derivable from the urge to self-preservation and racial continuity—as determinants of human behaviour. The soul of man, according to this conception, is the *locus* of an unceasing conflict for the conquest of the will which is directed in two apparently opposite directions, towards self and towards society, or community, as I term it in this book. In its application to the treatment of functional nervous disorders, in the form of psychotherapy, and in education, the Adlerian school of individual-psychology has deservedly met with enormous success and popularity.

If one wished to label Allers, one would describe him as a Catholic Adlerian ; he has managed to effect a, to my mind, satisfying synthesis between Catholic thought and all that is most valuable in individual-psychology. This book is on the theoretical side a unique combination of empirical observation and metaphysics, and on the practical side a brilliant exposition of how his Catholic-Adlerian characterological principles can be applied to the spiritual and mental hygiene of the child and the adult. Incidentally, he presents us with a social philosophy founded on values and the Thomist conception of the psycho-physical unity of man.

A synthetic exposition of this kind is admirable from the point of view of completeness of vision, but disadvantageous for style and arrangement ; I will revert to this point towards the end of this introduction.

In general, I find myself in sympathy with the author's method of approach and conclusions, so much so that I can afford to indicate a few of the points on which I would venture to disagree with him :

Firstly, in my opinion, Allers, in company with Adler and his disciples, orthodox and unorthodox, tends to underestimate individual, congenital idiosyncrasies, especially as applying to temperamental *differentiæ*. This is a fault in the right direction—if fault it be—for it emphasizes the fact that an infinitely greater number of both group and individual characteristics arise *reactively* (that is, in response to external circumstances), than was previously thought. But the point of disagreement is not merely of academic interest, as, according to my experience and that of many others, it is useful and expedient to conduct an analytical investigation in the course of psychotherapy only " down to the level of " a patient's temperamental make-up ; by that time the patient will have acquired sufficient insight into his hidden aims and motives to adjust his individual self to the needs of reality. Thus it is impossible by psychotherapy, or for that matter by any other means, to convert a schizothyme temperament into a cyclothyme variety ; [1] but skilful educational methods and re-educational psychotherapy, in accordance with the principles laid down in this book, can train the " will to community " in schizothyme individuals so that an essentially social character can develop in the soil of the schizothyme temperament.

If Allers has somewhat neglected the factor of temperament in his masterly analysis of that psychophysical unit, man, or if he has not fully understood Kretschmer's

---

[1] Those readers who are unfamiliar with these terms, and who are sufficiently interested, may consult *Physique and Character*, by E. Kretschmer (Allen & Unwin, London, Second English Edition, 1929).

conception of temperament as apart from character, it is partly the latter's fault ; for Kretschmer, who is a pure empiricist, nowhere draws a clear distinction, and, in my opinion, his great work, *Physique and Character*, should rather have been entitled " *Temperament and Character*."

Secondly, I find Allers's conception of sexuality somewhat restricted ; but this is not the place for me to indicate any modifications or emendations. In any case, Allers's views on this matter are a wholesome corrective to undiluted, uncritical Freudian dogmas (which raise the psychophysical energy associated with the sexual impulse almost to the rank of a kind of mystical life-force) and should be very welcome to Catholics.

I regard the publication of this book in English as an extremely important occasion, and I hope that it will help to overcome the Catholic indifference and hostility to modern applied psychology and to awaken an interest in the new science of characterology. It may also assist towards a closer co-operation between spiritual directors and Catholic psychiatrists in the interests of individual cases. It is much to be desired that more Catholic physicians should specialize in psychiatry, for, quite apart from the dangers associated with the psychological treatment of Catholic patients by non-Catholic practitioners, the latter can never properly understand the Catholic point of view, and therefore never really come to understand their Catholic patients.

It is hoped that this book will also have its appeal for the non-Catholic public, for it can afford to stand as a scientific, empirical work, without the support and confirmation of dogmatic theology. In any case, this translation is confidently offered to a wide English-reading public, specially to the clergy of all denominations, physicians, teachers and parents. I have already indicated that the construction of this book raises insuperable difficulties in style and arrangement. Practical observations and statements understandable to any reader alternate with closely reasoned and difficult philosophical arguments. The author calls attention to this point in his Preface, and trusts that the reader will not be discouraged in his study of the book by difficulties of this kind. I should like to add that, although it is in the interests of every reader to make the effort to grasp the author's meaning in the more metaphysical passages, he may safely confine himself to the more " practical " exposition of Allers's teaching.

Just as the future of medicine lies with preventative medicine, so must the efforts of psychic hygiene be largely prophylactic. Only a generation of children brought up on the sound psychological principles laid down in this book can hope to rescue the values still resident in our crumbling and tottering social edifice.

E. B. STRAUSS.

44, QUEEN ANNE STREET,
    LONDON, W. 1.
    January 1st, 1931.

PREFACE

THE PSYCHOLOGY OF CHARACTER

THE object of the present book is to interest a wider public in certain aspects of *character*, its nature, recognition and development.

As a physician, the author considers himself justified in undertaking this task, for the reason that his medical training enables him to form a judgment on certain aspects of his subject—such, for example, as the importance of constitution—and further, that his practical experience in psychotherapy has given him special knowledge of the factors determining the development of character. The author is by no means unconscious of the inadequacy of what he has written ; and if, nevertheless, he has been courageous enough to set out his views, the source of his courage was to a large extent the friendly recognition accorded to them in discussion, and the encouragement which he was fortunate enough to enjoy from expert authorities.

He must now make two preliminary observations, one of a fundamental, the other of a more technical nature. The lines of thought that will be followed in these pages have three main starting-points : the Catholic conception of the universe, the philosophical system of the *philosophia perennis*, and the empiricism of modern psychological investigation, especially as represented in the individual-psychology teaching of Alfred Adler, the Viennese physician. Admittedly Adler's teaching requires to be carefully freed from non-essentials which are foreign to its general nature ; but one of the objects of this book is to show that the positive content of his doctrines by no means conflicts with our two other starting-points, but rather confirms them. Naturally, in the following discussions, ideas of the most diverse origins will be found ; but it did not seem necessary to indicate their sources in every case by quotations or references to the literature, although sometimes these will be found in footnotes.

This book is addressed to a wide circle, and especially to educationalists, ministers of religion, parents and doctors— in fact, to all those who are interested in the problems offered by the individual and collective life of man. It has not been possible to make the exposition easy and simple throughout, owing to the difficult nature of the material dealt with, quite apart from the personal shortcomings of the author. It would be impossible to ignore all considerations of a general nature outside our special theme, for they form the basis of our practical teaching ; but their treatment in a form that would have made them intelligible to every class of reader would have required much space. Consequently the theoretical sections of this book contain many hypotheses that are not generally familiar. Nevertheless the author hopes that he will be understood even by those who do not immediately realize that such passages contain only hints or references to this or that philosophical opinion or empirical fact ; this incompleteness was unfortunate but unavoidable. But perhaps the author, who has sought to expound his deepest convictions most seriously and forcibly, may be permitted to ask his readers not to shrink from making some effort to grasp his meaning.

RUDOLF ALLERS.

FEAST OF ST. THOMAS AQUINAS,
March 7th, 1929.

CONTENTS

CHAPTER III.—CHARACTER IN CHILDHOOD AND DIFFICULTIES IN UPBRINGING

CHAPTER IV.—THE IDEAL OF CHARACTER AND THE OPERATION OF EXAMPLE

CHAPTER V.—THE CHARACTEROLOGY OF THE SEXES

CHAPTER VI.—LATER YEARS OF CHILDHOOD, SCHOOL, ADOLESCENCE AND THE PROBLEM OF SEX

CHAPTER VII.—ABNORMAL AND NEUROTIC CHARACTERS

CHAPTER VIII.—SELF-KNOWLEDGE AND SELF-UPBRINGING

INTRODUCTION

It will be generally admitted that an exhaustive inquiry into the nature of the development of man's character and the conditions determining it is important for two reasons. First, it is generally accorded that the object of education is not solely the imparting of theoretical and practical knowledge or even of rules of life, custom and tradition, but that it is also concerned with the formation of character. But if this task of character-formation is to be satisfactorily discharged, and if, moreover, guidance in it and knowledge of its methods is to be given to those on whom the task devolves, clear ideas must be given about the nature of character, its origins, and the influences that mould it. Secondly, the requirements of everyday life make the recognition of a man's character a practical necessity. In very many cases, and indeed in most, the appointment of a man to a particular post depends not only on his professional abilities in the narrower sense, his education or technical qualifications, but also, and essentially, on his character. That is so obvious that no examples need be given. Consequently, a knowledge of character is demanded by economic and social considerations. This requires the setting-out of basic laws and principles in whose light a knowledge of men can be taught, and of a technique by which the knowledge may be developed.

But the interest in a thoroughgoing knowledge of all that relates to character transcends these two practical considerations, important as they are. The formation of character is closely bound up with the nature of the moral and, further, of the religious life. The guidance of souls is impossible without an understanding of the character of those who are to be guided ; and in its absence, conversion is unthinkable. Finally, every serious-minded man desires to render account to himself and to God of what he has done and left undone, and for this purpose a knowledge of the science of character, if not indispensable, is at least of appreciable advantage.

Considerations of this kind are so obvious that they have never at any time been entirely ignored. But, oddly enough, previous attempts to present them more or less systematically have been only sporadic. In most cases, questions concerned with the formation of character have been dealt with only in pedagogic or ascetic treatises, and in systems of psychology the nature and basis of character have been regarded as incidental problems, if indeed any account has been taken of them. Apart from Theophrastus of old, his successor La Bruyère, and possibly Dr. Smiles, Bahnsen, the disciple of Schopenhauer, in the seventies of the last century, was the only person to publish a complete presentation of the science of character, until about twenty years ago, when an active interest in these problems first became apparent. Klages undoubtedly performed useful service in applying himself more seriously to the study of character, yet the growing attention paid to the subject does not depend on his influence, but is symptomatic of the intellectual tendencies of the present age. I cannot discuss this matter in detail, and must content myself with the statement that the newly awakened interest in the science of character runs parallel to new movements in biology, psychology and medicine, and to those currents which have been influencing all spheres of intellectual activity down to the most recent movements in philosophy. Evidence of the interest taken by the scientific world in the questions dealt with in this book is furnished in the works of Foerster, Kerschensteiner, Hoffmann, Haeberlin, Utitz, F. Kraus and Künkel, in many separate works emanating from the various schools of psychology and psychoanalysis, in the *Jahrbuch der Charakterologie* (of which five volumes have already appeared) and in many other works.[1]

It has not been possible to include a historical or critical survey of characterological literature in this book ; it has only been considered necessary to point out that this subject is nowadays much to the fore, and that both men of science and men of affairs are becoming conscious of the extreme importance of the questions with which it deals. Further, it is not my intention to discuss the methods of characterological investigation, the material it handles, or all the problems connected with the presentation of the various points of view in characterology. These matters belong more to theoretical characterology, even to a particular theory of characterology, than to an exposition of the applied science. Theoretical considerations cannot, of course, be entirely neglected. A certain elucidation of the concepts required for our work, and a general view of the subject-matter of our observations, must precede any exposition, however practical in intent.

Our first effort, therefore, must be to arrive at a working definition of character, or at least to obtain some idea of its nature. On such an idea depends the intelligent investigation of the development of character and the factors concerned in it.

[1] Some works may here be mentioned, which admittedly, for the most part, only contain their authors' theories, without a general survey of their teaching. Only Hoffman in *Der Aufbau des Charakters* (Berlin, 1926) gives a good summary of the most important characterologists. P. Haeberlin, *Der Charakter* (Basel, 1924) ; L. Klages, *Grundlagen der Charakterkunde* (Leipzig, 1926) ; and *Persönlichkeit* (Das Weltbild, Vol. II, Potsdam, 1928) ; A. Utitz, *Charakterologie* (Charlottenburg, 1925). The best exponent of psychoanalysis is H. Hartmann, *Die Grundlagen der Psychoanalyse* (Munich, 1926), of individual-psychology, E. Wrexberg, *Individualpsychologie* (Leipzig, 1928), and, in a more personal application, F. Künkel, *Charakterkunde* (Leipzig, 1929).

CHAPTER I

THE NATURE OF CHARACTER AND THE METHODS OF CHARACTEROLOGY

1. THE MEANING OF THE WORD "CHARACTER"

An invariably useful starting-point is the meaning and common use of words. However unscientific may be the ideas underlying ordinary speech, there is always some profound reason why a particular meaning is assigned to a word or phrase in popular usage either to-day or in the past, for the history of a word is often enough the history of an idea.

The word "character" is of Greek derivation. It is related to a noun χάραξ, meaning "post," and a verb χαράσσειν, meaning "to cut," "saw up," "notch," and the like. χαρακτήρ seems originally to have meant the markings on a boundary-post—the sign that served to mark off the fields of Kleon from those of Timon—a sign that was generally used by individuals within a community ; finally, the sign was understood as delineating territorial boundaries between adjacent communities themselves. The meaning of the word therefore is "a generally recognizable and understood sign."

Although the intermediate stages in the history of the word may not be traceable, the meaning apparently widened, coming to connote a recognizable sign of anything. But it should be remarked that originally the term was not applied to something general, but had a quite particular application—the field of the individual Kleon, the territory of this or that πόλις. The word then came to be used for

4

the actor's mask, which in the Greek theatre was rigidly fixed, one particular form of mask being invariably used for a particular rôle.

The *dramatis personæ* of the Greek theatre represented types more or less. This is not peculiar to Greek drama ; in the *commedia d'arte* of Italy, which still survives in part even to-day, the stage figures and their fortunes are fixed once and for all, and the same is true of the Punch-and-Judy show. Even when, later, dramatic personages became more individualized, the old tradition was by no means overcome. Evidence of this is to be found in Molière's *Avare*, in which the player of the title-rôle is called Harpagon, which simply means " the miser " ; and similar evidence is to be found in Hamlet's speech to the actors. The same tradition has survived into modern times ; for instance, Ibsen introduces minor characters as " the stout man," " the thin man."

When, about the time of Shakespeare, and largely owing to his influence, these stylized figures of the drama became more and more individualized, the meaning of the word " character " changed accordingly. The " characters " of Theophrastus and La Bruyère were delineations of type, and the character was something common to a number of men ; the new meaning of the word " character " was something peculiar to an individual and " characteristic " of him.

The meaning of the word " person " has undergone a similar change. Originally it denoted the actor's mask, through which his voice sounded (*personare*).[1] Later it came to mean the man who spoke through the mask.

As we are discussing words, mention may be made of one that has been greatly misused by even the greatest stylists. " Personality " (*personalitas*) etymologically can only mean

[1] *N.B.*—The primary meaning of *personare* is " to sound through," *i.e.*, through a space (cf. " *tuba personat salutaris*," in the *Exsultet*).

the " being person," in the same way as " honesty " connotes the " being honest," of a man. To make personality and person (or character) practically synonymous is absurd ; and it is still more absurd to regard his personality as a part of the complete man, as is frequently done.

Character in ordinary speech denotes something in a person that is individual and peculiar to himself, limited in time to himself, and incapable of repetition. So the adjective " characteristic " denotes a feature belonging peculiarly to any thing or image. To say that the shape of a mountain is characteristic is to imply that only one mountain has that shape. If the word " characteristic " be sometimes used to qualify a plurality, it is only when the plurality is for the time being regarded as a unity. Thus, in ordinary speech it is more correct to say that some quality or other is characteristic of " the officer " (or the officer class) than of " officers." There are, then, characteristic features of " the mountain range," " the large city," " the revolution," etc.

There is one other conclusion that can be drawn from the usage of ordinary speech. We speak of a man as both *being* a character and *having* a character. This dual phraseology corresponds to a dual meaning. To say that anyone *is* a character is to give expression to a judgment on him in which character is given special importance. That one *has* a character is self-evident, for the phrase " without character " categorically implies an estimate of value. It is also obvious that the possession of some kind of character is a distinctive natural attribute of man ; but it is equally clear that man and his character are not one and the same. We cannot say that man *has* person ; he *is* person, and, as such, has personality in the sense already indicated. The word " person " plainly connotes the whole being of a man ; character, on the other hand, if indeed we can rely on language as a guide, must be something connected with the man or the person. Exactly what that something is must now be investigated ; for the character can be the quality of the person, or a part, or at least an aspect of him, and as such it provides a definite method by which he may be regarded, observed and judged.

2. THE NATURE OF CHARACTER

The nature of character raises issues that are fundamental and decisive in all our subsequent discussions. It would be idle for us, and opposed to our original scheme, to make use of the various theories of earlier writers ; they are so contradictory that a selection and an apologia would be rendered necessary. It seems more worth while to attempt an independent inquiry.

In order to appreciate the character of a man, it is necessary first of all to concentrate on what he *does*. Admittedly, we all more or less assume that the words in which he expresses his views, aims, and sentiments will conform with his actions. But experience teaches us that many men consciously—and probably, as we shall see later, a much larger number unconsciously—fail to act up to their declared principles. That fair words can cover an ugly disposition is a common enough experience. The ugly disposition will eventually express itself in deeds. Hence one has always stressed the deeds of a man as an index of his disposition, his real thoughts—in fact what is ordinarily called his " character." But the concept of an act or deed must not be unduly restricted ; it must be made to include not only deeds in the special sense of the term, but also all movements, gestures, expressions, looks, postures and lineaments,[1] his behaviour in various situations. In short,

[1] Recently a valuable contribution to the knowledge of character derived from these factors has been made by J. Vance in his small book, *A Mirror of Personality* (London, 1928).

all the factors that go to make up the general term "conduct," form the basis of the estimation of character.

All conduct is, however, in its very nature, deed or action. It is true that there are also involuntary forms of behaviour ; examples of this are the motor responses to a sudden violent and unexpected stimulus, such as the involuntary gesture that betrays perturbation on being startled, the blush of shame, the pallor of fear, and so on. Although such phenonoma can in a sense be brought under the head of action, their further discussion would lead us too far astray.[1] Provisionally, we shall content ourselves with the establishment of the fact that actions provide an essential index of a man's character ; and we shall assume the validity of the statement that a man's whole conduct may be regarded as being built up in the same way as his actions in the strict sense of the term.

There is indeed strong support for the view that a man's conduct at any given moment, his every action, is an expression of the whole man, and that a single observation should enable us to interpret the man. It is unnecessary here to discuss the plausibility of this contention in detail. In the first place, there are undoubtedly forms of action that reveal a man's nature to us as if by a flash of lightning ; secondly there are some especially gifted and experienced observers who are able to obtain a complete picture of a person from a very brief observation. " If," Goethe once said to Eckermann, " I have heard a man talk for a quarter of an hour, I will let him talk for two hours." By this he obviously meant that in such a brief period the nature of the person would become sufficiently clear to him to enable him to predict and calculate with reasonable accuracy his conduct in all possible situations and his attitude to all

[1] Compare my observations on the comprehension and methodology of interpretation in O. Schwarz's *Psychogenese und Psychotherapie körperlicher Symptome* (Vienna, 1925).

possible questions. For there is, he thought, a "certain consistency" in character by reason of which definite primary dispositions inevitably lead to secondary effects. If, as commonly, in order to arrive at a further understanding of a man or his character, we are compelled to observe him over a long period of time (possibly for his whole lifetime for a complete understanding), this is mainly due to lack of skill on our own part, and to our inability to deduce what is truly "characteristic" from a single action.

The fact that the observation of many separate actions is required, according to general conviction, for a full understanding of a man's character, implies that character is a factor of each single act, or in any case one that is common to every act.

Before we try to determine this common factor in man's actions, a further point must be made. There are certainly some traits of character (using the term in its ordinary sense) that leap to the eye without the necessity of lengthy observation. Such are sternness or mildness, determination or weakness, and the like, which often enough can be read in men's faces. Often, however, one may be mistaken, for appearances are sometimes more ambiguous than separate actions ; many an act that seems to spring from good nature may actually be coldly calculated ; a deed that may strike the observer as harsh or even cruel may be dictated by love ; a cold and aloof manner may conceal over-sensitiveness and weakness ; a wolf in sheep's clothing may have the most attractive manners. Long experience, acuteness of observation, regard for apparently trivial details, may to a large extent obviate such errors, but they will constantly recur. The real question is this : when we have diagnosed either physiognostically or by means of the apparent unequivocality of certain conduct, have we really recognized the character of this one particular individual ? Have we not rather been made aware of a type of character that contains something common to the characters of other men, and enables us to classify it and bring it into a group, as it were? That is really the fact. An individual character, peculiar to one person and to him alone, can hardly be physiognostically deduced. Furthermore, any number of individual traits do not make up character; it is not, as will be shown later, a mosaic of separate traits or elements of any kind. Character is a unity and a whole, not a mere aggregate.

3. THE TRANSMUTABILITY OF CHARACTER

Having now made our point that any constructive understanding of character must rest on a knowledge of diverse actions and behaviour, we may apply ourselves once more to the *nature* of character; we must seek a factor common to all modes of man's actions and conduct. From the outset of this task we encounter a further difficulty. Up to now we have tacitly assumed that the character of an individual remains throughout his life unaltered in its essentials and fundamental traits. This assumption seems likely, possibly obvious; but though it may very often prove to be valid, it cannot be accepted uncritically. The fundamental unchangeableness of character is not proved by the fact that no change, sudden or gradual, has been observed; that would only indicate the actual persistence of the character, without disproving its potential transform-ability. On the other hand, the establishment of a single case of change of character would suffice to invalidate the theory of the unchangeableness of character once and for all, and to degrade it from a law to a statement of the most frequent way in which character appears to us. Now, experience offers us many more than a single case of change of character. Its various forms will be described later; we must first seek to reconcile the transmutability with our assertion that a man's character can only be grasped if we have knowledge of his action and conduct over a long period of time.

Such probing into a man's conduct throughout his life may indeed reveal the fact that his character has undergone a complete change in the course of years. Such a statement may have two meanings. It can mean either that two or even more characters have manifested themselves successively in the same person, or that one and the same character has undergone a gradual transmutation. If the latter interpretation is correct, a comparison of the man in the earlier and later stages of his life might well give the impression of a real multiplicity of characters ; this impression would be only partially modified by consideration of the temporal relations and phases of the transformation. It is indeed open to question whether these two interpretations are in fact distinct ; it is possible that an apparently sudden change of character represents fundamentally the same process as a gradual transmutation, the difference depending merely on the rapidity of the succession and the duration of the transitional periods, and that between the two extremes there is every conceivable intermediate form. Nevertheless, this does not dispense us from the obligation to regard a man's life as a whole, so far as is possible, if we are to gauge his character. Often enough the understanding of the " new," *i.e.*, the later-manifested, character depends on a knowledge of the original character, from which circumstances have evolved it. This is the case, for example, when the new character can be described as at least in certain respects the antithesis of the old. " *Courbe ta tête, fier Sicambre, adore ce que tu as brûlé, et brûle ce que tu as adoré.*" These words, addressed to the Duke of the Franks by the bishop who was baptizing him, lead us to consider the first kind of essential change in character.

The most impressive evidence of the possibility of such a fundamental change is furnished by the phenomenon of conversion. Not every conversion implies a change of character, although every one is a change of disposition, a μετάνοια. Even in many conversions that seem to transcend mere change of disposition, and in which it seems possible to perceive an entirely new character, some elements from the old life remain in the new. This can be explained in two ways : either these elements are the expression of qualities peculiarly deep-rooted in the nature of the *person* [1] —so deep-rooted that they must break through and modify the man's character and life in its every manifestation—or they attach themselves to the new character as they did to the old, in order, as one might say, not to undergo extinction.

Two examples may be given. When the son of Bernadone, the rich merchant of Assisi, was moved by the grace of God to change his life, the young man of the world became in many respects an entirely new person. Before, he had been kindly ; now he not only retained his natural kindliness, but became even kindlier than men deemed possible. But that is not the most striking feature of his change of character. St. Francis—the " little poor man of God " in the loneliness of Monte Alverno, the beggar in the Italian streets, the penitent, conscious as no one else of the insufficiency of human nature in face of the demands made upon it and the grace vouchsafed to it—remained throughout a troubadour. As God's player, " *il guillare di Dio*," he was able, in a way unheard-of in those days, to interweave his life of penitence and service to God with songs praising His greatness and—perhaps more remarkable still—the glory of the creation, from Brother Sun to Sister Death. It is as though this desire for song, poetry and acting was so firmly

[1] " Person," as we may recall, and as we shall see more clearly later on, must in no circumstances be regarded as identical with " character."

implanted in the soul of St. Francis that he was compelled to express all that was dear to his heart, all that was important in his life, in song and poem.

We will contrast him with another man of the world who became a saint, and who, like St. Francis, did not seek to fulfil his vocation in a monastery, but maintained his contact with the world, in which he saw his field of action— St. Ignatius of Loyola. In his case, too, there was an abrupt change of life, bearing, and mode of thought ; he, too, retained in his new life something that had been a feature, possibly a specially " characteristic " feature, of the old. St. Ignatius remained a military leader, a knight, a Spanish nobleman ; the Order he founded was called the Company of Jesus, and throughout, for good or ill, its organization was conspicuously military ; in the Saint's book of discipline we can detect something of this soldierly spirit, and perhaps also something of the Spanish noble of those times—one is reminded of this in the *Meditatio de duobus vexillis.* Nevertheless, the case of St. Ignatius impresses us quite differently from that of the Poverello. We rather feel that St. Ignatius used his military experience and system of enlistment because it served the purpose in hand, and that his militarism was not an integral part of his inner being ; it was not bound up with his very essence, and could have undergone extinction. His life provides many episodes, actions and incidents that show nothing of this martial spirit ; this in no way conflicts with his previous conduct, but shows that the two attitudes were not of necessity dependent on each other. But there is no episode in the life of St. Francis of Assisi, no legend, however trivial, in which there are to be found no traces of the singer and poet. Even if nothing were known of his singing, is there anyone who could have overlooked the rhythm, harmony and melody in the soul of the man who, as we learn from the stories in the *Little Flowers*, addressed his " brother " the wolf of Gubbio, with the same love as his " sisters " the swallows in the market-place?

There is a special problem presented by the fact, represented in both these instances, of the carrying over into the new life of elements that had belonged to the old. The point to stress here is that a complete transmutation of character *can* occur as the result of religious conversion. It is not only *conversio* in the special sense that can bring about such a change of character, but every similar disturbance of the psychological equilibrium ; there are instances of conversion to evil, if the phrase is permissible.

In the psychical sphere, the change of life and conduct resulting from successful psychotherapy is very like conversion—so much so that Kempf [1] says : " The principle of psychotherapy is conversion." In these cases, too, the change is sometimes radical, as when a man in response to psychotherapy, in a strikingly short time turns the rudder of his life and reorientates himself completely. Such cases are rare, but in any case, here we find a change of character which is a direct contradiction of the thesis that character is unchangeable—a thesis which is commonly accepted as self-evident.

This widespread, almost universal, belief in the untransmutability of character—even if the belief is modified by the admission of the possibility of change through constant gradual development—leads most people to regard sudden changes of character resulting from " conversion " with a certain amount of distrust. It is not only that they are inclined by common sense to regard such a change in a fellow man as pretence, or at the best as self-deception— a change neither seriously meant nor lasting—but that there is something inherent in the minds of most men, something

[1] E. J. Kempf, *The Autonomic Functions and the Personality* (New York, 1921).

never very clearly formulated, which leads them to suspect the genuineness of such a sudden and far-reaching change. Is it because such an admission seems to destroy the sense of security in their own lives, with its implication that perhaps they cannot with full assurance count on the permanence and unchangeableness of their own characters? We do not propose to pursue this further. But one circumstance is worthy of note and fuller consideration—the readiness of man to believe in a change for the worse rather than in conversion in the strict sense of the word. However that may be, it is an undoubted fact, which can be confirmed by every experienced student of mankind, and more especially by every experienced psychotherapist, that outside the religious life there are occurrences that are identical with or at any rate very similar to the psychological order of conversion.

Apart from these two types of change of character, there remains a third group of phenomena, which would provide striking evidence for the fact that a man can show a multiplicity of characters in the course of his life, were it not for the fact that the value of this evidence is somewhat diminished by its derivation from the sphere of psychopathology. It is a mistake to underestimate the value of the pathological as a means of obtaining knowledge about the normal, but it must be borne in mind that knowledge so derived can be regarded as truly reliable only when it is supported by similar observations in normal subjects.[1] The physical or psychical phenonoma of human life are of far too complex a nature to permit of a simple uncritical transfer to healthy individuals of data derived from the observation of the mentally abnormal. Every observable manifestation of life is variously conditioned, and the

[1] M. Scheler, in *Wesen und Formen der Sympathie* (Bonn, 1923), has vigorously protested against the hasty application to normal psychology of conclusions derived from psychopathology.

apparently simple can prove in reality to result from most diverse and conflicting factors. This fundamentally important fact, which must always be borne in mind when we come to employ the data of psychopathology for our present study, holds good for many other aspects of character, its genesis and formation. To emphasize it yet once more : Illness can be recognized and judged only in relation to health ; health is the final criterion for disease, and, as I have expressed it elsewhere, normal conditions the norm.

Subject to this reservation, we will now turn our attention to those remarkable cases described as multiple personality, splitting of personality, *état second*, etc. As will be made clear later on, they should properly be called cases of multiple *character*, for the misuse of the term " personality " in this way, as already stated, is an offence against clarity of ideas and purity of speech. The assumption that there are multiple persons in one and the same individual is inadmissible, at least as long as it remains a question of human entities ; we will disregard the phenonoma of demoniacal possession. But it should be mentioned that T. K. Oesterreich [1] believes in the possibility of a " metaphysical " division of the ego, and the actual co-existence of several egos in the individual. How far these egos can be called persons needs careful examination, as does the propriety of such an assumption. We will not describe here these interesting cases of divided and multiple ego, but will merely point out here that sometimes quite remarkably different and anomalous characters can co-exist and alternate with each other in one and the same individual.

The ætiology of these remarkable abnormal states is uncertain. They belong undoubtedly to the group of psychogenic disturbances, and are not due to organic lesions

[1] *Das Problem der Einheit und der Spaltung des Ich* (Stuttgart, 1928).

of the nervous system ; but their exact causation is difficult to establish.[1]

Observations of this kind show that one and the same individual not only can pass from one form of character to another, as happens in the case of conversion and related experiences, but can exhibit an alternation of vastly different characters.

The following important conclusions may be drawn from these facts : In the first place, the principle of the mutability of character has been established beyond dispute ; secondly, it has been demonstrated that an individual is not bound up with a definite character which is permanent in essentials and only capable of change within narrow limits. But this opposes to the doctrine of innate character an obstacle which cannot in any way be overcome theoretically.

Those who maintain the immutability of the innate character can object to the evidence provided by the phenomena of multiple " personality " (*i.e.*, multiple character) on the grounds that the evidence is derived from abnormal psychology, and is therefore not applicable in the case of the normal. Before proceeding to make deductions from what we have already said about the nature of character, or to arrive at a conception of it, we must discuss the validity of this objection.

Deep-seated changes of character, which result in a man's being altogether changed, occur also in other conditions ; namely, in organic mental disease. The term " organic disease " is applied to those mental disturbances in which macroscopic or microscopic examination of the brain, or the clinical findings, demonstrate the existence of destructive processes in the central nervous system. Examples of organic mental disease are : dementia paralytica (commonly called

[1] A summary of the earlier observations is given by T. K. Oesterreich *Die Phänomenologie des Ich* (Leipzig, 1910).

general paralysis of the insane or G.P.I.) ; the mental disorders associated with arterio-sclerosis ; senile dementia ; true epilepsy and the resultant morbid mental symptoms ; the various mental disorders grouped together under the terms " schizophrenia " or " dementia præcox."

Whilst we are on the subject of organic mental disease, we should here mention a fact that is of importance for the theoretical basis of our views. In G.P.I. a steady progression of the disease is the rule, but it has long been observed that incidental bouts of fever may not only arrest the mental disintegration, but even lead to a great improvement in the condition, amounting sometimes to such a marked abatement of the symptoms as to constitute a cure ; occasionally such remissions occur spontaneously without any apparent cause. We are indebted to the long researches of the Viennese psychiatrist, Julius Wagner von Jauregg, for the method of treating general paralysis by means of artificially inoculated malaria, a method of treatment which is surprisingly successful, especially in early cases of the disease. These cases of cure, whether spontaneous or in response to malarial therapy, raise issues that require further discussion.

In general paralysis the patient at first appears completely different from what he was in normal times. Not only is his demeanour completely changed—so much so that he becomes unrecognizable, a different man—but the change can be so far-reaching as to justify the use of the words " complete decay." It is unnecessary here to describe the behaviour of such a patient ; a description of the disease will be found in any text-book of psychiatry. It is, however, important to emphasize here the fact that during a period of remission or after recovery, such patients may show themselves exactly as they were before the onset of their illness ; all the symptoms of decay, the disagreeable changes of character caused by the disease, disappear, and whereas during the illness the nature of the true man was quite obscured, after recovery it reappears quite unchanged. This recovery can be so complete—happily such cases do occur—that it is impossible for the most careful clinical examination, with all the most refined psychological and psychiatric tests, to detect any defect.

From this we may conclude that the person himself, the possessor of character, the mainspring of all action and behaviour, *cannot be affected by destructive cerebral lesions*. Disease of the brain only checks the development and means of expression of the person, and cannot alter, still less destroy, the kernel of man's being. Further, although G.P.I. and other organic mental diseases are different in respect of their pathology, the fundamental process within the collective whole, the living man, is identical in all such diseases. It is our ignorance alone that is responsible for our present inability to treat epilepsy, schizophrenia, and the other organic mental diseases with the same success as general paralysis. From what we have said, it is clear that the character that underwent such a change during the course of the organic cerebral disease cannot be identical with the person of the patient, which remains fundamentally unchanged throughout ; we are given full justification for a strict separation of the fundamentally distinct concepts " person " and " character "—a separation that is demanded by the facts. Indeed, I believe that much of the obscurity in psychopathology, characterology, and even pedagogy and psychotherapy, may be ascribed to the confusion of these two concepts.

In this matter, clinical observation and experience lead to the same conclusion as an analysis of the phenomena of normal healthy life. If this claim holds good in the case of far-reaching forms of disease, which are responsible for such profound changes in the organism and its functions, we may claim even stronger justification for the contention as to the fundamental transmutability of character in the evidence provided by mental processes which are indeed abnormal, but do not affect the organism regarded as the embodiment and unity of bodily functions. It is therefore quite certain that pathological organic factors no more determine those remarkable cases of multiple "personality" (character) than they may be assumed to do in cases of conversion or character-mutation brought about by psychotherapy. The attempt to reject the evidence that tells against the doctrine of innate character as irrelevant because it is derived from pathological sources must therefore be considered unsuccessful.

How little that doctrine is supported by the facts will be repeatedly shown in the course of our discussion. For the moment, it suffices to have demonstrated that *character represents a fundamentally variable "something" common to the actions and behaviour-pattern of a man, something that must be regarded as an added property of a person rather than as something congenital, simple and unchangeable.*

The *person*, the actual kernel of man's being, remains, as we saw, even in organic disease of the brain, unchanged and restricted only in respect of its outward means of expression. General metaphysical principles, not empirical fact, force one to the conclusion that the person is unchangeable. If, then, the person remains unchanged, but the character proves to be fundamentally changeable, it follows not only that the character is not co-equal and hence identical with the person, but also that the character cannot form a part of the person. Far from being an integral component of the person, it is not even a quality of it.

If this be so, a man's character can only be grasped by an analysis of his actions, for it is by action alone that character finds outward expression, thereby providing us with criteria for its evaluation. The evaluation of character in the light of more or less speculative theories of the nature of man and his metaphysical place in the cosmos is probably false, and can certainly lead nowhere.

4. THE FACTORS DETERMINING ACTION

In order to understand character, a clear conception of the factors antecedent to and determining action is required. This is of such basic importance for all our subsequent discussions, whether we are dealing with theory or the applied science (as, for example, education or psychagogics), that a more or less exhaustive exposition seems necessary, even though it appears to take us away from our main subject. It is impossible to avoid a certain prolixity, the more so as we are dealing with very difficult matters which cannot be explained as clearly as might be wished.

Every action implies a movement, or at least the taking up by the ego of a position in relation to the non-ego. Each separate action affects the general structure of the cosmos and of the non-ego shaping it. Even the most trivial action—the picking up and pocketing of a box of matches— changes the appearance of the world ; temporarily at least, a mere gesture or play of facial expression effects such a change. If one takes memory and the continuity of individual experience into consideration, even the mere gesture may perhaps be reckoned strictly as a true change affecting the cosmos. The subjective taking-up of a position, the decision, the intention, the opinion : these do not apparently change the world, although even they, inasmuch as they are consciously and arbitrarily affirmed in the mind, could very well be brought under the head of action or conduct. It must be borne in mind firstly that these subjective events do not remain without effect in the external world, inasmuch as they are and must be the antecedents of acts, the **basis of** a position of the ego *vis-à-vis* the non-ego ; and secondly that the conception of the non-ego must include much more than the visible world of men and things. The realm of ideas, of verities and values, is itself a world, the world of the non-ego. This world is " changed " by every judgment, every attitude, every feeling, every direction of the will, not because this ideological realm as such is especially susceptible to change, but because such dispositions bring ideas into the realm of real space-time.

Every " action," using that term in the wider sense already indicated, is thus a relation, the formation of a nexus between the ego and the non-ego ; as a relation it is determined by two parts—*terminus a quo* and *terminus ad quem*. Regarded simply as a relation, action is, so to speak, the obverse of perception. In the latter, the movement is from the non-ego, the thing perceived—for example, the thing seen in the external world, together with its realized content or value—to the ego as the percipient. Moreover, the place of man within the cosmic continuum can be defined in one way by means of a cycle described from the world (the non-ego) through the man back to the world again. The world intrudes upon the ego as something that is perceived, or grasped in some other way, and this intrusion, this urge to movement, which, of course, can be understood only in the figurative sense, returns into the world in the form of action. But every action, since to some extent it refashions and alters the world of the non-ego, provides a new occasion for perception ; and so this hypothetical cycle can never cease as long as human life endures.

We have already seen that character cannot possibly be an integral part of a person ; hence it can only be of the nature of a *formal factor*. To determine character it is necessary to seek for a formal sign common to all the man's actions. The most common *form* of action is relation. A formal characteristic common to all a man's actions must therefore be apparent, above all, in its relational aspects ; it will show itself as a determinant bearing the special impress that distinguishes the relation, the " action," of this one man. In order to discover this formal factor, we must work out the structure of action more precisely. The assertion that every action is manifested objectively as a relation of the ego to the non-ego, of the person to the world, of subject to object, indicates only the most general formal characteristic ; looked at more closely, action has several aspects. The detailed exposition of this fact requires some brief consideration here. Insofar as every action or disposition of a man causes a change of the world, affecting the whole cosmic structure, it becomes *cause*, and as such is charged with consequences and effects. This aspect of action increases the responsibility involved in every deed and action by a responsibility that may be called external, inasmuch as it is concerned with the change of the non-ego caused by the action of a man.

The rest of the responsibility, which may accordingly be termed internal, depends upon the fact that through his conduct man assigns to himself or achieves in a manner determined by the nature of his actions a status in the general continuum of being to which he belongs. For as a physical organism he forms a part of the inorganic and organic natural realms. As a human being he belongs to the realm of persons, to the community. The community may take the form of large or small groups—the family, social class, State, nation, and so on—but in every case the group bears its communal impress. As an intelligent being, he has his part in the realm of mind—the ontological order of mind does not concern us here—which comprises ideals and mental potentialities that have not yet been realized or made their contribution to the world's general fund of culture ; finally, as an immortal soul predestined to the final resurrection, as a member, actual or potential, of the *corpus Christi mysticum*, and as the vessel of divine grace, he belongs to the realm of the supernatural. The position that man makes for himself in this general continuum of being is determined by the nature of his actions ; and from that results his incorporation in these realms of being. The fact that he is able himself to determine his position within these cosmic continua, to which he necessarily belongs in virtue of his ultimate nature, to accept or reject his natural membership of them—although he can never rid himself of them as objective states—is what primarily makes possible the mystical basis of freedom of the will and responsibility. The second aspect of action, then, may be termed the representation of a person in the realms of being which constitute him.

Whilst by action man unites himself responsibly (we can leave aside cases of irresponsibility or lessened responsibility) to an objective system of being—completes the representation of himself in an objective realm—there is coincidently a reflexion of this objective event on the subjective plane, so that in the completion of an action, and especially subsequent to it, man acquires self-knowledge. For just as we know or understand little of our fellow-man, so we can experience little that is essential about ourselves except from our actual deeds. If the saying " by their fruits shall ye know them " be true of that aspect of action which we have called the objective representation of a person, then Schiller's lines, "The deed completed bears a different look from what it had before 'twas done," apply to the aspect of action under consideration. This third aspect of action is concerned with the *subject* of responsibility, whose manifestations, according to experience, are self-approval or self-condemnation, the sense of duty done or guilt incurred, ease of conscience or torturing remorse.

Whereas the first two aspects of action remain wholly objective and the third is subjective self-objectivization, the two last aspects are purely subjective. The fourth aspect, in which action appears as *expression*, is indeed in a certain measure midway between objectivity and subjectivity, inasmuch as expression is directed towards and extends into the external, the non-ego. For every action, together with its objective content, is also expression, in which it is shown that the action derives from a particular person, and also that it emanates from that person in the psycho-subjective state existent at the actual moment at which the deed is done. Note that this aspect, which may thus be properly called "*physiognostic*," belongs not only to the deed as a psychic event, but also to the enduring effect of the deed— that part of it which is more than momentary—the product ; fundamentally every product of man has a physiognostic aspect. Admittedly the product is no way exhausted in the process of its expression—a hypothesis responsible for the naturalistic-psychologistic error of various current theories —for it is further defined by the validity of the " idea " realized in the product, and by the medium in which the idea is realized. Our excuse for making this observation, apparently a side-issue, is that it will prove to be of some importance later, when we come to consider the estimation of character. For as in a certain sense every action takes place in some medium—it may be that of one's own body— and is always obedient to some idea, even if that idea be merely a primal urge, so the deliberation required for the product reacts in a measure on the action itself. From the subjective standpoint, the line of demarcation between " mere " action and product cannot generally be drawn with any accuracy. The implication is that such a line does not exist at all ; that in the subjective realm it is impossible to discover any reliable criterion by which to distinguish between the product and that aspect of action which is momentary conduct. For responsibility attaches not only to actions that leave some visible impress on the world, and so bear the distinctive features of " work," but to all conduct. So, inevitably, the concept of responsibility is important to the science of characterology. This brings us to the main thesis of this introductory section, namely that a merely descriptive system of characterology—a sort of natural history of character—is impossible, and that theories of character that fail to include, or are not founded on, the conception of " values," remain only fragmentary and incapable of fulfilling their proper functions.

The fifth and last aspect of action, which remains wholly in the subjective sphere and is hence especially perceptible by means of psychological investigation, is that of *completion*. Every action not only completes objectively the cycle described above—from the world through the subject and back again to the world—but constitutes in the event itself a kind of conclusion. We are forced to say " a kind of conclusion," and not simply " a conclusion," because, in point of fact, no event has a conclusion ; every moment connects one thing with another, and every element of experience—if this highly unsuitable term can be applied to something that is instantaneous—is part of a continuous chain. In each perception there is the germ of a deed ; each experience strives after some kind of manifestation ; every effect seeks an appropriate outlet, every thought its formulation in speech, and so on ; no impulse, whatsoever its source—perception, emotion, or idea—comes to rest until it is brought to a conclusion in action or conduct. Often enough this kind of tension is a recognizable content of the event itself ; it is hardly necessary to adduce examples. It is inherent in the nature of experience, even when it is not consciously realized that it is disconnected from its expression, manifestation and action.

We have shown above that all action is in its very nature *relation*, and that every relation has two components, the ego and the non-ego, between which the five aspects of action above enumerated are so divided that two of them belong to each of the two components, while one, in a sense, connects them. To put it briefly, we may call the five aspects *effect*, upon or in the non-ego ; *position* or place, in the various realms of being that unite in man ; *representation*, of oneself and for oneself ; *expression* ; and *conclusion*, in the sense just described. The division between the two members of the relation can then diagrammatically be represented thus :—

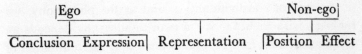

It must be pointed out that these five aspects are only aspects, incapable of independent existence. At no time does any particular action show only this or only that aspect ; they are all essential to all conduct whatsoever. Consequently, it is to be assumed from the outset that character as a formal factor common to all the actions and conduct of a man will be encountered in all the five aspects of action, even if at first this formal factor does not appear to impress itself everywhere in the same way. That character cannot manifest itself identically in every case will be apparent from the following example. We have seen that a product can be regarded more or less as frozen action, action that has become concrete in form from the point of view of expression—physiognostically, as we termed it. But the " expressiveness " (if we understand that word in its original sense) of different products may be very different.

Thus in a hand-made article, as it leaves the hand of the craftsman, one can detect characteristic features of various kinds, indicating hasty workmanship or loving care bestowed upon it. In a machine-made article, though the machine is controlled by the human hand, the personal note is almost undistinguishable ; for that reason one often hears complaints of the lack of individuality in machine-made articles as compared with the corresponding hand-made products. A scientific or mathematical treatise shows little trace of the kind of man the author is—although even here there must be some personal note : see H. Poincaré's remarks on types of mathematical thought. In some circumstances, a work on chemistry is more likely to give us some information about the author ; a historical or biographical work bears in a much higher degree the stamp of the author's individuality ; and as for philosophy, we may say with Fichte that " a man's philosophy depends on the kind of man he is." Thus we see that the evaluation of a product physiognostically, and even, consequently, from the standpoint of action, is not altogether straightforward.

It can well happen that one or another aspect of action renders the discovery of that formal factor for which we are looking, and which should be called " character," easier than another. This is due to the fact that it is difficult for an observer to grasp all five aspects simultaneously. As further discussion along these lines will inevitably lead to an investigation of the sources of characterological knowledge, we have only touched upon that point. It seems likely that this formal factor of which we are speaking is most discernible in that aspect of action which we call " representation " ; for the association of the action with the subject and of the latter with the object seems to act as an equilibrating factor, and it is in this aspect that the two members of the relation seem to meet on the same plane of values.

5. ACTION AND VALUE

If we wish to elaborate the last statement and use it as a *motif* in further discussion, it is necessary to investigate action from this, the more psychological, point of view, because this aspect involves the representation of self for oneself. However, in so doing, it must never be forgotten that psychology by itself is unable to provide a complete analysis of action. It must always be remembered that the relation to the non-ego must also be mirrored or represented in the psychological, and that the phenomenon concerned, being a representation of the non-psychic, can never be adequately defined in terms of psychology. Volitional action—what we call "action" or "deed" in the strict sense—always presupposes knowledge of a particular situation as the actual one, and of a second as a possible one. Without the pre-existence of such knowledge, at least in germ, no action ever takes place. Every deed of mine is the attempt to change a particular situation by my intervention ; that is, I must realize, however dimly, that an effort at change is desirable. Even when this wish for change is entirely formless, and expresses itself only in a sense of dissatisfaction, it is ultimately based on such realization. Since this realization involves—as is at once apparent when rational deliberation is involved— a comparison of the possible future and the actual immediate situation, it manifests itself as a recognition of a relation, and often finds expression in a comparative judgment, in this form : " It would be better if . . ." Consequently, *every action is preceded by a comparison* which, as the phrase just quoted shows, is one of *value*. The old dictum, *omne ens appetit bonum*, " every being seeks a ' good,' a ' value,' " is justified by psychology. It is certainly obvious that this *bonum*, this value, is a subjective evaluation of the kind mentioned above, and by no means of unconditionally objective validity ; but it is also clear that an analysis of action divorced from considerations of value is impossible. And in another respect—more formally—the introduction of the concept of value seems to be inevitable. We have seen that every action, looked at from the standpoint of the subject, is impressed with the quality of completion, that is, the conclusion of some chain of external and internal events. In every action there is a completion of a part-whole within the comprehensive whole of the lived-through and experienced continuum (Dilthey) or inner life-history. But every whole, as such, is necessarily of greater value than its parts ; all that is fragmentary is unsatisfying, and strives towards completion as a whole. Thus it is that in this most general feature which is always present, every action contains its relative value within itself.

The possible situation, which is conceived of as of greater value and which is realized in action, appears in experience as the appointing of a goal. But it is a mistake to suppose that action can be simply described as a series of stages : knowledge of the unsatisfying present and of the more satisfying possible future situation ; the appointing of the latter as a goal ; performance. The structure of the phenomenon " action " is more complex. For in the mere knowledge that an existing situation is unsatisfying, and that a change is therefore desirable and perhaps possible, there is no really adequate stimulus to action, to personal interference. The whole experience remains at the level of " it ought to be "—of a theoretical knowledge of something better. At this theoretical level, the recognition of the *difference of value* between the actual and the potential is more or less impersonal. Only a strengthening of the urge to personal interference—or at least to the taking-up of some personal attitude, the germ of which certainly exists in the theoretically realized " ought to be "—takes us beyond this rather impersonal stage. One can catch a glimpse of this even in those cases in which personal action is objectively impossible, as when a man not actively engaged in politics discusses the political situation. Often, in a case where adequate participation in the matter in hand is objectively impossible, one can see how the urge to personal action may find relief in side-issues ; one has only to think of the passions involved in tap-room politics.

A second phase, in which there is a special relation between the realization of the necessity for change and my own person, first takes us out of the plane of merely theoretical knowledge. This second phase, which itself passes through many stages which need not here be more precisely described, culminates in the internal attitude of *tua res agitur*.

6. THE CONCEPTION OF CHARACTER

We will now consider two possible forms of conduct, either of which we can choose. Either we can remain indifferent to a stimulus to a deed—saying, for example, " What is that to do with me ? "—or we can " make it our business." For this latter case, W. Grühn [1] has coined the excellent term *Aneignungsakt*, " act of appropriation." This internal acceptance, this affirmation of the situation which is brought about—and this really means affirmation of the value implied in it, which is made possible for the first time—is the real origin of the deed. The man who cannot bring himself to the point of making a choice simply and forcibly, and saying " Yes," never performs a deed, or at the best performs only a half-deed. We shall have to consider these matters in greater detail in a later discussion dealing with the ability to take decisions, hesitation, and similar phenomena. For the moment it is unnecessary to carry the analysis of action further ; for our present purpose,

[1] *Werterlebnis* (Leipzig, 1925).

the obtaining of a conception of character, it is enough
to have shown that it springs from such an "act of
appropriation."

In the realm of values of objective validity, there are and
must be definite laws of preference and rejection ; it is
inherent in the nature of a value that it has a definite place
in a scale of values. Whether and to what extent we may be
in a position to recognize the objectively existing system of
values is a question of theoretical axiology, and must be
left out of consideration. That there must be something
corresponding to an objective scale of values, which is
consequently directly binding upon all mankind, would be
obvious and of general acceptance were it not that by many
philosophers this very assertion is accepted only with great
distrust, or even entirely rejected. Certainly the attempts
to clear up this point and to establish an axiomatic system
of values are few in number ; perhaps the future holds a
surprise for us in this respect. In any case, since Scheler's
monumental criticism of Kant's formalistic ethic of duty,[1]
interest has been reawakened, and a new kind of interest
has developed in philosophic thought on the problem of
values. But indeed the fact that at all times, and in all places
and in all civilizations, the twin concepts of " good " and
" evil " have existed, points to the general acceptance by
mankind of universally binding laws of value. At least no
one doubts that all human actions are guided by the
principle that the (subjectively) higher value has precedence
over the lower. *Every law of preference in accordance with which
an individual determines his course of action is nothing else than
what we call his " character." The character of a man, then, is the
justification of his action, something in the nature of a rule or maxim.*
And inasmuch as this rule embodies the general form of the

---

[1] *Der Formalismus in der Ethik und die materiale Wertethik* (Halle, 1914). See
also Kolnai, *Der ethische Wert und die Wirklichkeit* (Freiburg, 1927.)

person's preference for and rejection of values,[1] character can also be called " the individual categorical imperative," to adapt Kant's famous term.

It is not our intention—indeed it would be unreasonable —to assert that this principle or rule, this individual law of value-preference, is in every individual case capable of formulation or even expression in words. There may be characters, or at least character-types, of relatively simple structure, which allow of such formulation—such a type is Spranger's [2] " economic man," whose every action is determined by the central value, " utility "—but in general, and especially where individuals are concerned, such formulations are hardly practicable. But it is not important that we should be able to express the character of a man in a simple formula ; what concerns us is the determination of the nature of character. According to our definition, character is not an integral part or distinctive feature of the person—we have already demonstrated the impossibility of this—but something belonging to the order of judgment, principle, or rule.

As every judgment takes the form " S is P," a predicate P being related to a (grammatical) subject S, so every principle of value-preference that constitutes character involves the relation between two members, the subject (taken in this case in a real rather than a grammatical sense) and the object, the non-ego, the world. This completes our hypothetical cycle.

The non-ego, with which in action the agent, the ego, enters into an objective relation, affects this subject in the measure and manner in which it is recognized ; for thereby

[1] I have written further on this subject with reference to psychotherapy in the reports on the *Relations between Psychology and Psychotherapy, Psychotherapy and the Science of Healing, Will and Perception in the Formation of Character* (in the three vols. of *Berichte der ärztlichen Kongresse für Psychotherapie*, Halle, 1926).

[2] *Lebensformen* (Leipzig, 1927).

it appears as something postulated or is seen as something rejected.

We have previously remarked that the conception of the world, or non-ego, must on no account be confined to what is commonly called the external world. Rather is it true, as we have seen, that all the concatenations of value and truth that are properties of the non-ego, or are contained or inherent as value in any other existing being or event, constitute a world, even if their place in the scheme of existence escapes us.

7. CHARACTER, ENVIRONMENT, INHERITANCE

Consequently, for the establishment of the law governing an individual's choice of values—in other words, character —two factors are of decisive importance : first, the person's predisposition ; and secondly, the mode and manner in which he represents to himself the world, or rather the collectivity of worlds to which he, like every other human being, belongs. This shows the importance, which can never be overestimated, of environment in the formation of a man's character.

This in no way implies the acceptance of a naturalistic " milieu-theory," like that of Taine and his successors. According to such theories, the person's disposition or character is the resultant of various external influences— climate, nationality, or social, political or economic environment. Man would thus be comparable to a completely passive medium, like a lump of wax, which receives its shape and impressions from various dies. Such a theory completely ignores the first member of the ego:non-ego relation, and forgets the fact that the reaction of a man to external influences is always a *reactio*, though, of course, it always retains its nature as *actio*. The converse error is made by those who assign decisive importance to such constitutional factors as hereditary peculiarities, especially those of the body, and all those factors which are grouped together under the vague terms "talent" and "predisposition." Such views entirely leave out of account the second member of the relation.

If character is at bottom an objective relation of the ego to the non-ego, it is obvious that character and disposition must be co-determined. This especially influences the mode and manner in which the collectivity of worlds is represented to a man. It is as decisive for the directions along which a man will develop—the possible directions that may be followed from the outset will be discussed in detail later—as for the extent of his progression in these directions. It is, however, a mistake to maintain that the factors depending on individual disposition, which assist in the formation of character, must be to any extent recognizable from the first.

Some believe that they can reach conclusions about the elements of character from the study of a person's natural disposition, his heredity and family history, including a careful comparison of the dispositions of his ancestors and direct ascendants with those of his descendants. But it has not been realized that underlying all such attempts there is a *petitio principii*, for such analyses are only reasonable when the inheritance of definite characters or characteristic traits has been established—a thing that must be proved, not merely assumed.

It is very often possible to satisfy ourselves that much that at first sight appears to be obviously inherited is in reality acquired. The fact that timid parents have timid children seems at first to imply the transmission of a quality, timidity. But if we take into account the upbringing of such children, and consider how strongly they must be impressed by the demeanour and conversation of their parents, it is obvious that they can only grow up timid. The unimportance of the hereditary factor can be deduced from the observation of an orphan child in the care of unusually timid foster-parents in no way related to the child, who acquires an excessive degree of timidity.

The determination of constitutional and hereditary factors in such a way is unsound ; for their establishment we must apply a process of exclusion. It is a mistake in method to start to investigate the importance of constitution and heredity without first having determined the elements in the character under investigation that might have been generated reactively, as the response to experience. For we can obtain the kinds of action and conduct which are conditioned by a man's experience and lot, and by the manner in which he reacts to his surroundings and the world in general. On the other hand, congenital factors, such as hereditary and constitutional influences, can be determined, described or established only with a minor degree of certainty ; here, as in natural science in general, a really vital understanding is excluded. The saying of A. V. Hallers, *"Ins Innere der Natur dringt kein erschaffner Geist,"* " no created mind penetrates into nature's innermost," has acquired a new and deeper meaning since the reawakened interest in philosophic thought in recent years, and in particular the intense and unprecedented preoccupation of philosophy with human and biological problems. An elemental deep-seated need in the nature of man urges us to seek to understand the world in accordance with the " scheme " that underlies our understanding of man and the works of his spirit.   One thing is certain, namely that man is susceptible of understanding to his very depths, and that this understanding is limited only by accident, not restricted by principle. There is one exception : the inner-most kernel of a human being, that metaphysical something which lies at his very roots, that something which is absolutely unique, is recognizable only from the fact of its existence, and it is impossible adequately to determine its nature. This limitation obtains not only in our understanding of others, but also in our understanding of ourselves. Fundamentally, our ability to understand ourselves is, quantitatively, so to speak, the same as our ability to understand others. Later we shall have to conduct an inquiry into the empirical restrictions of such knowledge.

Already the fruits of the intellect, all that we call culture, or the mind made " objective," [1] is less intelligible to us than the works of the spirit that are " subjective." If such works are considered from the physiognostic standpoint, as biographical documents, so to speak, our understanding can be very considerable ; but even here we find some products that are incomprehensible to us. I doubt if even the greatest authority on ancient Egyptian art would be able to deduce anything about the personal disposition of the artist from the sculptures that are preserved for us, especially those in the hieratic style. We also find ourselves in the same position with regard to the works of exotic and primitive cultures, such as negro plastic art or Mexican works of the Maya period. When we abandon the physiognostic method and seek to grasp the work in itself, in terms of itself, our understanding immediately reaches barriers that it seeks in vain to cross. In our attempt to understand the phenomena of nature we encounter such insuperable obstacles from the outset. Our appreciation lags far behind our vivid understanding of cultural or even human

---

[1] In our use here of the term " objective " as applied to mind or spirit, we naturally do not wish to imply acceptance of that unfortunate trichotomy of body, soul and spirit which derives from Gnosticism and plays such a part to-day in all conceivable philosophies and doctrines. " Objective spirit " means for us merely the congeries of values that have become objective in the world of space-time, without any definite metaphysical implications. Cf. H. Freyer, *Theorie des objektiven Geistes* (Leipzig, 1927).

phenomena ; we are compelled to content ourselves with mere statements and descriptions. Nay, natural science can never do justice to the phenomenon with which it is dealing in all its fullness, for, being necessarily descriptive and bound to the quantitative method, it leaves quality wholly outside its sphere. Although natural science can show the greatest practical successes, its range is somehow limited to the surface of the natural world. It represents what T. Haering [1] aptly calls a " resignation-stage " of human understanding.

If an object is susceptible of understanding in a manner other than understanding at the resignation-stage, it seems entirely mistaken to give this inadequate " resigned " mode of understanding preference over the more vital manner of comprehension. Resignation is forced on us soon enough. So long as we are not compelled to resign ourselves in this way we will force our understanding to its utmost limit. *Only when we cannot proceed any further on the path of true understanding are we entitled to content ourselves with the merely descriptive and recording methods of natural science.* Applying this assertion to our study of character, we may say that *it is inadmissible to postulate natural laws before exhausting every effort towards a vital understanding.* Only what seems ultimately to escape our understanding may be regarded from the standpoint of natural science, and considered in the light of pure biology, constitutional biology and genetics.

I call this methodological principle the *principle of the greatest possible application of the reactive factor.* Failure to recognize it is one of the most fatal of the errors apparent in many characterological and educational treatises, for it is clear that the greater importance we attach to congenital and constitutional factors the more restricted will be our efforts in psychotherapy and education.

Incidentally it may be remarked that while the rejection

[1] *Philosophie der Naturwissenschaft* (Munich, 1923).

of this principle commits one to pessimism in the spheres of education and psychotherapy, and even, if we are consistent, to nihilism, its recognition, on the other hand, furthers an optimistic attitude towards man and his potentialities, an attitude that, like optimism generally, has its proper place in practice.

It is worthy of note that, despite all the talk about an immutable congenital predisposition dependent on individual inheritance and the like, every educationalist acts fundamentally as if he were convinced of the opposite. For should we not all be compelled to fold our hands and leave the young to work out the factors inherent in them, if we did not all believe that man in the depths of his being can be other and better than his actions and conduct lead us to suppose? In point of fact, every admonition, every exposition, every criticism, every punishment, is in its deeper sense evidence of our trust in the better nature of man. This trust should be stressed in our educative dealings with children, adolescents and adults. Even the mature should be made aware of this trust that is placed in them.

(The pessimism frequently experienced by the teacher or doctor in individual cases or after a long, and on the whole futile, life-work devoted to therapeutics or education, is often enough attributable not so much to a fruitless struggle against insuperable difficulties inherent in the nature of the task as to personal incapacity and, above all, to an inadequate knowledge of the necessary principles and technique. In fact, in the great majority of such cases we are dealing with an effort not misdirected, but made with inappropriate means.)

This confidence in the possibilities of human nature— and we must never forget that human nature is " wonderfully fashioned and still more wonderfully restored " by God—a trust that is natural and hence naive in the best sense of the word, leads us to a second important conclusion, which is deducible from our theoretical speculations on the nature of character, and, in our opinion, lends our theories further weight. Possibly it is a good test for the soundness of an opinion arrived at theoretically if its conclusions correspond with naive and natural conceptions.

If we believe that admonition, the indication of faults and the teaching of the right principles of life, can help man to build up a desirable character, and if above all we believe that man can learn by experience, then we simply are expressing our conviction that it is knowledge that plays the leading rôle in character-formation. In other words, we are thereby asserting the primacy of the Logos.

8. CHARACTER AND THE INDIVIDUAL APPRECIATION OF VALUES

If character, then, is the factor determining an individual's choice of values, the general principle underlying his actions, that is, his aims, then the manner in which the individual appreciates values determines his character. But the appreciation of values implies a prior perception and a subsequent conception of the existence of values and things of a like order. This is not the place for an inquiry into the genesis of the appreciation of values and its place in the realm of psychical phenomena. It need only be said that in the act of seizing upon a value, something—the value—is conceived of as the object of this act, which must be regarded as a becoming-aware of this object. Consequently, this grasping of values must not be considered as emotional in the strict sense, for it does not function in the affective sphere. We shall be satisfied if we can demonstrate that in the grasping of values there is a special kind of act which we can leave to psychology to describe more fully. But inasmuch as in such acts a value becomes apparent to a man as valid or as appertaining to a thing or an event, the grasping of values can be considered only as a special aspect of perception. Incidentally, no one doubts that when we regard a possible situation as being better than a particular actual situation, we are concerned with a realization, a perception. This judgment of the relation of the two situations, the actual and the potential, is founded upon a grasping of values and is itself one.

Against the view often put forward that all values, psychologically—not ontologically—speaking, are ultimately traceable to the pleasure-principle, we must point out that the very statement of this view contains its own contradiction, and the exact opposite is true. For a value does not owe its validity to the circumstance that pleasure is associated with it. *The purpose of an action is the realization of a value, and not of a pleasure.* Pleasure can be the goal of an action only because it represents a particular kind of value which has its place in the general scale of values. The sense of pleasure that we experience on doing the right thing is not the purpose of the action, as we learn from introspection into such modes of conduct ; the purpose is rather to do the right thing. If pleasure accompanies it—the association is not invariable—it is incidental to the whole complex : perception, purpose, and execution. The pleasure is the reward.[1] The determination of what is and what is not value, and of the place of a value in the scale of values, is the function of judgments. But judgments are the criteria for the true and the false, and judgments of value can be true or false. Consequently, actions are either right or wrong.

" Ye shall know the truth, and the truth shall make you free." " Free from what ? " asks St. Augustine in his homilies

---

[1] I am aware that this view conflicts with many current theories, particularly those of Klages and von Haeberlin ; but a critical examination of the opinions of others is not here purposed.

on the Gospel of St. John, and he supplies the answer, " from sin," that is, from the doing of what is wrong, from the realization of that which is not-value.

9. FREEDOM

Before we bring these introductory remarks to a close, there is one question to be discussed. This question does not belong to characterology proper, but it must be considered here if we are to avoid criticism based on a misunderstanding of our views. The objections we anticipate arise from the assumption that the doctrines of the primacy of understanding and of the freedom of the will might clash. The critics might contend that if human action is determined by insight or understanding, the will cannot be free ; for in that case, right understanding brings right action with it automatically, as it were, and the responsibility inherent in the free exercise of the will is thereby taken from man, and the Socratic view, that virtue can be taught and is up to a point identical with knowledge, again obtains. This thesis substitutes ignorance for guilt, and error for sin.

Now even the strictest exponents of the doctrine of the freedom of the will admit that often enough error and ignorance are responsible for obviously faulty behaviour, rather than evil intentions and the deliberate rejection of the recognized good. The fact that we have the conception of an erring conscience and make a distinction between formal and material sin is sufficient evidence that we take serious account of the possibilities of error and ignorance. In practice it happens with extreme frequency that lack of insight is responsible for misconduct, and that the recognition of the truth is often sufficient to rid a man of his faults.

On the other hand, it must be conceded that a man fully imbued with understanding, and contemplating the Good, is not a free agent. In the *visio beatifica* there is no freedom.

From this it follows that there is a direct proportion between the determining action of knowledge and perfected (so to speak, pure) human nature, and that the resistance to understanding—*video meliora proboque, deteriora sequor*—belongs to that imperfection which we are taught to regard as an attribute of fallen human nature, and as a symptom of inherited guilt. But the degradation of pure human nature is in no way restricted to a part-function or part-aspect of that nature. It would be quite wrong to suppose that the " will " is concerned alone or only in the first instance. Rather must the change brought about by the Fall have affected human nature in its entirety, in its capacity for understanding as well as in its volitional faculty. In other words, firstly, the apprehension of the objective scale of values can never be wholly adequate, and, secondly, the transition from realization to action can never be quite complete. The question of " freedom of the will " is somewhat one-sided. It is not the will as a psychological function but the whole human person that is free. Decision is not on the plane on which the will comes into play as a psychologically determined function, but rather on the plane where that internal affirmation, the " act of appropriation " (*Aneignungsakt*) has its place. Freedom to assent or refuse may be called freedom of the will, so long as one bears in mind that it then has a different connotation to the one it usually bears in psychology.

Speech is so unsubtle that the elucidation and comprehension of these ideas is rendered very difficult ; the ambiguities of ordinary language encourage the multiplication of concepts of every kind. One must pick and choose one's words when dealing with subtle questions. E. Husserl has shown that no less than fourteen different meanings can be given to the word *Vorstellung* (introduction, presentation, representation, remonstrance, conception, notion, idea, image, etc.), and the same is true of the words *Einsicht* (inspection, examination, insight, understanding, discernment, judgment, opinion, cognizance, etc.), *Erkenntnis* (knowledge, perception, discernment, intuition, understanding, cognition, recognition, etc.), and *Wille* (will, volition, intention, etc.).[1]

There are at least two kinds of understanding (*Einsicht*) that I should like to distinguish : (*a*) theoretical, and (*b*) experienced. This distinction has often proved of practical utility. Not infrequently does it happen that we perceive something, grasp the import of a concatenation of things or events, or recognize a value without all this " understanding " (*Einsicht*) having any importance for our action. How often do we honour a third person's deed of heroism, self-sacrifice or self-renunciation, and recognize it as a guide to human conduct in general, and in theory, therefore, as of personal application, and yet are not personally actuated by it to similar deeds ? But no less frequently does it happen that a man finds in an example of this kind a stimulus for his own action ; in this case the knowledge has transcended the mere theoretical, and led to a practical result. The process may be difficult to describe psychologically, and possibly also difficult to grasp, but it is not without analogy in other fields. Such an analogy is to be found in the purely intellectual sphere, as, for example, in the understanding of a proof or in the solution of a problem. We may have gone over the demonstration of a proof many times without having " understood " it ; suddenly it dawns on us—" Of course it is so "—and it is at once quite clear. Again and again we may have taken great pains to solve a problem—a geometrical construction, for example—and not succeeded ;

---

[1] The translator hopes that the reader will bear this in mind before he passes judgment on the exactness of the translation. The translation of philosophical works and treatises dealing with abstract matters in general is always difficult, but the German language, with its wealth of synthetic words, offers peculiar difficulties which are sometimes even insuperable.—TRANS.

suddenly the solution is clear to us. In many other elementary operations we meet with the same thing. We have the experience in a striking way in the apperception of shapes when we are attempting a jig-saw puzzle. Our gaze may pass quite indifferently over a curiously shaped piece of wood, when suddenly we see that it fits into some place for which we have been seeking the right piece.

As an idea enters into a series of ideas enlarging or completing it, or as the little piece fits the gap in the puzzle, so apparently with the operation of some sudden enlightenment, the true nature of which is still admittedly a mystery, does a particular realization fit into the general pattern of our experience and conduct, and exert an influence. And as the piece in the jig-saw puzzle, at which we have often looked, somehow seems to be new and different at the moment it is recognized as fitting into its particular place, without, of course, undergoing any change of form, so does the content of the hitherto only theoretical, abstract realization assume a new kind of character, which is living and personal, without undergoing any real change. But in applying the term "understanding," "realization" or "knowledge" (*Einsicht*) to both the theoretical and the vital or experienced kind of realization, we run the risk of failing to recognize the essential difference between them.[1]

The same is the case with the word "will." Perhaps there are few words which are so misused. So far as I can see, the word "will" is used in the following senses: (1) Will, in the strict and precise sense of the term, is that psychological function or that psychical phenomenon which initiates and accompanies an action. A will to seize something really only arises at the moment when I stretch out my hand towards the object which is to be grasped. So

---

[1] Newman in his *Grammar of Assent* deals with some of these problems, but with a somewhat different end in view.

long as I do not make this movement, it is wrong to speak
of willing in the specific sense. (2) Will also denotes an
intention to perform, or possibly only an anticipation of,
some future act. " I will go to Italy " has the same meaning
as " At some future point in time it is probable, it is to be
hoped, it will perhaps be the fact, that I shall go to Italy."
As far as this meaning is concerned, it is instructive that in
colloquial English " will " often means nothing more than
the future " shall." (3) Closely connected with this last
meaning is the use of " willing " in the sense of " wishing "
or " liking," which we find in the German language.[1] The
confusion of this meaning of the word " will " with the first
given above is often significant. Many men deceive themselves about what they " will," believing that it is sufficient
for them to wish for anything. St. Ignatius, in his
Meditatio de tribus classibus s. binariis hominum, refers to this
type of man. (4) We also use the word in the sense of
decision, resolution or intention. How little the latter is
really " will " we learn from the proverb about the good
intentions which pave the road to hell. Decision and
intention are only *schemata* which may sooner or later be
realized by an act of volition ; they are in no way identical
with the will itself.

This ambiguity—and we have not exhausted all the
possible senses of the word—deters us from the hasty use of
the term " willing " as applied to the particular function of
the will in every case. The analysis arising out of this
digression contains points which are of some importance for
our further speculations. For if the assertions of a man as to
his willing and its purposes are to be accepted with reserve
on account of their terminological ambiguity, where shall

---

[1] The author gives several examples of the use of the word " *willen*," the
point of which would be quite lost in translation. As an example of a similar
use of the word in English, cf. the alternative title to Shakespeare's *Twelfth
Night—What You Will.*—TRANS.

we find a criterion and a test of the direction and the purpose of the volition of an individual man ?

This question is obviously of fundamental importance in all judgments of character. If character is the principle of individual value-preference, if the values most deeply treasured by a man in his innermost being are at the same time the goals towards which he strives, then it follows that the discernment of these goals is the only reliable criterion for a knowledge and understanding of character.

10. KNOWLEDGE OF CHARACTER

Character is the principle of action. Action is the relation between the ego and the world, from the ego to the world. It involves a definite, even if very transitory, reshaping of the world. How can the real meaning of action, with its teleological principle and its value-content (*i.e.*, the value regarded by the individual as the higher one in accordance with his ruling preference) declare itself otherwise than in the cosmic change that action brings about ? It is not a man's expressed words, thoughts or feelings, nor his professed intentions, even though he be subjectively honest, that enlighten us as to the direction of the will that quickens and informs him, or help us to grasp the principle that really guides his course of life ; we can really learn about these things only by the actual results, the fruits of his actions and conduct.

Recognition of this fact is implied in a passage from a famous book : " More readily does the body obey the slightest dictates of the will and of the soul, and move its limbs at their beck, than does the soul hearken unto itself and accomplish its will merely in the act of willing. Whence and wherefore this inexplicable fact ? . . . The mind commands the body, and it obeys forthwith ; the mind commands itself, and is resisted. The mind commands the hand to be moved, and the movement is accomplished with such readiness, that one can scarce determine where the command ends, and where the execution thereof begins. Yet is the mind mind, and the hand is body. The mind commands the mind to will, and yet, though it be itself and none other, it obeyeth not. Whence and wherefore this inexplicable fact ? Again I say, it commands itself to will, and would not so command, unless it willed ; yet is that not done, which is commanded. But it willeth not entirely ; therefore it commandeth not entirely. For would it but will in entirety, then would it not need first to utter its command ; its will would be accomplished, because it was already accomplished. In part to will, and in part not to will, is not an inexplicable fact ; rather is it a sickness of the spirit, that raiseth not itself to its full stature, sustained by the truth but weighed down by custom. And thus are there two wills, and neither is entire ; the one possesseth that which the other lacketh. . . . I neither willed entirely, nor yet was I entirely unwilling. Therefore was I at war with myself, and divided against myself. And this division took place against my will ; but that bears not witness that I house an alien spirit within myself. . . . One and the same soul it is, that with half itself willeth this and with its other half willeth that."

These words are quoted from the eighth book of the *Confessions* of St. Augustine. We shall have to bear in mind many times this psychological fact of the existence of a " second will." It must, however, be noticed in parenthesis that St. Augustine uses the term " will " in a wide sense, making it almost synonymous with inclination, striving, and the like. This does not, however, in the least detract from the correctness and profundity of his observations.

We will paraphrase these words of St. Augustine in a language less impressive, but more suitable for a characterological treatise. First, a man's actions and conduct are the outcome of volition ; secondly, this act of willing, which is the mainspring of his conduct, can remain unknown to the individual concerned. Thus, this passage from the *Confessions* contains the first expression, implicit if not explicit, of the idea of the " unconscious," and also the first presentation of that aspect of human action which we call today " finalistic." In modern scientific literature, especially that dealing with education and the prevention and correction of mental abnormalities, these ideas are especially well represented in the school of " individual-psychology," founded by Alfred Adler. Adler's views will often prove of use to us ; in fact, they form to a large extent the basis of the opinions expressed in this book ; even if we have modified them and altered the form in which they are often taught today, their essential content is retained.[1]

For the moment we are only concerned with the fundamental principle of methodology, namely that *the real motives of a man can be deduced only from his actions*, and indeed only from their actual results. The term " actual result " needs some explanation. It is not to be understood as meaning what is made apparent as the direct effect or consequence of a deed, nor yet only as what seems to be its immediate purport. Human actions can really only be understood if they are regarded as belonging to an integration of greater or lesser complexity. If, in judging certain actions, we were to look only at the immediate outcome, we should be led into making quite grotesque mistakes, and in very many cases we should be compelled to admit our complete

[1] A. Adler, *Der nervöse Charakter* (Munich, 1929) ; *Theorie und Praxis der Individualpsychologie* (Munich, 1926) ; *Menschenkenntniss* (Leipzig, 1927) ; E. Wexberg, *Individualpsychologie* (1928) ; *Handbuch der Individualpsychologie* (Munich, 1926). For elaboration and criticism, R. Kronfeld, *Psychotherapie* (Berlin, 1926) ; R. Allers, *Charakter als Ausdruck* in the *Jahrbuch für Characterologie*, 1925, vol. I, and the works mentioned in the footnotes on p. 8.

inability to understand the actions. If, in time of war, a soldier deliberately shoots himself in the hand or foot—if, that is, of his own volition he inflicts on himself an extremely painful and slow-healing wound, which will considerably restrict his earning capacity in the future—such an action is quite unintelligible, so long as it is looked at only as a deed in itself, and not with reference to its further consequence, that the action renders him unfit for active service. But when due regard is paid to this, it becomes understandable that a man should take the consequences of his action in order to escape the miseries and dangers of service at the front, and the likelihood of serious wounds or death. We can make a further deduction : as far as the man is concerned, the self-mutilation with its physical suffering and inevitable social consequences are insufficient to outbalance the dangers that threaten in the future, although there is only great possibility and no certainty of these dangers eventuating. We recognize this self-mutilation as a self-defence mechanism, a safeguarding from danger ; but the reason for the evasion of the dangers cannot be deduced with any certainty merely from the quality of the action. It would be over-hasty to talk simply of cowardice, for there are other possible interpretations. In other and less crude cases, the immediate acceptance of the seemingly obvious explanation is still more mistaken ; for almost invariably there are a number of possible explanations of one and the same action, so long as it is not regarded as belonging to a more comprehensive integration.

In order to grasp the purport of human action, it is therefore necessary to have a clear view of its operation over a longer period of time, and to include in one's survey not only its immediate results, but also its later consequences. We can also see that the question of the purport of an action can in some cases be conveniently formulated as follows :

What were the inevitable consequences, if the person concerned had not acted as he did ? The self-mutilator, for instance, would, but for his deed, have had to go to the front. That is a very simple case. But, to continue deriving our examples from the war, it has not infrequently happened that men have quite unexpectedly volunteered for service at the front quite contrary to the expectations of their acquaintances. In many cases that was undoubtedly dictated by patriotism or the desire to emulate the loyalty of others. In other cases it might have been the wish to avoid appearing poor-spirited or cowardly before one's fellows (perhaps collectively, or perhaps an individual such as one's betrothed). But there have also been cases when this seeming act of heroism has in reality been a gesture, which with a fuller knowledge of the circumstances we should be compelled to describe as a " desertion to the front." Large numbers of men have volunteered for active service owing to domestic quarrels, unemployment, threatened professional failure, imminent financial loss, and so on. By their action they have made two gains ; first, escape from immediate and seemingly insuperable difficulties ; secondly, the esteem and admiration of their fellow-men. They have as it were, from being cowards in one sphere of life, become heroes in another. I have known a number of men who did remarkably well in the war, both as officers and privates, winning approval, distinction and fame, who on their return home were failures in ordinary everyday situations, and unable to tackle the most trivial tasks. The fact that a man can be a hero in war, or achieve the most daring feats of mountaineering, by no means proves that he is fundamentally courageous. Great problems and occasions often more or less solve themselves, and it is rather that they drive a man to decision and action than that he decides on his own account. It is not in these great occasions, but in the little situations of daily life that character most of all proves itself, if we may, for this once, use the term " character " with an implication of value.

The basic principle that actions are to be judged by their actual results may be further extended as follows : A man's conduct is often dictated not by the situation of the moment, but by its analogy to other situations which are of importance to him. This may be made clearer by some examples, starting with a somewhat unusual but illuminating instance. A man fears, or imagines he has reason to fear, danger from a personal enemy ; he fears even that the latter may take the opportunity of a shooting-party to kill him. It is open to him to avoid going out shooting with his enemy. But he can also, in order to conceal his apprehension with regard to that particular man, entirely give up shooting. On what he bases his decision to give up shooting is unimportant ; what is significant is that he gives up shooting entirely, while in reality he is afraid only of shooting in company with his particular enemy. In the same way, the hare has only the hound to fear as the latter rustles in the under-growth ; but in order to make sure of bolting on the rustling of the hound, he must also bolt when it is only the wind or a crow. Or when a man shirks a particular task for any reason, he may say to himself that he is " by nature " too lazy to make the effort demanded by that task. But as there is no such thing as laziness in respect of particular tasks, but only general laziness in all circumstances, he will fail to accomplish other tasks which are to his taste and within his capacity, on account of his laziness.

With regard to the judgment of an action or its actual result, it should be noticed that this result very often, perhaps as a rule, does not only show itself in the particular domain in which the particular action is directly initiated. For example, it is well known that one may help a fellow-man in order thereby to injure a third person ; I can strike at an opponent by helping *his* opponent. The first impression one receives is that the purpose of the particular action is to aid a fellow-man, whereas, in reality, it is to injure another. How often is philanthropy actuated not by a love of one's neighbour or a sense of social obligation, but by a wish to outdo others and annoy them. It is therefore of great importance for the understanding of human action to explore beyond the obvious and immediate results. I will not adduce other examples at this point, because they will recur at a later stage of our discussion.

In judging cases of this kind, great care must be taken— as in characterological investigations in general—to avoid falsifying purely descriptive observation and interpretation by the introduction of judgments of value. To take up this critical attitude to one's fellow-men is very easy and consistent with a fundamental tendency of human nature ; in fact, such an attitude is unavoidable in everyday life. But it should be confined to the facts of action, which it should judge by their material nature—to borrow a term from moral theology—and not according to their formal nature. Good and evil deeds must be recognized and distinguished as such. The dictum, "Judge not that ye be not judged," cannot be applied here. However, it is hardly possible—and in my opinion it is quite impossible—to decide whether a man in the depths of his being is good or evil. But the temptation to make this kind of judgment is very great. The relation of morality and behaviour to this question is of no importance. Characterology, however, regarded as a science whose function it is to ascertain the principles of practical character-formation, must stand aloof from such judgments of value. They must also be left out of account when, in the course of our observations, we are compelled by inner necessity to encroach on the domain of morality, as in considerations of responsibility for or the imputability of individual actions.

Nevertheless, the form of judgment that includes an estimate of value is of theoretical importance, especially for the understanding of those forms of action which we have just mentioned. The actual results of any action are apparent in more than one direction. If forms of conduct that are good or valuable in themselves can at times be put to uses that are out of harmony with their real nature, their good or proper nature cannot be destroyed or even weakened by the fact that a particular individual always distorts or perverts them. To make this clearer by an example : One can misuse the love of truth by means of aggression. It is an enlightening fact that the phrase " to tell anyone the truth about himself " almost invariably has an unpleasant connotation. There are people who " cannot refrain from speaking the truth," and whose utterances of this kind are always tinged with disapproving criticism ; this " truth " is never appreciative, appraising or admiring. Clearly, the love of truth in itself and the value belonging to it and inherent in it is in no way impaired by this ; but neither is it lawful to assume that people of that kind are diligent in truth *only* in order to be able to be disagreeable towards their fellow-men under the cloak of righteous indignation, to belittle them by their criticism, and mercilessly expose their weaknesses on the pretext of well-intentioned candour. There are plenty of more effective ways of exercising their hostile, dispraising and envious disposition. Why, then, does a man " choose," so to speak, this alleged love of truth ? In such cases everything will depend on the man's behaviour in other respects ; and one must first of all ascertain how his love of truth fits in with other situations. The matter is clear if it turns out that he is only " truth-loving " when criticism can be disguised as candour. But if apart from that he really does love truth, then there are two possibilities : either his love of truth is genuine and only on occasions and up to a point does he give it false expression by making it ancillary to less worthy sentiments, or else the true *raison d'être* of his love of truth is to be able to indulge, and at the same time mask, his aggressiveness and contemptuousness ; in this case he exhibits his love of truth at other times only in order to be able to justify his attitude of " always speaking the truth " both in his own eyes and in those of other people. It will be seen without further explanation that in these two cases, which are not inventions, but familiar to all those who take an interest in factors underlying human conduct, two totally different mechanisms are discernible. In the one case we have a man to whom truth in itself represents a value for which he strives, but who is deluded into the belief that he is striving after this value, when actually, unknown to himself, a different goal has been substituted. In the other case, truth has no independent value for the man, but is of importance only as an instrument or means to compass his original and dominant end, supremacy over others. But in cases like the latter, we ask ourselves why the love of truth should have been " chosen " as the weapon in the struggle for supremacy. Sometimes we can find an answer to this question in the influences of the man's early environment and the principles that were instilled into him in childhood. Sometimes it is exceedingly difficult to arrive at a real understanding of the inner concatenation of motives. There is still a further problem which requires solution : If a man of this type has once made it a rule to speak the truth, and does so when he is not actuated by motives of aggression and even in circumstances when speaking the truth is disadvantageous for him, should not his love of truth be an object of esteem ? At this point we must have recourse to the ethical method as an aid to characterological understanding. I believe, indeed, that an attitude that in practice manifests itself positively, even if only on occasion, cannot have purely negative sources. But I will not hazard a decision on this difficult point, for its further pursuit would entangle us in problems of finality and the ultimate. It seemed, however, necessary to point out that a theory of character that is entirely divorced from ethics cannot be really comprehensive, even if the scope of ethics in these matters be strictly limited in the manner already indicated. The author doubts his competence to enter upon an ethical discussion.

It appears in practice that even the apparently simple methodological rule, that an action must be judged by its actual results, is by no means so simple in its application. Rather must we assert emphatically that *isolated examples of action and conduct must never be taken as the basis of an estimate of character*. There is nothing isolated in human life ; all the events and experiences of a person's life form part of a continuous chain.

Before we bring these introductory observations to a close, there remains one more question of vital importance to settle : *How can we arrive at an estimate of a person from his potentialities*, the person who is the agent, so to speak, in all action and conduct ? In our discussion of the conversions of St. Francis of Assisi and St. Ignatius Loyola, we regarded it as a permissible assumption in the case of the former saint that the troubadour quality was not only inherent in his conduct (*i.e.*, his character), but part and parcel of his innermost being. It was perhaps more a tentative suggestion, a " feeler," rather than an assertion. But can we really recognize a person, and if so, to what extent ?

That we can in some manner catch a glimpse of the person, and that men of all kinds and at all times have cherished this conviction, is beyond dispute. For, as we have already remarked, this is presupposed in every attempt at education, psychotherapy, improvement or instruction in rational living. Over and above this, there are several striking experiences in which the person, the inner nature of a man, is in a measure revealed to us. Many have had such experiences ; the psychotherapist, professionally concerned with men of abnormal character who are out of harmony with life, and unable to meet its demands, has such experiences daily. We encounter men who are narrow, circumscribed and enfolded within themselves, incapable of facing the smallest difficulties of life or of coping with the simplest situations ; such people regard themselves as totally unequipped for the battle of life, and are judged by others as being inefficient, futile, or even half-wits or idiots. If we study such persons more closely, we inevitably receive the impression that all this is merely superficial, and that in reality they are much better, more capable and efficient, more talented, more active, more resolute and more vital than their behaviour would lead us to believe. How can we justify this view ? On what do we base it ? What do we see in such a man beyond his demeanour of the moment ?

These questions are not easy to answer. Indeed, we must assume from the outset that the person, the innermost principle of a man, must somehow be taken for granted by us. For if we regard character as the guiding principle of action, as the relation between an ego and its appropriate non-ego, and if we are in a position to form an estimate of character, then we should also be in a position to form a certain estimate of the two members of the relation. I shall not here consider the psychological functions that make this possible, or the ontological foundations of such knowledge. I will only state that in my opinion Scheler's assertion that we can have direct perception of a person without recourse to self-identification, analogies and the like, seems to hit the mark.[1] Even if we are not in a position to analyse this achievement more fully, we must accept the fact of such direct external perception, and the possibility of viewing the external ego in its existence and, in a measure, in its nature. The fact is simply there, and is at bottom neither more nor less mysterious than any other kind of objective knowledge.

If we assume that it is in fact possible to acquire a knowledge of the person of a fellow-man apart from the appearances and manifestations provided by the sum total of his actions and conduct, and by the guiding principle regulating these (*i.e.*, his character), we must ask ourselves further : what it is that we actually know of this person. We know, as we have already seen, that it can be richer and more vital than appearances would lead us to believe, and that the principle guiding his actual conduct does not, so to speak, do justice to one member of the relation, the ego. We perceive, therefore, possibilities of self-expression in the person. All self-expression involves action, using the word in its wide sense, and all action passes over into the realization of values. *We perceive, then, value-potentialities in the person.*

The term " value-potentialities " has, in the sense in which it is used here, a double meaning—or perhaps it would be more correct to say that it has significance in two directions. First, the person possesses possibilities of realizing certain definite values by means of action. We may express it thus : values that are real, but belong to the realm of ideas, can by means of human action be brought into the world of space-time, and thus for the first time fulfil their functions in the cosmic continuum. Just as the general form

[1] See *Wesen und Formen der Sympathie*. P. Schilder also writes from this standpoint in *Medizinische Psychologie* (Berlin, 1925).

in which a man brings about this realization of values is identical with what we call character, so does this itself belong to the sphere of value-realization and forms part of that totality which we call "mind made objective" or culture. At bottom, this is only another means of expressing the statement that character is determined not only by the ego, but also by the non-ego, a statement upon which emphasis must always be laid. Finally, we are faced with a mystery of awe-inspiring depth, namely, that the non-ego with which a person is brought in contact is again in some way dependent on the person himself, who can accept or reject the riches of the "worlds" that are there for his taking. Thus a man's character becomes in a twofold sense his own "work," since he comes into relation with the wealth of the non-ego which lies before him but exists independently of him, in accordance with the measure of his own understanding, and, further, because he himself determines the amount of this wealth, now made his own—an act of ultimate determination which takes place in the innermost recesses of his being.

Secondly, the possibilities of the realization of values, as these acquire shape, appearance, and duration in concrete deeds and works, are at the same time possibilities of making values "real" in the person himself. In this context, there is a vague uncertainty in the words "real" and "possible"; one is hardly able to avoid this vagueness and gain more in precision. For the person as such is "real," as are all his latent possibilities, and yet these only attain to reality if they express in concrete conduct and actual performance the automatic incorporation of the man in that realm of being to which from the beginning he belongs as his birthright. The dictum, "Become what thou art," paradoxical as it is in logic, exactly expresses the case.

We must not proceed further with our speculations arising

from this preliminary survey ; but the fact that all the avenues of approach to the study of human character lead ultimately to problems of the kind we have been considering, shows how little characterology is entitled to rank as a self-contained science, and how much it requires to be supplemented by—and indeed based upon and justified by —other branches of philosophy. If it is to do justice in its own field, *theoretical characterology must be founded upon a theory of values and ultimately, therefore, upon ontology and metaphysics*. A working theory of character, therefore, needs the constant support of ethics, which is the science of the realization of values ; thus, characterology itself must refrain from determining values, but cannot exist without paying regard to them. The further implication is that since, for every one of us, all that there is of value can only culminate in, as it originally arose out of, a *summum bonum, the science of charac- terology must ultimately be bound up with religion*. A naturalistic system of characterology is inherently impossible.

In these closing remarks, I believe we have sufficiently touched upon the limitations as well as the assumptions of characterology. Admittedly we have had to content our- selves with mere hints. An immense task, an inexhaustible subject, remains for the speculations of philosophers. The mystery of the problems arising out of the study of character will probably never stand revealed in the clear light of science. Necessarily, therefore, in practical application, innumerable problems remain unsolved or insoluble. But that should not deter us from applying all the available garnered knowledge and practical experience in an attempt to render for us the nature of our fellow-men as intelligible as our own, and to assist us to discharge as worthily as possible the task with which we are saddled, the task of developing that nature. The educationalist, the leader of every kind, is in duty bound to examine carefully all that the psychologist and the characterologist believe they have discerned, and to make use of this store of knowledge, so far as it is established, for the furtherance of his task. It is inadmissible to reject any new knowledge without careful consideration and evaluation of its content. Many a truth appears first in repellent guise and mingled with much that is false. The nature of gold is not affected by the ore in which it lies ; gold remains gold even in a muck-heap.

We shall therefore attempt to select from the wealth of modern contributions in psychology and allied fields, all that seems to us to be of value for the theory and practice of the science of character. But we are fully aware of the inadequacy of our knowledge, and have no doubt that, within a short time, possibly much will appear to us in quite a different light from what it appears in today.

CHAPTER II

THE GENESIS OF CHARACTER

1. PRELIMINARY OBSERVATIONS

HOWEVER strongly we may insist that every human person enjoys the attributes of being a separately existing and unrepeatable entity, and of possessing therefore, strictly speaking, a unique character, it must on the other hand be admitted that there are certain features in a human person whereby he may be distinguished *qua* person. All sorts and conditions of men must share certain features and qualities in common, for the reason that no individual man exists in absolute independence. For he is, as we have already pointed out, a member of the continua or realms of being of animate and inanimate nature, of a community, and of the spiritual and supernatural worlds. In the same way, or even in a higher degree, the world in which an individual person lives and moves, to whose influences he is exposed, and to which he responds through his actions, displays certain constantly recurring features and events. Consequently, man's modes of conduct show close similarities, when a set of such external circumstances as recur in all our lives evokes a response from some fundamental trait peculiar to human nature, and therefore found as an attribute of everybody. By searching for similar reactions in similar external situations, we are provided with a method of acquiring a knowledge of those fundamental traits. Such knowledge is of the greatest importance, if we are to understand the individual and non-recurrent factors of human behaviour, and be able to segregate these from what is common to all mankind.

For this reason, the reproach of over-systematization or stereotyping must not be levelled against a method of characterology that endeavours from the outset to elucidate many diverse modes of human conduct in the light of a few fundamental features common to them all. The only possible way of understanding the particular is by previously establishing that which is general.

2. THE PRIMITIVE URGE TO SELF-ASSERTION

We may start with the assertion that every human being shows that one fundamental urge, known in biology as " the instinct of self-preservation " or something similar, which is common to every living creature and possibly to the whole order of creation. The tendency of an entity to preserve its status in its own particular order of creation may rightly be regarded as the fundamental characteristic of all beings of whatsoever kind ; Spinoza expresses it thus : " *Omne ens in suo esse perseverari conatur.*" This conservative tendency, this urge to self-preservation, may, however, only be perceptible when the being is faced with forces that threaten its existing state or life itself. The urge to self-preservation is directed towards the maintenance of stability in the face of hostile influences. By their nature, such influences can make themselves felt only in the particular order of creation to which the being in question belongs. As we have repeatedly said, man is a member of four different orders of being. Consequently, in man, the tendency to self-preservation must manifest itself in various different ways. These modes of manifestation are not of equal value for the formation of character. The development of man and the form of his activities depends not merely on existence and the bounds set by the mere fact of existence, but also on consciousness—not only on the conditions of his life, but also, and in a special measure, on his experience.

But bound up with this, his position in one of the already-mentioned systems of being—*the subservience of man to and within the community*—possesses a natural prominence over the others. Man's environment is in the first instance the communal world, the world of his fellow-men. Consequently the tendency to self-preservation acquires paramount importance in the form in which it is directed towards the community. As will be shown, the predominance of its communal relations, both positive and negative, is so important that their proper direction is the pre-requisite for the satisfactory formation of man's relations to the other spheres of being. It is clear from the start that an active participation in cultural matters, in the realm of " mind made objective," cannot exist independently of corresponding relations with the world of the community. Even the connection between man and the realm of ideas, truth and values is unthinkable without the mediation of the community of his fellow-men. We shall also see that his connection with the supernatural could never have developed adequately unless his relations to the community had first paved the way. This concatenation, which will later be explained in more detail, finds expression in the words of that second Commandment which describes the love of one's neighbour as being " like unto the first." The above-mentioned connection between membership of the community and communion with the supernatural may be better expressed analogically as a mirroring of the relation of the two Commandments established by divine teaching.

Regarded in and by itself, every tendency to self-assertion must, in the last instance, lead to the making absolute of the being which is asserting itself. This is objectively impossible in the first place, because the human individual is not, and by his nature cannot be, an isolated being, and, secondly, because this tendency is limited in many ways. Subjectively, however, according to experience, the movement towards self-assertion is directed in the long run to this goal of absolutism. Within the communal environment, the tendency to self-assertion and self-preservation acquires a quite specific form which is admirably expressed as " *the will to power*," a phrase of Nietzsche's used by Adler in his *Individual Psychology*. This will to power is unquestionably a fundamental trait of human beings ; we constantly encounter its presence and effects in the lives of individuals and of groups and of peoples in history, although, admittedly, it may be so strangely disguised as to be apparent only to the most wary observer. As we shall become sufficiently acquainted with these transformations and disguises of the will to power in the further course of our speculations, we need not consider them more closely at this point ; here we need only sketch them in general terms.

Were it not for the limitations imposed upon it by human organizations and the conditions regulating individual and collective life, the will to power would drive onwards indefinitely uncontrolled. It is really identical with what the Greeks called $\H{\upsilon}\beta\rho\iota\varsigma$, the ultimate fate of which is illustrated in the story of Prometheus. Obstacles to the free development of the will to power are not set as a check, but rather as a stimulus to more powerful activity. So long as this activity remains within the limits imposed by nature and morality, the will to power has always been and still remains the great impetus which brought man out of the condition of primitive savagery and to the state in which he was capable of making those contributions to culture, technology and science which cause us to marvel at the history of the human race. Force is the most primitive method by which the will to power tackles every obstacle placed in its path.

3. THE NATURE OF IMPULSE

Before we proceed further with our discussion of the development or limitation of the will to power, it seems right to interpolate here some remarks on the concept of impulse, and the part it plays in characterology and psychology in general. Up to now we have intentionally spoken only of a " tendency " to self-assertion, of a " will " to power, and carefully avoided the term " impulse," although we started with the biological conception of an impulse or urge to self-preservation. In biology and psychology, the two concepts " impulse " and " instinct " play an important part. We must, however, put the following question to ourselves ; its answer will be shown to be decisive for our grasp of characterological problems. How important and how far applicable are these concepts to the problems of human existence, even if they have their place in biology ? This question is not merely of theoretical interest and of importance for the establishment of our views ; it must be answered in order that we may take up a critical position towards other theories which have made the idea of impulse their corner-stone, or at the least depend on it to a very large extent. We will, however, content ourselves with mere indications of this controversial matter, without actually indulging in criticism. We must first of all state that an impulse, as such, never becomes an object of observation. There are only certain particular modes of conduct that can be observed and, from their resemblance to one another, related to an impulse. *Impulse is a hypothetical idea* introduced for the purpose of explanation. In logic, the concept of impulse is on the same level as that of force in physics. Whether an impulse or impulses " exist " is a question that can never be answered with absolute certainty. It is only phenomena, modes of conduct, that "exist," and for the sake of clearness are related by us to an impulse. There is no need for us to justify the assumption or indicate the value of its claims as an explanation. Whether or how far it can do justice to all the facts must be the subject of further investigation. The assumption of impulse, as such, is not here called in question ; the questionable attitude is rather that which regards as a fact what should only be termed " hypothesis " or " theory " ; we are too easily misled by the long use and varied applicability of the conception. One pictures impulse in an organism as being in a continued state of readiness for self-expression ; one assumes its presence although it cannot be manifestly observed ; it is in a sense lying dormant, possessed of latent energy. When impulse is not manifested, we can explain the fact either by postulating obstruction by obstacles which for the most part can themselves be conceived of as partaking of the nature of impulses, or by assuming its temporary satisfaction. The simile of the accumulator has frequently been used ; the accumulator can be discharged and must later be charged in order to produce a difference of tension ; so the impulse is discharged in its manifestations, and likewise requires a certain interval for the restoration of tension. As we have said, this is a permissible and even plausible hypothesis, but nothing more.[1]

The assumption of the existence of impulse even in the absence of its expression or manifestation involves the danger from which many theories of human conduct have not escaped. It is this : the impulse is assumed in some way or other to have acquired independence, and is no longer regarded as a member of the whole organism, or person. But it is to this membership of the whole that it owes its existence ; hence the real idea of collectivity is

[1] A criticism of the idea of impulse is to be found in A. C. Garnett's *Instinct and Personality* (London, 1928), which also throws doubt on the existence of impulse beyond the period of its manifestation.

lost, and gives way to a conception according to which the organism or person appears as a summation of relatively independent parts. This gives a stimulus to a purely physical construction, which is in no way adequate to explain the uniqueness of living creatures or of persons, and opens up the way for any naturalistic teaching.

The existence of impulse apart from its manifestations is an unnecessary assumption, as may be seen from a brief consideration of a group of phenomena which—without its being found necessary in biology to assume analogous constructions—bear a great similarity to the phenomena of impulse. What we have in mind is all that is described as "reflex" in the physiology of the nervous system. By a "reflex" one understands the stimulation of a particular area of the body, sensitive thereto (the receptor organ), and the production of an appropriately typical response without the intervention of consciousness, or even of the higher levels of the central nervous system, such as the cerebral cortex. Reflexes are conducted along definite "paths," which are fibres connecting the point of stimulation with the nerve-centre (*e.g.*, the spinal cord) ; the impulse[1] is further conducted, through "shunting-stations" which are sometimes extremely complicated, along a path connecting the centre with the effector organ, for example, a muscle, which then contracts. The following examples may be given in illustration : a blow upon the tendon of the extensor muscle of the knee, which produces a sudden stretching of this muscle, gives rise to an impulse, which reaches the spinal cord and is then conducted by means of another set of fibres to effect a brief twitching of this muscle ; this reflex, which is of great clinical importance, is known as the knee-jerk or patella reflex. Illumination of the retina of the eye stimulates certain groups of cells in the

---

[1] In the following brief account of reflex action, the word "impulse" is used in its strictly physiological sense, *i.e.* the nervous impulse, without any psychological connotation.—TRANS.

mid-brain, whence the impulse is conducted along the third cerebral nerve to the muscle-fibres of the iris, effecting a narrowing of the pupil. Foreign bodies that invade the conjunctiva give rise to irritation which is conducted and shunted in a similar manner to effect an increased secretion of tears. All these reflex phenomena presuppose that the mechanism, the so-called reflex arc, is unimpaired and in working order—that is, in a condition to respond to the stimulus in a normal way. In order to explain reflexes, there is no need whatsoever to assume the existence of a special "impulse." With an adequate and appropriate stimulus, the corresponding reflex apparatus is brought into activity ; in its absence the apparatus, although present, shows no " urge " towards activity.

The analogy with impulses is at once clear. If one ignores the fact that the impulse is somehow experienced—a fact whose importance will be shown later—both cases are at bottom identical : a particular situation gives rise to an appropriate reaction. A distinction seems to arise from the fact that the situations that give rise to the impulse or its manifestations need not come wholly from outside. Impulsive reactions are also caused as the result of internal changes in the organism : thus the feeding impulse is activated by an insufficiency of nutrition in the tissues ; the rest impulse is a response to chemical changes in the muscles ; the sexual impulse depends to a certain degree upon the activity of the ductless glands, etc. In reality these things differ in no particular way from ordinary reflexes. There are many reflexes that are brought about by the result of changes occurring entirely within the organism ; for example, the opening of the pyloric muscle, which shuts off the stomach from the intestinal tract, is caused in this manner, as are also the increase or diminution in the frequency of the heart-beat or the secretory activities of the suprarenal gland.

Regarded purely descriptively, the impulses do not seem to differ from the reflexes. They are only more complex reactions synthetized from many reflexes, which follow one another according to definite laws and are interdetermined. But the more complex the mechanism, the more specialized are the situations it tackles. Therefore, the fact that the impulse can arise only in response to highly differentiated situations, whereas the reflex is elicited by relatively simple stimuli, does not imply a difference between them. So long as impulse is conceived of, and the term employed, for descriptive purposes only, in relation to the behaviour of animal organisms, there is no need to postulate special mechanisms essentially different from the reflex. Impulse means nothing more than a reflex action which is more complex and therefore operating under more or less specialized conditions. The boundary line between reflex and impulsive activity is therefore not traceable. Who can say if the flight-movements of the decapitated frog are reflexes or the expression of an impulse to flight or self-preservation ?

But the conception of impulse does not arise from simple observation and description of animal behaviour, in the sense of " behaviourism," a doctrine much in vogue in the United States ; it is rather a transference of man's experience to the phenomena of animal reactions. Here we seem to come across a far-reaching distinction between reflex mechanisms and impulsive reactions, namely that the former operate at least to a large extent unnoticed, whereas the latter somehow make their way through consciousness. The impulse, then, seems to lie somewhere between the reflex mechanism, which remains at the organic or physical level and conforms to its own appropriate laws, and the actual will. An attempt has been made to explain this apparently intermediate position by regarding impulse as a kind of primal form or preliminary stage of the will ; and many people even conceive of the will itself as being merely an impulse, and an inhibitory one at that. In these various conceptions of the relation of impulse to will there is, so far as I can see, much obscurity. Any system of characterology demands clarity on the factor of " impulse," and for this reason we must occupy ourselves further with it.

The fact that one often relates impulse very closely to the will is shown in the expression *involuntary action*, a phrase not infrequently used in psychology, psychiatry, pedagogy and criminology. The term is obviously intended to cover a man's active conduct that in its externals is similar to consciously controlled action—where consciousness seems to be present at the moment of the act, or, if the act gives the impression of being " automatic " or the result of habit, to have been present at some time and still to be underlying the act—but internally lacks some of the factors proper to volitional action, and replaces them by others. An investigation of this idea will prove necessary for an understanding of the relation between will and impulse, and of the part it plays in human action regarded as a collective whole.

In this connection it must be noted that involuntary action is often differentiated from voluntary action on the one hand, and from instinctive action on the other. The description of an " action " as occurring from or by reason of instinct is certainly to be avoided. It would be more correct to restrict ourselves to the use of the term " instinctive reaction." (Of course the same hypothetical character and dubiety attach to the idea of instinct that we have just noted in the case of impulse.) By an involuntary action is usually understood one in whose motivation the impulsive quality plays an important part. What is the part it plays ?

Many hold the opinion that in the last resort all impulse is directed towards " satisfaction " and the pleasure inherent therein. According to this view, the impulse comes to rest at the moment of the attainment of its object and its accompanying desire for satisfaction. This certainly applies in some degree to the nutritional or sexual urges. There are, however, other forms of pleasure that may also be regarded as being grounded in impulse. K. Bühler[1] has quite rightly emphasized the great importance that attaches to another form of pleasure (besides the desire for satisfaction), which he very aptly designates *Funktionslust*, " the pleasure in right function." Bühler also correctly imputes independence of the others to a third form of pleasure, namely " the pleasure in creation." Its nature is such that the impulsive action is not brought to an end by the pleasure it generates, but creates out of this pleasure a new stimulus to activity. The most illuminating example of this kind of impulse and the pleasure in right function connected with it, is the play impulse. But apart from this it must be noted that there are other forms of functioning to which the impulsive quality is generally ascribed ; this applies especially to the impulse of self-preservation. To have escaped danger may well be a source of pleasure ; but this pleasure neither has in itself the quality of the satisfaction of impulse nor does it bring the impulsive tide to rest, as occurs with satisfaction of the nutritional urge ; nor does it connect up so directly with the final situation as happens in cases of desire for satisfaction. Hence, the contention that all impulse is based on pleasure cannot be right. Behind this opinion there is no weight of biological conviction or theory ; it is only a certain definite conception of the universe or at the least a definite interpretation of the factors underlying moral conduct. At bottom, this theory of the nature of impulse, though alleged to be biological, is a projection of the hedonistic ethic on the plane of biology. It is characteristic of hedonism to regard pleasure

[1] *Die Krise der Psychologie* (Jena, 1928).

as the only possible goal of action. In the first chapter of this book we have already shown that this assumption finds no support in the phenomenology of human action ; a more or less complicated distortion of a set of facts is required at times in order to justify the contention that pleasure is the goal striven after. We are convinced, as we have said, that it is not true that any possible situation that offers an unconditional promise of pleasure is the goal of action, but that pleasure shares with other possible goals of action the fundamental characteristic of realizing in experience a definite value, one of a series of vital values.

Every impulse properly so called is activity, and as such is directed to some future situation that is to be realized. Impulse and conduct share with true action the same mechanisms in common. If in the consideration of this mechanism we have convinced ourselves of the fundamental principle that the actual event is the starting-point, this principle must now be applied. The actual event, the situation realized by action, is, as the goal attained by the action, always the realized value, the understanding and the recognition of whose " worthwhileness " always precede the whole action-complex. We have then to ascertain the values sought after in the so-called impulsive actions.

The answer to this question is easily provided. *In impulsive actions, only vital values are realized ;* whatever the outcome of such actions may be, it never goes beyond the sphere of individual and organic life. It cannot be argued that the sex-impulse does in fact do this, since it " serves the continuance of the species " ; this connection between sexuality and generation is obviously indisputable, but in the experiencing of the impulse its connection or relation with the procreation of children plays no part. So far as this factor does enter into sexual experience it comes from knowledge, which is quite a different sphere, and as a motive for action it derives from regions that lie right outside the impulsive sphere.

The form in which impulses are expressed or made manifest is simply *the manner in which the series of vital values presents itself to experience*. The frequently alleged irresistibleness, or at least compelling force, of impulse, which renders resistance so difficult, is to be understood from the position accorded to vital values in non-reflective conduct.

This position is characterized by two factors. In the first place, the realm of reality within which these vital values, which are the goals of the impulses, become concrete is the substantial body of the agent. Therefore the agent in a purely impulsive act is not in a position to overstep the bounds of his individual sphere. I believe that whenever apparently impulsive actions encroach on a realm of reality other than somatic, the situation is complicated by already existent ties with the non-impulsive. In the second place, the vital values have a special potency—one might say power of conviction—which does not correspond to their objective position in the scale of values. Why this is so, why it appears " more natural " to give these subjective impressional values precedence over the higher objective values, is a question that is outside the range of characterology— one that philosophic anthropology can tackle as a theory of the nature of man. (This, it may be noted, is very closely bound up with the problem of the Fall of man and of hereditary guilt.) But for characterology it is important to establish the legitimacy of substituting in the place of a theory that asserts the existence of permanent impulses in man—like some kind of dynamic organization enjoying relative independence—another conception, which interprets the so-called manifestations of impulse as the realization of definite, that is, of vital, values.

This somewhat tedious digression on the conception of

impulse was necessary, first, because its elucidation appeared to be an indispensable preliminary to the question, to be discussed later, of the part played by the constitution in the formation of character, and, secondly, because the concept is intimately bound up with that of the will to power, a phenomenon which formed the starting-point of the whole digression. For it might well be asked why this should be called a " will " to power, if it is, as we assume, an essential constituent of man's nature and a general and fundamental feature of it. One is in fact inclined to regard all general constituents as being directly rooted in the psycho-physical organism, and therefore to bring them into the same category of what is usually connoted by the word " impulse."

In order to protect our limitation of the conception of impulse against all possible criticism, we should have to test all the various forms of impulse described in the literature in order, and see whether they conformed to our definitions. This, however, would cause us to overstep the limits that we set ourselves in this work, and the fuller argument must be left for elaboration elsewhere.

But if it be correct that everything we call impulse, or the manifestation or expression of an impulse, is only the manner in which the vital values are represented to experience, and if it be true that the realm of reality in which and by which these vital values can take concrete form is always limited to the physical body, then power, as a value that indisputably belongs to the realm of the non-ego, can never be the goal of mere impulse and at the same time the realization of a pre-existent value. In that case an " impulse " to power must be meaningless, and the " will " to power must imply more than a special modification of the impulse to " self-preservation " or " self-assertion."

The reason why the " will to power " is something more

than, or something different from, a somehow modified manifestation of impulse, follows from man's membership of the various continua of being, not as a divided but as an undivided entity. He is not a member of the realms of animate and inanimate nature simply by reason of his bodily substance, nor a member of the realm of spirit merely in virtue of his mind and soul ; he belongs to each of the four realms as an undivided whole or unity. Of course man's membership of the natural realm is made especially visible in his body, but even here he is seen to be not merely a natural being, when we consider the fact that alterations occurring at the other levels are not without influence on the state and functions of his physical organs. So, at bottom, there is no pure quality of impulse within that complete being called " man," because such a quality would be limited to the physical, natural realms, and have no part in those of the community, spirit, and grace.

Such considerations apply logically to all human conduct, even to those forms which we are inclined, or may be accustomed, to regard as purely " impulsive." It is therefore quite impossible to interpret impulse as a kind of " preliminary stage " of another and " higher " form of conduct ; this is a point on which emphasis must be laid, but without going into any further detail. Certainly the organic aspect and consequently that functional aspect included under the term " impulse," are the foundation of the higher achievements, inasmuch as these, in view of the one and indivisible body-soul nature of man, derive from it ; but they must not be understood as " proceeding " from it by means of a transformation, a mechanism which is often enough assumed but never made intelligible. Even if this point has not been dealt with in detail, the consideration we have paid to it relieves us of the necessity of the detailed examination of all those characterological conceptions according to which impulse is made the chief element or primal stuff of all human conduct.

One observation still remains to be made : although, in all the modes of human conduct—whether these lie at the organic level, like the organic physical functions in health or disease, or attain the level of the highest spiritual achievements, including even union with the supernatural power—the whole and indivisible man is active and functioning in all the possibilities and aspects of his being ; this fact by no means renders superfluous a classificatory division of these various actions and reactions according to their appropriate aspects. So far as the person presents himself to our consciousness more or less clearly in one of these aspects, we have the right to speak of " organic " (bodily), " social," " cultural " or " religious," provided we keep clearly in mind the fact that in the strict sense there are no " pure " categories of conduct. The sublimest thought, inasmuch as it is in some way derived from a perceptible image, is by its very nature dependent on expression, that is on speech, which is a bodily function, cannot therefore escape its connection with the physical, however much its content may belong to the spiritual world ; it is equally related to the social level, because expression always means expression to others. Again, inasmuch as the thought embodies truth and value, it has its place in the realm of truth and of the *summum bonum*. In the same way, no form of conduct can escape from its manifold unity, from the *unitas quadruplex*, which, according to our thesis, defines and constitutes the nature of man and his place in the general cosmic order.

4. THE WILL TO POWER

We have said that the environment that primarily and preponderatingly exerts an influence on man's conduct is that of his fellow-men. It is to this environment that that fundamental attitude or tendency which on that very account we describe by the term " will to power " is mainly directed. History teaches us that rule over one's fellow-men—or, still earlier, their conquest—was established long before the advent of the control of nature or the mastery of the things of the spirit.

We are now clear as to the postulates that will enable us to start and conduct our consideration of the will to power, its modes of manifestation and the conditions of its development.

We have said that the will to power is a primitive tendency of human nature and that, left to itself and in the absence of restricting forces, it would overstep all bounds. In point of fact, this will encounters a twofold limitation. On the one hand, it comes up against obstacles arising from its environment, and, on the other, there are in man himself conditions, also of a twofold character, that inhibit free and immoderate development of the will to power. First, man possesses a second tendency as primitive as the will to power, but antagonistic to it ; this tendency, which we shall understand more clearly later under the term " *the will to community*," is part of man's deepest nature. Secondly, there are in man certain definite dispositions that render an unrestricted development of the will to power impossible from the first.

We need not waste many words on the external obstacles to the will to power. They result from the competition of the will to power of other men, from the resistance of inanimate nature—which technology can indeed circumvent, but does not know ultimately how to convert into allies— and the laws of value laid down by custom, tradition, law and economics. This is not the place to speak of the bounds set to the will to power by subordination to the commands and laws of supernatural origin which are regarded as binding, nor of the restrictions imposed by the consciousness existing deep in every soul of the finiteness and limitations of the created being, nor again of the voice of conscience. These things are by their very nature outside man, although they are experienced as being operative within him ; they can therefore be more properly discussed when we come to speak of the walls erected in the inner life itself, which the will to power assails in vain.

If this will to power is in fact a primal tendency and as such a characteristic and constituent of man's deepest nature, we should expect it to be apparent even in childhood. Indeed, we could assume that its manifestations would be particularly intelligible in childhood, especially in the first years, because the various influences that repress the will to power or compel it to adopt various disguises will not as yet have made themselves felt.

5. THE PSYCHIC LIFE OF EARLY CHILDHOOD

This expectation is justified by experience to an extent that at first is perhaps unexpected. An exhaustive study of child conduct and motives yields a remarkable number of conclusions helpful to an understanding of the bases of character and of the factors largely responsible for its formation. Since all human conduct can be summed up as the relation between the ego and the non-ego, between the person and his environment, and is essentially dependent on the second member of the relation, the first question to be answered deals with the specific nature of the child's environment.

The opinion sometimes put forward, as, for instance, recently by E. Spranger,[1] that the psychic life of the child is fundamentally unintelligible to the adult, or, as one might

Psychologie des Jugendalters (Leipzig, 1926).

say, that it is impossible for the adult to " feel himself into " the inner life of the child, can, I think, be held only if and because one has not tried sufficiently to make clear the peculiarities of environment as it is represented to childish experience. In agreement with K. Bühler's illuminating psychology of childhood,[1] I am disposed to maintain that there is no such unbridgeable gulf between the forms of experience of the adult and of the child. Moreover, the recent investigations into the sociology and behaviour of the young child carried out under the direction of Charlotte Bühler [2] support this contention, quite apart from the experience gained in educational discussions and in schools by doctors and teachers, who have investigated the matter from the individual-psychology point of view and have made pronouncements to the same effect.

What are the distinguishing features of the child's environment ? So far as I can see, there are four that may be regarded as fundamental :

(i.) *The child's smallness*, which always directs his gaze upwards, and undoubtedly implants a sense of inferiority, although this feeling, like most of the experiences of those early years, does not attain to a clear or rational under-standing on the child's part. The fact that we use the words " inferior " and " inferiority " in a metaphorical as well as in a spatial sense, reveals the connection of ideas, which is brought out clearly when we recall the fact that at all times those in authority have made practical use of the symbolism of position in space, and have occupied literally higher positions than those over whom their authority is exercised. It is unnecessary to give examples.

(ii.) *The child's physical weakness*, in consequence of which the world's resistance to all efforts of the little ones to carry

[1] *Die geistige Entwicklung des Kindes* (Jena, 1925).
[2] Collected in *Kindheit und Jugend* (Leipzig, 1928).

out their will or realize their wishes is immeasurably greater than those encountered by adults. Just as many objects are beyond the reach of the little arms so eagerly outstretched to grasp them, so many ideas cannot be realized because the obstacles are too great.

Both his smallness and weakness are brought home to the child's consciousness especially by the behaviour of the adults in his environment, who are wont in their talk to stress these things more than is necessary or useful. We shall see later what mistakes are made in this respect, and what undesirable consequences ensue.

(iii.) *The unreliability of the child's knowledge.* Children attempt very early to frame general laws and to develop comprehensive conceptions of things, following in this the primal disposition of man ; and like adults, they do this chiefly on a basis of analogies, which in the case of children are necessarily connected with what is incidental and therefore soon proves to be deceptive. Thus a child may get the idea that yellow glittering metal is called " gold," and delight in that knowledge—for the increase of knowledge is as a rule very delightful to children—only to find a few days later that there is such a thing as brass. By such disappointments, the confidence of the child in the completeness of his understanding of the universe is often badly shaken. To this must be added the variation in the meaning of words, and the diversity of their syntactical usage, which soon strike many children.

(iv.) With the incompleteness of the laws and generalizations evolved by children, there is closely connected the fact that *the universe gives them the impression of being unaccountable*. Their " confidence in the regularity of events " is small ; therefore it is as easy for the child to believe in miracles—for example, that the badly written exercise will on the way to school change itself into a masterpiece of tidiness—as to be in complete ignorance of the next event. The laws of cause and effect, which to us seem so obvious and inviolable, do not at all possess these attributes for the child. He is in fact less inclined to believe in these laws, because he soon discovers that many of them admit of exceptions, which to us, indeed, are only apparent exceptions, but appear to the child as actual violations of the rule that is presented to him as unalterable. For example, it happens that a glass falls to the ground without breaking, when the child has always heard that breakage occurs in such cases. Even time, the succession of the days of the week, is not altogether certain to the child's mind. A five-year-old child once said to his father on December 22nd, a Monday : " Don't go away ; it might suddenly be Wednesday—Christmas Eve."

This disbelief in the strict operations of cosmic law is strengthened by the behaviour of adults. " One never knows," a girl of eight or nine years once confided to me, " what grown-ups will do." Unfortunately the child was right, and not only from her own standpoint. Inconsistent behaviour on the part of the teacher or parent is a fundamental evil which may influence the formation of character very unfavourably.

Many actions of adults must indeed seem to the child to be unintelligible and hence unaccountable ; and in point of fact, adults are guilty of much that, regarded even objectively, seems quite unaccountably inconsequential. How often does it happen, when visitors are present, that the child is rebuked for something that ordinarily would pass unnoticed ; the child can see no necessary connection between the fact of the visit and the rebuke. I must admit that I also cannot see it. Behaviour that is good enough for father and mother ought to be good enough for strangers. If we ask what will be the total effect of those fundamental facts of childish experience and environment just set out, which are in my opinion certainly the most important, there is no doubt about the answer : it must be an all-permeating uncertainty. This uncertainty is not always—indeed, very rarely—present to consciousness ; in fact, consciousness of it already indicates a departure from the normal course of development. The contention that uncertainty is an essential feature of child life will presumably be met by reference to the many familiar sayings that speak of the " security " in which the child lives : " Ah ! did I but know the way back. . . . Why did I seek my fortune and leave my mother's side ? " But security is felt, experienced, desired only by the man who knows himself to be somehow insecure ; security means simply that the fight against injustice and difficulty, the responsibility for what we do and what we leave undone, does not depend on us, or at the least not entirely on us, but is taken over and fought for us by others. Security is the correlative of insecurity ; the latter presupposes the former.

This insecurity arising out of the nature of the child's environment—or rather of the environment as experienced by the child in virtue of his own nature, the weakness of his body, and his lack of knowledge—raises serious obstacles to the will to power, obstacles which are original and inherent in it, rather than antagonistic. The will to power, as one might say, feels itself from the very beginning doomed to failure. Therein lies tragedy ; for the person's will to power, self-preservation and self-development must not be arbitrarily judged from the purely negative standpoint. When directed towards proper goals, it is indeed the great impulsive force that first renders possible all personal, historical and cultural development. In every case, therefore, there is always the danger that the experience of limitation in the development of power not only will prevent an excess of that

will and the development of morally and culturally undesirable manifestations, but will also choke the source of all
positive achievement and check all moral and personal
progress.

Therefore, as will be more clearly shown later, the dictum
that " the child's will must be broken " is altogether perverse. For the will is needed for all striving for the good, and
resistance to evil ; and how can one expect a man to make
use of a will that has been broken in the years of childhood ?
We shall not, however, deal here with the practical educational conclusions that could be drawn from what we have
just said, but will consider the circumstances or conditions
that tend to make the limitation of the will to power still
more considerable and impressive, restricting our discussion
to limitations that result from internal causes and are
inherent in man's nature and experience.

We have already indicated that words like " experience "
and " impression," applied to the psychic situations of childhood, are not to be understood in the sense of something that
is clear, conscious and intelligent. It must be clearly recognized that the " second will," of which St. Augustine speaks
in the previously quoted passage, is one that man himself
for the most part knows nothing of, and must discover by
laborious self-examination in order to understand it and its
aims. This second will is nourished by the impressions that
enter into our souls without our thinking about them and
even without the intervention of consciousness. For our
present purposes it is not necessary to occupy ourselves with
the concept of the " unconscious " ; the question how it is
to be conceived need not detain us ; but we must assume
the existence of something of that order. It is therefore
entirely wrong to believe that events that the child becomes
aware of, talk that he hears, actions he observes, do not leave
their impress on the little soul, because, as one says, " he

surely does not understand " or " he does not yet understand." For impressions to be effective it is not necessary
that they should be understood ; their mere existence
suffices.

Thus, circumstances of many kinds, which we adults
would gladly believe to have no effect on the child, may be
of decisive importance, in that they ultimately raise insuperable obstacles to the will to power. The will to power
provides the means by which and through which the real ego
can assert and express itself ; it is of such moment that, if we
are to acquire that measure of self-confidence which shall
permeate our whole experience—and this is requisite for our
maintenance and progress—it must not be wholly destroyed.
It is absolutely essential for man not merely that he should
be something that exists, but that he should carry meaning
and value. This sense of incorporating a personal value need
not, any more than the sense of bodily health, which is
indeed in many respects analogous, form part of the content of conscious experience ; but its lack or weakening
unfailingly produces its train of effects, as in the case of
bodily illness, although it is not experienced as a disturbance
of bodily function in the same way as the latter. Often
enough, one feels unwell without being conscious of any
particular illness.

It is a peculiarity of man that he is continually measuring
both his external and his internal situation against some
norm, and comparing himself and his achievements with
some ideal standard, which has two different origins. First,
every man possesses a vague but none the less effectual
knowledge of " what he can and should be " ; in some really
mysterious way we know our ultimate possibilities, the
potential values inherent in and realizable through us,
which, as possibilities, mean to us what we can be, and, as
values, what we should be. Secondly, we construct an ideal

for ourselves on the basis of experience, especially that of others, but also that resulting from our own activities. More will be said later on this setting up of ideals and the part it plays in character-formation. Here it is important to note that the same tendency exists in children, impelling them to contrast themselves and their position in the world with the pictures they make for themselves of other persons and their position.

It would therefore be of the greatest importance if we were in possession of more accurate knowledge of the mode and manner in which children, at any rate very young ones, picture adults and children of their own and different ages—a point on which we know extraordinarily little. Perhaps we have not realized the great importance of this question sufficiently well to investigate it thoroughly. Admittedly it is a matter about which it is by no means easy to obtain information. Something nevertheless can be said, thanks in part to the work done in individual-psychology, and in part to reliable inferences drawn from the manner, above described, in which the child experiences his environment.

We have said that every child, even under the most favourable conditions, feels himself to be insecure. He sees security, or fancies he detects it, with the adults to whom he takes flight in order to find safety ; and he has reason for his belief, because in many instances the adults have helped and protected him and smoothed his path. His insecurity compels the child to seek " safety " ; his will to power makes him experience this necessity as a sign of inferiority and inadequacy.

6. THE FEELING OF INFERIORITY DETERMINED BY PHYSIQUE

Consequently everything that leads to an increase of the child's sense of insecurity operates to the detriment of his sense of personal value, and promotes the " feeling " of insufficiency. In individual-psychology this is termed the " inferiority-feeling," an expression that has now passed into current use.[1] The use of the word " feeling " in this connection, a word of many meanings, is open to criticism ; it is always desirable in scientific discussions to restrict the use of a term within narrow and clearly-defined limits Inferiority as a content of experience involves the realization of a relation to a value, measured against which a person deems himself to be inferior ; that is to say, the experience is founded on the recognition of a relation, which recognition may be vague and not attain the level of a formulated judgment, though nevertheless based on one. Whether the term " feeling " can be properly applied to such a class of experience is open to doubt ; in any case, it seems wiser to speak of a vague knowledge or experiencing of one's own insufficiency and inferiority rather than of a definite feeling. In contrast, the term " inferiority " is well chosen, because it takes account both of the insufficiency experienced and also of the fact that it is caused by a comparison—the measurement of oneself against others and against an ideal. On the other hand, every impression that serves to deepen the experience of inferiority increases the sense of insecurity in which a person finds himself, thereby leading to a vicious circle and in far too many cases bringing about deformations of character, which later have to be corrected with difficulty —and then not always with certainty of success.

The factors responsible for an increase in the sense of insecurity or an accentuation of the experience of inferiority derive either from the personal make-up of the individual child or from the attitude taken up by his environment towards him. (In reality these two factors, however much they can be conceived of discretely, are very intricately

[1] The German term is *Minderwertigkeitsgefühl*, which is usually—and, to the translator's mind, wrongly—rendered in English as " inferiority complex."—TRANS..

interwoven.) Though we cannot provide an exhaustive enumeration, we will now consider the most important of these factors and their mode of operation. This will also give us an opportunity of bringing out many points of fact and criticism that are of significance in characterology.

The general physical make-up.—This is commonly called " constitution," although strictly speaking that term ought only to apply to innate and unchangeable factors, not those which are acquired through illness and the like. As the scientific problem of the origin of this make-up is, in the present connection, irrelevant, we can speak without hesitation of " constitution " in the current sense of the term. We have in mind constitutional types that may be simply distinguished as weak or strong, and also anomalous forms, diverging from the " normal type " in some direction or other, which have suffered from the effects of disequilibrium of the organic functions or developmental anomalies.

The meaning of constitution or physical make-up for the development and moulding of character can be conceived of in many different ways. According to the most current view, the constitution is of primal importance ; there is a simple, inevitable bond between constitution and character, the nature of the former determining the particular form of the latter. It is true that Kretschmer, who in recent years has carried out the most vigorous and valuable investigations, in his work, *Körperbau und Charakter*,[1] speaks only of an " affinity " between certain physical types and forms of character ; but even he regards constitution as an essential factor in character-formation.

We must dissociate ourselves from this point of view.[2] If it were right, there would be an inconsistency between the

[1] 7–8 Edition (Berlin, 1929). Cf. also Kretschmer, *Medizinische Psychologie* (Leipzig, 1924).
[2] More on this subject will be found in my contribution to *Medizinische Charakterologie*, and again in *Psychologie und Psychiatrie* (*Beiheft der Wiener Klin. Wochenschrift*, 1927).

unchangeableness of the constitution—for it is unchangeable, or at least capable of variation only within quite narrow limits—and the fundamental transmutability of character. But in view of the arguments elaborated in the first chapter of this book on the mutability of character, we are unable to accept an inevitable interdependence of this kind determined by a rule of natural causality. We know of cases of the most profound change of character occurring in persons of markedly abnormal constitution ; psychotherapy can undoubtedly effect such changes without, of course, in any way influencing the constitution. To this it must be added that in a group of people suffering from a uniform and pathologically determined change of constitution—such as occurs in endemic cretinism, a condition invariably secondary to disease of the thyroid gland—we find persons of the most diverse character.

We must therefore seek for some other method of approach. It cannot be denied that physical factors exert an important influence on character, and that certain affinities appear at first sight to be causally determined. The interpretation of bodily factors as primary causes, and of moral phenomena— and hence character—as effects rests on a particular assumption of the nature of the body:soul relationship. According to this particular view of the relationship, which is known as the theory of psycho-physical reciprocity, body and soul are regarded as independent entities, which are only accidentally and to a limited extent interconnected. It is not possible to demonstrate here that this theory is as little able to do justice to the facts and to provide a satisfying philosophical theory of the problem of body and soul as the doctrine of psycho-physical parallelism—a fact that is becoming more and more recognized.[1] But a careful consideration of all the known

[1] For a comprehensive discussion on the theory of psycho-physical parallelism, see H. Driesch, *Das Leib-Seele-Problem* (Leipzig, 1924). Cf. also H. Bergson, *L'Energie spirituelle ;* also A. Kronfeld, *Die Psychologie in der Medizin* (Berlin, 1927).

facts, in my view, leads us inevitably to a theory that asserts not a psycho-physical nexus, but a union of body and soul in man, who is by his nature indivisible. Such a theory—resulting, as I believe, from the examination of the most weighty modern opinions and of all the facts, and therefore to be as strongly emphasized as possible—is in remarkable accord with the views held long ago and with good reason by the scholastic philosophers. Also, be it noted, within this theory no controversy need arise on the subject of the reciprocal interdependence of physical and psychical conditions and functions ; but the problem of cause and effect assumes a different complexion.

One of the problems that led to the theory of psycho-physical parallelism was that in which the body, or a change in its state, was regarded as a " cause " of psychical issues. It is true that the introduction of the idea of causality is thereby avoided, but the inconvenience involved in such problems by the causal conception can be avoided by making it clear that in addition to the connection of cause and effect another connection is imaginable. We must distinguish between *cause* on the one hand and *occasion* on the other. The experiences we have and the impressions we receive are occasions for action. If we could look on a man's bodily make-up as a part of his experience, it could then be regarded not as a cause, but as an occasion of his actions or of an attitude adopted by him. Moreover, one can also imagine that the actions of a man, or the principle underlying them (his character), can undergo a cataclysmic change despite the absence of constitutional alteration ; for not only his condition at the time, as such, but also his attitude, valuation and significance, which belong or are assigned to the whole complex of his experience, exert an influence in the determination of action.

Now, such a view is quite plausible. It is by no means too

bold to assume that *man in some way has experience of his bodily make-up*. We know that general physical states—either those within physiological limits, such as fatigue, or those outside them, such as disease—can alter our behaviour. Often we do not grasp—and perhaps it surprises us—why today or recently we are or were " not the same as usual " ; but if we can ascertain the occasion of this state of being " not ourselves," we find that it is to a large extent in our power to give way to it and " let ourselves go," or to free ourselves from it. As we sometimes feel too tired and slack, too weak to put up a resistance, and so on, so at times we may feel ourselves to be well equipped or less well equipped for the battle of life, and somehow have the experience of having reached the end of our tether when we are still capable of further efforts. It is by no means strange, or at any rate no stranger than other phenomena of human nature, that we should have knowledge of the limits of our capacity for effort—a knowledge that as a matter of fact we have constantly. A burden seems heavy because it approximates in oppressiveness to what cannot be borne, not merely because it is in fact a much greater burden than one whose oppressiveness we should not feel. All great impressions, like all great achievements, are judged by us in relation to a maximum, which, however, to be used as a standard of reference, need not have been experienced. This very important fact—important for the psychology of sense-perception as well as for the elucidation of many other problems—demonstrates to us (although we cannot here discuss the matter fully) that such awareness of the limits and of the maxima of our capacity for effort is a fundamental quality of our experience. Consequently, it is not only not absurd to make an assumption of such knowledge, even in respect of experiencing our own " bodiliness," but apposite and illuminating to do so.

We maintain that man, from the very beginning, knows himself as an organism, more or less well equipped or endowed with the capacity for resistance. His attitude towards life or towards himself is in correspondence with this knowledge. The body is, so to speak, the instrument used by the person in the struggle for self-assertion. Just as one feels insecure if in a scramble over rocks the stick on which one relies for support shows signs of bending, so does one lose confidence if on account of fatigue, illness, or some constitutional weakness, the trusted instrument of the body fails to respond to the demands made upon it.

This knowledge of our capacity for achievement and of the state of our own bodies we call " *vital consciousness.*" It colours all our experience ; it permeates all our deeds and motives like an impregnating dye.

From this survey we can now readily understand that all bodily weakness and misfunctioning and all constitutional anomalies undermine man's sense of security and emphasize the knowledge of his lessened powers of resistance in the stress of life, and therefore his inferiority. The subjective corre-late of such knowledge and such a sense of insecurity takes the form of a lack of courage—for a sort of buoyant courage is an inherent quality of man—or, better still, of *discouragement*.

Consequently, all constitutional anomalies endanger the normal development of character. Children of abnormal constitution require the application of special educational methods, and failure to pay attention to such requirements is the cause of many educational failures, and results in the acquisition by the child of undesirable characteristics.

It is therefore to be desired that in all cases of children who are difficult to bring up an experienced doctor should be consulted—one who is as competent to deal with anomalies of character-development and the factors deter-mining them as he is with physical abnormalities.

It would be tempting to conduct a detailed investigation into the connections between definite physical, organic disturbances on the one hand, and definite characterological dispositions on the other. Thereby it would be shown that many apparently ideopathic variations of character can be intelligibly regarded as appropriate responses to organic change or constitutional anomaly, in the sense of perceptible reactions to some particular experiencing of the person's own bodily state. Such an inquiry, however, belongs more to the field of medical or pathological characterology, and we are unable to devote space to it here.

7. COMPENSATION

We must now elaborate another idea, whose formulation was amongst the greatest contributions to psychology made by Alfred Adler—the operation of *compensation* and *over-compensation*.[1] In fact, this forms the real starting-point and corner-stone of the whole body of doctrine of individual-psychology. Put briefly, it is this : if an organ is ineffectual —that is, inferior in some respect—the organism develops a tendency to stimulate that organ to greater efforts, or to strengthen some other part of the organic system connected with the inferior organ, and to increase its development and effectiveness, so that the total operative capacity of the organ in question attains a normal level (compensation) or even exceeds it (over-compensation). We need not consider in detail all the relevant facts ; we need only say that this thesis is based on sound biological and pathological grounds. As a matter of fact, it was known to a large extent before Adler, although it was not presented in any systematic scheme. The importance of Adler's conception is, however, twofold ; first, it expresses the " finalistic " point of view—

[1] This idea is developed in its main lines in *Studie über die Minderwertigkeit von Organen* (Berlin-Vienna, 1907 ; Munich, 1927).

that is, *the decisive rôle of the purpose or task* in the realm of organic functions—and secondly, the principle of compensation is with much acuteness and success transferred by analogy to human conduct in general.

This transference may be described as follows : If that sense of physical fitness which, as we have seen, colours the whole of our experience is reduced, and if that reduction does not exceed a certain limit, the first effect of it will be an increase in the tendency to self-assertion—in other words, an exaggeration of the will to power.

This principle provides a theoretical commentary on very diverse phenomena connected with normal and abnormal forms of character, phenomena which in its absence would be difficult to interpret ; to this we shall return later. Here we need only point out that the above formulation contains an idea already touched upon, namely, that restrictions of the will to power give occasion not to inertia or resignation, but to enhanced efforts. *The doctrines of individual-psychology provide us with a possible method of synthetizing organic, psychic, and hence characterological, events in accordance with a single fundamental principle.* This doctrine, which always emphasizes the unity of human nature, must not be held to imply that man's conduct in general, and intelligent action, especially when directed in accordance with purely organic laws, can be " explained " in terms of the organic or regarded as a by-product of it. It must be rather understood as meaning that in the law of compensation we can perceive a special illustration of that comprehensive philosophical (and, in fact, metaphysical) thesis termed in scholastic philosophy *analogia entis*, the analogy of being.[1]

---

[1] It must, however, be admitted that the school of individual-psychology usually fails to pay much attention to the philosophical assumptions or consequences arising out of its doctrine. In my opinion, indeed, its point of view is often upside down. The " metaphysic of the person " upon which I insisted in the treatise cited in footnote 1, p. 49, is not regarded by this school as a methodological necessity for the constructions of its system. This, however,

Applied to the problem with which we are immediately concerned—the significance of constitutional defect or the experience occasioned by it (a diminution of vital consciousness)—the meaning of the idea formulated above is as follows : an internal situation of the kind in question will lead immediately—in a first phase, so to speak—to an increase of the will to power, augmented efforts, and a corresponding attempt to make oneself effective, to get to the top and to " make good."

Other bodily factors have the same effect as constitutional weakness or disequilibrium of the whole organism—a decreased operative capacity, resulting from the " inferiority " of individual organs or groups of organs. Smallness of stature is an example. It may well be that because of his consciousness of this, a man who regards himself as inferior to others in this respect is spurred on to special performance by way of compensation. Quite a number of small men can show remarkable muscular accomplishments—for example, distinguished mountaineers. Amongst famous generals we find unusually small men, like Eugene of Savoy, or Napoleon, or men otherwise physically defective, like Narses.

It will be noticed as a general rule that efforts at compensation are made in the particular quarter in which the insufficiency is experienced. As a classical instance, we can point to the great Greek orator Demosthenes, who, as is well known, suffered from an impediment in his speech ; he was not satisfied with attaining the same facility in speaking as other people, but won his successes and triumphs in that very field in which he had appeared to be condemned to inferiority. One must not push this idea to the trite

does not detract from the credit due to individual-psychology for its methodologically pure idea, and for its main tenets. The recently published and somewhat aggressive polemic of Kunz (*Zeitschr. für die ges. Neurol.*, Bd. 116, 1928), based for its own part on quite unproved assumptions, does not go to the root of the matter.

conclusion that of the original factors that cling to a person nothing remains over. Impediments of speech do not, of course, give one a claim to oratorical distinction. But the process of compensation is of great importance, especially because its working is so transparent.

If compensation is not obtained in the same sphere as that in which there is inferiority, it will frequently be sought elsewhere. As the simplest case, we may notice that many remarkably small men—of course by no means all; overstatement is especially deplorable in such instances—speak unusually loudly, as though to say " Stop! Don't overlook me ; although people might fail to see me, they shall at least hear me." Perhaps one might discern a similar motive behind the child's habit of talking and crying more loudly than necessary, although this is certainly to a large extent to be interpreted in terms of " the pleasure of right function." Further, the trivial fact that almost everyone imagines that by loud speaking he emphasizes his words or commands, points to a similar connection. This mechanism of compensation, occurring in a different field from that of the inferiority, accounts, at any rate partly, for the frequently noted intellectuality of hunchbacks, as in the case of Moses Mendelssohn, or for their malice and love of intrigue, as with Thersites. A very remarkable instance is that of Shakespeare's Richard III, to whom we shall return later.

It seems unnecessary to enumerate the various organic inferiorities. But one conclusion of the greatest importance to education may be drawn from our discussion—a conclusion that should be self-evident, but unfortunately is far too frequently ignored. A child's attention should never be drawn in a disparaging way to a failing for which he is in no way responsible ; he should never be allowed to overhear pitying and dubious remarks about his future, length of life, ability to earn a living, and so on ; otherwise, he is in danger of losing all confidence, even when attempts are made to encourage him to realize his potentialities. In a publication [1] by Ella Lynch, an American Catholic, and director of the Teacher Mothers' National League, we find the following striking warning, which should be taken to heart. All children, and especially those who are physically handicapped—or even mentally ; but in judging this, great care is needed—should be taught thus : " I am only someone, but I *am* someone. I can't do everything, but I can do something. That I can't do everything is no reason for my not doing what I can." That is a motto that many an adult would do well to note and adopt ; it really contains a lesson that could have been inferred long ago from one of our Lord's parables, that of the talents.[2]

With this reference to the perversion of the natural means of the will to power in that remarkable disguise which has been aptly termed " the means for weakness," we shall discontinue this discussion for the time being. It will be resumed later, when we have learned more of the other conditions that serve to increase the child's sense of insecurity.

8. INFERIORITY-EXPERIENCES CONDITIONED BY EXOGENOUS FACTORS

In addition to the enhanced sense of insecurity that is constitutional, inasmuch as it is determined by some organic insufficiency, we must consider that form which may be called exogenous or situational, so far as it is conditioned not by endogenous, personal factors, but by a man's attitude to his fellow-men and to his environment. Let us remark at the outset that these situational factors are very important ; and of the utmost importance is the grave responsibility

---

[1] *Training the Child at Home* (New York, 1922).
[2] *Mat.* xxv. 14.

devolving upon parents and teachers and those persons generally who form part of the child's environment. *We lay the blame*—if indeed one is entitled to talk of blame in matters depending on the exercise of human judgment— *for an exceptionally large number of cases of characterological defect or anomaly at the door of those concerned in the upbringing of children.* It must not be assumed that their errors, for the most part made in ignorance, remove all responsibility from the shoulders of the child. Judicial authorities and ecclesiastics can determine the degree of responsibility according to their respective standards ; but in the light of the present state of our knowledge, it is no longer justifiable, in a remarkably large proportion of cases, to fall back on the convenient assumption that a child is naturally bad or defective in this or that respect. In these cases we ourselves, parents and teachers, have usually every reason to cry " *Nostra maxima culpa !* "

The situations that tend to increase a person's natural sense of insecurity can be divided into those which are impersonal, and exert an influence as such, and those which owe their significance exclusively to persons forming part of the environment ; the distinction is analogous to that made with reference to constitutional weakness and the like. In speaking of impersonal situations, which can exert an unfavourable influence in virtue of themselves alone, we do not mean to imply that their undesirable influence is unavoidable. On the contrary, such influences can almost always be balanced by appropriate educational adjustments, and made innocuous. Situationally determined inferiority-experiences respond even more fully to educational correctives than those which are determined by constitutional factors and the like, but the responsibility is proportionately greater ; this has already been emphasized.

The first group of situations is produced by the child's sex, by the presence or absence of brothers and sisters, and by his order of birth in relation to them. As the whole conduct of man, and hence also the principle that directs it (his character), is in part determined by the non-ego, the following questions must be of great importance : whether the child has or has not brothers or sisters ; whether it is the first, last or middle member of a family ; whether it is a boy or a girl ; whether it comes between two children of the opposite sex ; whether it mixes with older children ; and so on. It is quite common for parents to express surprise- - " We have brought up all our children alike, and they are quite different ! " or " Only this one has turned out different ! " This is simply foolish. The grievance is often enough the result not of peculiarities of disposition, but of difference in the position in the family—for example, as eldest or youngest child—which proves to be of greater importance than uniformity in the upbringing. As the children do not live in the same conditions, they cannot all be brought up on the same plan.

Since we propose in the following chapter to give a detailed description of some typical " situations " of practical importance in education and character-formation, it will suffice here if we give only a few brief indications.

Particularly noteworthy are the situations arising out of the child's position in the family as the only child, the eldest, or the youngest. This is brought out by the following fact, among others : of the children with whom the educational consultant specialist, and of the adults with whom the psychotherapist, is brought in contact, i.e., neurotics and hysterics, an overwhelmingly large percentage is made up of these three classes. A like importance attaches to the fact that despite the really large number of men that suffer from neuroses—obsessional neurosis, anxiety-neurosis, hysteria, and what-not—the frequency of such disturbances is even greater amongst women. Since the various forms of neurosis must all, as we shall see, be jointly regarded as special accentuations of characterological abnormalities—for this reason they must be given some attention, however brief —the observed nexus must be accorded characterological significance.

The second group of situations decisive for character-formation is dependent not on some special set of concrete circumstances, such as numerical order in the family, but on the conduct of the people forming the personal environment, and, in the first instance, those concerned in the child's upbringing. The noteworthy factors are : unequal treat-ment of brothers and sisters (*i.e.*, favouritism or neglect, excessive severity or undue mildness or pampering) ; incon-sistencies, such as alternating severity and leniency, the result either of the teacher's lack of skill or self-confidence, or of his own moods ; and, finally, bad example on the part of the upbringer. We must also here mention the custom, which often works out unfavourably, of entrusting the elder children with the upbringing of the younger, or at least delegating to them some share of the parental authority.

The neglect—or conversely the favouring—of one child in relation to its brothers and sisters is harmful to the favoured as well as to the neglected child. Such a situation—especially the favouritism of one child—need not of necessity arise out of any fundamental dislike of the other children, although this occurs more frequently than one imagines ; it can frequently be explained intelligibly, although this does not make the practice any more reasonable. The child may be a constant source of sorrow and anxiety to his parents on account of weakliness ; in such a case he is, in many respects, very much in the same position as the youngest child.

A similar influence is clearly exerted by sociological situa-tions that affect the child's position adversely. There are orphans who feel their state, and the disadvantages entailed by it, from an early age ; there are step-children who, even if they enjoy every possible kindness on the part of the step-parents, are made to suffer on becoming aware of their special position through the unguarded talk of others, the remarks of their schoolfellows, or their own reading ; there are children whose oppressive poverty is brought home to them by comparison with the better lot of their more fortunately situated contemporaries.

The characterological abnormalities so often shown by illegitimate children, and many of the so-called " weaknesses " of childhood—such as bed-wetting—are not congenital or inherited, but are determined by environmental factors, defective education and, above all, by the realization, often only too soon acquired, of being unwanted by the mother. Also, children born before marriage are often, even in spite of the most conscientious efforts of the parents, worse situated than children born in wedlock. The same also applies to children who owe their existence to a breach of the mother's marriage vows—a subject that has been sufficiently well dealt with in novels and fiction of every kind.

The children of divorced parents are equally endangered. Often, when both parties are equally to blame, or are divorced by amicable agreement, there is a stipulation that the children shall share their time with each of the parents in turn. As divorced parents are unlikely, save in the most exceptional circumstances, to seek to bring the same set of influences to bear on their children, such children are the victims of antagonistically opposed methods of treatment. In their bewilderment, their sense of insecurity increases, and they easily develop either a shallow opportunism or the ability to wear a mask in the presence of the parent for whom they have the lesser regard, or for whom they entertain feelings of strong prejudice with all the attendant consequences.

Of quite special importance is the question of severity and leniency in education ; in view of its directly practical bearing, it requires to be somewhat more fully discussed.

9. SEVERITY, AUTHORITY, PUNISHMENT AND " SPOILING "

The application of severe educational methods combined with punishments is commonly justified by maintaining that the child must learn submission from an early age, that a proper respect for authority, especially that of the parents, must be inculcated, and that the bad disposition and inclinations inherent in the child must be met by firm repression. All this is a mixture of right and wrong, if these principles are understood in the commonly accepted sense. It frequently happens that advocates of severity and harsh punishments in the upbringing of children find their justification in biblical admonitions, which are especially to be found in the Old Testament. If it is proposed to base one's educational methods on such dicta, there are two quotations from the writings of St. Paul which should not be forgotten : " The members of the Church "—and every child is just as much a member of the mystical body of Christ as the adults— " ought to subject themselves one to another " (*Eph.* v. 21). " Fathers, provoke not your children, that they be not discouraged " (*Col.* iii. 21). The first exhortation of the Apostle clearly teaches us to remember the respect due to the child as a person ; in the second, we are warned that bounds must be set to strictness, or the child will run the danger of being robbed of his courage. It is in no way contrary to the spirit of religious and moral education, even the Catholic spirit—it is indeed entirely in accordance with that spirit—to emphasize the grave dangers and disastrous consequences of excessive strictness in the upbringing of children. Severity and lack of sense can permanently destroy a man's ability to fight the battle of life ; people emerge from such an upbringing as moral cripples. Anyone who is made daily aware of these facts will realize their importance, and will agree that no remarks will appear too strong nor any demand too energetically urged where the remedy of these errors is concerned.

As a preliminary, we must meet an objection that is always raised when anyone dares to criticize the principle of severity in education. It is customary to point to some distinguished person or other, preferably from a bygone age, who after an extremely strict education became a moral paragon. Also, teachers frequently assert with pride that by great severity they have succeeded in rooting out some " evil tendency " in a pupil. On this point several things may be noted. First, though a pupil, on going out into life, may leave the hands of the educational " powers " as a seeming incorporation of the educational ideal, what is decisive is his later conduct of his active life, in his profession and in his marriage. Of this the teachers know extremely little, partly because the pupils disappear from their ken, and partly because they do not live to see the catastrophe, which often takes place relatively late. Secondly, it is frequently doubtful whether the pupil's conduct—the sort of conduct that is striven after and ultimately attained by such educational methods—is genuine ; often it is a mere pretence, adopted for reasons of opportunism, fear, weakness and the like ; the young person may come to believe in the genuineness of his attitude, but sooner or later the mask is torn from his face by the realities of life. Thirdly, the citation of isolated cases is inconclusive here as elsewhere. Nothing warrants the conclusion that the person in question became what he was *because* of his education ; it may well be that he developed favourably *in spite of* it. To answer such questions, a far more thorough knowledge of all the circumstances involved is required than is usually available. Fourthly, it is very weak to support the argument by adducing the educational principles of bygone centuries and their favourable results. We must not forget that the ultimate purpose of all education —the adjustment of subjective estimates of values to actual objective values—remains unchanged by times and places ; but the forms in which and the means by which this end can be obtained depend on the general level of civilization. Examples offered by the lives of the saints confirm this. The saintly life, as an ideal goal, is unchangeable and completely summed up in terms of itself ; but compare the style of life, if one may use that term, of a St. Simeon Stylites, a St. Benedict, a St. Francis of Assisi, and a St. Ignatius Loyola one with the other, and, as a group, with that of St. Clement Maria Hofbauer ; or—which is perhaps more striking, since they were both members of the same Order—compare the style of life of St. Teresa of Jesus with that of the " little " St. Theresa of the Child Jesus. It must be noted that we are not dealing here with individual characterological differences —at least only to a small extent—for all these saints are in some way or other typical products of their age and civilization.

When we speak of the evil results of excessive severity, we have in mind not only those extreme cases in which the power to punish is exercised with a harshness bordering on brutality. There is a detestable kind of severity which yet eschews corporal punishment, or at least all corporal punishment of a harsh kind. As often as not *the fundamental spirit of severity is primarily an exaggeration of the distance*—in itself natural and inevitable—*between the child and the parent*, or anyone *in loco parentis*, and *secondly, a lack of regard for the individual nature of the child*. Such an attitude in education arises, in my opinion, out of a mistaken conception—though the mistake is made entirely in good faith—of the nature and meaning of authority, a concept that must once and for all be clearly grasped and stripped of factors accidentally imposed on it in the course of history.

The word "authority" is derived from *auctor*, which is itself derived from *augere*, meaning to "increase" or "enlarge." *Auctor rei publicae,* "an enlarger of the State," has at all times been a ruler's title of honour. It is of the nature of authority that it exists for the sake of those over whom it is set, and not for its own sake. The purest conception is to be found in the title borne by all the successors of St. Peter since Innocent III : *Servus servorum Dei,* "Servant of the servants of God." When authority makes itself absolute and rules for its own sake, it degenerates into tyranny and incurs that tragic guilt and destiny which, as history teaches us, is the lot of all tyranny. The position of authority seems inconsistent, or if one prefers it, paradoxical, for the ruling over others and the serving of them at the same time seem mutually exclusive. Such antitheses can be reconciled only on a plane higher than that on which they first become directly visible ; and the paradox of authority solves itself when viewed from a higher standpoint. To make it clear, an analogy—of the conception *opus operatum*—is useful. As is well known, this principle lays down that the efficacy of a sacrament does not depend on the person of the minister ; that is, it is not an *opus operantis*, but is determined solely by the nature of the completed sacramental action, as *opus operatum*. The rôle of authority is to be understood in the same way. It is not bound up with the person who exercises it, but with the task imposed upon him. The military salute is not accorded to the person of General X., but to his rank ; the obeisance is not to the ruler, but to the "throne" or "crown" ; and so forth. Clearly there is a fundamental moral obligation for the person to be worthy of his position, and grave guilt is incurred when this is ignored ; but the value of the position is not contained in its holder. A position that by its nature involves authority creates a series of heavy responsibilities for the man who holds it, amongst the most important of which is the recognition that all the privileges and powers are invested in his position and not in his person. No less important is it that he remain always conscious of the danger and likelihood of his abusing his position either through inefficiency or by diverting his rights and powers to his personal ends. Moreover, it must never be forgotten that the authority belonging to a position is self-limited. The limits are of various kinds : in part they are imposed by the definite natural rights of the " subjects " or " inferiors " ; in part also by other factors, the chief of which is time.

Authority can rightly claim jurisdiction in certain matters for those placed under it, but only for as long as the latter are not in possession of or have not yet developed the ability to decide for themselves.[1] Only in the case where years of discretion can never be reached is authority unlimited in time. Consequently, a man never outgrows the authority of the Church, which with the authority of the ever-living Christ proclaims those truths and laws which man as such and unaided cannot perceive. Further, the establishment of a certain set of circumstances can justify the abolition of a certain kind of authority. The Roman consul and dictator, Lucius Cornelius Sulla, vacated his almost omnipotent position on the re-establishment of tranquillity in Rome and the revival of the constitution. Few in history have done as he did ; fewer still in the little circle of their own jurisdiction and authority. The unwillingness to relinquish a power over others that external circumstances no longer justify, on account of the subjective pleasure [2] associated with pomp and

---

[1] " The children stand," says St. Thomas, " under the care of the parents until they have the use of free will." (Sum. Theol., II–II, q. 10, a. 12).

[2] " Whence come the evils in thy monastery," writes St. Gregory to an abbot, " save that thou hast too great a love of power ? " (Cited by Cl. Aquaviva, S. J., Industriæ ad curandos animæ morbos, Rome, 1615).

power, is the more reprehensible in that others are made to suffer for an individual's sinful pride.

That authority must be, is an intuitive belief, somehow deeply rooted in human nature, in the truth that " anarchical " forms of communal existence are neither practically attainable nor theoretically unassailable ; but this intuitive belief is from the beginning no more explicit and vivid than any other. It must first be developed, elaborated and vitalized, if the acceptance of authority—and this ultimately involves recognition of the hierarchical system—is to be genuine, and not merely externally imposed and hence incapable of resisting the buffets of reality. While a person is still in a state of innocence and freedom from responsibility, and naively a law unto himself, it is a mistake to imagine that the brutal imposition of authority is the best method of inculcating a respect for authority in general and that of the parent or teacher in particular. Authority must be constructively built up in the childish soul, not imposed upon it ; and love is its only possible architect. Only when it is sustained by love does it become authority in the real sense ; only then can it look to the love of God as its foundation. The authority that exists only for its own sake, and serves only for the glorification—a term that, rightly understood, is sufficiently indicative—of the individual wielding the authority, derives from the devil ; Satan it was who spoke the fateful " *Non serviam* " and scornfully promised our first parents " *Eritis sicut dii.*"

Now, *excessive severity almost always originates in a false idea of authority*. Men may believe honestly enough that they exercise severity only for the good of its victim, yet we find on close examination that their conduct results from an over-estimation of their individual ego, which, in this case, as always, brings forth evil fruit.

The great pedagogues have never ignored the fact that

severity is neither the primary nor the perfect educational method ; so that we often receive the impression that severity is only a means imposed by pedagogical incompetence. The excessive stressing of authority arises from weakness. The leader who is really sure of his position does not need to make violent demonstrations of his authority ; that is but weakness masquerading as strength.

Pronouncements against severity in upbringing are to be found in the works of the most various writers, in St. Marie Madeleine Barat no less than in Don Bosco. The following instruction was given by a representative educationalist to the Sisters and teachers of the house she directed : " One must not be overbearing with the children . . . one must never be harsh with them, and must treat them with as little severity as possible. If it is necessary to correct them, it should be done in love and kindness, since our Lord never treats us with harshness. We must strive to follow the example of our holy Founder, and win over these little ones by humility and gentleness. . . . If we went about our office as handmaidens of the Lord, we should receive the divine light and grace to speak and act aright on behalf of the children entrusted to us by Him." These words were spoken by Blessed Marie de Sales Chapuis of the Order of the Visitation, who at the beginning of the nineteenth century worked with great success in many of the schools and convents of her Order.

Unwarranted and exaggerated authority (arising out of a misconception of its nature), like immoderate or wrongly applied severity, as we have already said, results in an increase of the child's sense of insecurity, enlarges the gulf between him and the adult, and diminishes the sense of his own value. The child sees an enormous gulf between adults and himself, whilst somehow guessing and frequently hearing that he too will one day grow up. " Wait until you are big " is a phrase that is used equally as a promise and as a warning ; a promise, because it sets before him knowledge, achievement and pleasure ; a warning when it is intended to indicate the damage he is doing to his life in the future by the present sins of commission and omission. The adults, the parents, seem to the little child to be crowned with a nimbus of omnipotence and omniscience, so that he is inclined to doubt the possibility on his part of ever attaining such heights. One would do well, therefore, at the earliest possible moment, to point out that the omnipotence and so forth are not very far-reaching, and to seek above all to eradicate the naive opinion that restrictions imposed upon volition apply only to children. Children are disposed to idealize ; if they once discover the striking contrast between the idealized picture of their parents and their parents as they really are, it may well happen that both the ideal and the parents will cease to be of any account in the child's mind.

It is not wholly true that severity is by itself responsible for a widening of the gulf and a deadening of legitimate self-esteem. They are just as much a consequence of a similar disposition in the child. Here, as elsewhere, a vicious circle develops. Anyone who imagines himself to be very much superior to the child, who is pictured as a still incomplete human being, fondly contrasts his own wealth of experience with the child's inexperience ; he is also inclined to exaggerate his own size, importance and value— largely owing to his own insecurity—and to depreciate others, among them the little child ; he is also therefore unwilling to accept the latter's natural claim—to say nothing of his supernatural claim—to recognition of his person and his dignity. Such a person—and teachers are especially liable to belong to this group—is necessarily compelled to adopt an attitude of severity in education, because he puts a distance between himself and his pupil, and severity is the only available means, once one is thus " working at a distance."

Severity may show itself in various forms, positively as punishment or a general attitude of disapproval, negatively as a withdrawal of praise and a lack of tenderness.

(i.) *Punishment.*—The essential connection between wrongdoing and punishment is directly apparent even to the small child. There could be no greater mistake than to dispense with punishment in a child's upbringing. For the receipt of punishment is most closely interwoven with the process of contrition, the recognition of wrongdoing and the resolution to avoid it in future. There has never been an age or a civilization in which the concept of atonement was lacking. We are unable here to start a psychological discussion of conscience, penitence, atonement, and the remission of guilt by punishment ; and even later, when we come to deal with conscience, we shall have to refrain from an exhaustive examination of these problems. In order that punishment may fulfil its natural function, a function in full accord with the whole organization of moral consciousness, namely, that of being a factor in moral progress—the dialectic of guilt and contrition, the intolerable strain of which is ended by an act of penance—certain conditions are necessary. These seem so obvious that their exposition is often met with impatience. Yet breaches of these conditions by those charged with the upbringing of children are so extremely common that it is far from useless to call attention to them.

Punishment must be just and proportionate. Everyone knows this ; but what is overlooked is that this rightfulness and propriety *must be understood from the standpoint of the child*, not from that of the adult. In detail this means that above all things there must be a present *consciousness of subjective guilt*. In education, punishment must not be inflicted in accordance with a systematized penal code or set of regulations. Where these apply, it is a principle that ignorance of the law is no excuse. In education the theological conception of sin must be taken as the example. Just as only the *peccatum formale*, the act done with the knowledge of its sinfulness, and not the *peccatum solum materiale*, the act committed in ignorance, is imputed to man as an offence against God, so in relation to children—the relation is obviously analogous of that of God to us, to whom " he gave power to become the children of God "—there is no room for any other conception of guilt. It is therefore the bounden duty of the parent or teacher to make absolutely sure of the presence or absence of this subjective factor, guilt. If a child does something wrong for the first time, it is entirely mistaken, and often disastrously so, to punish him summarily, merely because *materialiter* a wrong act has been committed ; one must first of all be satisfied that the child was conscious of wrongdoing. In the alternative case, instruction should take the place of punishment.

Further, the idea, borrowed from legal procedure, that the punishment should be quantitatively regulated in relation to the harm done, is entirely erroneous. It is a quite natural reaction to punish a child more severely for breaking a fine porcelain plate than for breaking a common earthenware one. How can a child know the difference between the two acts or between the values of the two articles ? The same applies to modes of behaviour that are not so easily comparable. Above all, the child does not understand how behaviour that, if not actually permitted, is at least tolerated in the home circle, is regarded as " naughtiness " when strangers are present. The possibility of the standards of right and wrong varying to suit the social situation is too subtle for the child's understanding.

A child's experience is neither very extensive nor very

complex ; this fact must not be lost sight of in the application of punishment. All observers who have made a special study of the psychology of children are agreed that the child lives chiefly in the present. The manner in which children experience time is different from that of adults, probably because of their undeveloped or too often disappointed faith in " the regularity of the world." Broadly speaking, it can be said that the formula corresponding to the childish conception is this : a single act of wrongdoing = a single act of punishment. Children are completely unable to understand a single transgression being atoned for by a punishment lasting for days and weeks.

But *it is most important of all that the punishment*, generally speaking and in each particular case, *shall be made intelligible to children*. If this be neglected, three serious consequences can result, which unfortunately are met with only too often. The child loses more or less completely that understanding of punishment and its necessity which, as we have said, he originally possessed ; he loses faith in the justice of the parent or teacher, and hence takes refuge in deceit—almost all conscious lying originates in fear of punishment. Further, there is a general loss of confidence, which increases the distance between the child and the adult to an unhealthy extent ; by this endless obstacles are erected in the way of education—especially in the critical years of puberty—and the sense of security of the growing man is shaken to an extent that is perhaps irreparable.

Further, *the punishment* must be recognizable *as a demonstration of confidence*. This at first sight appears paradoxical, but is in reality a truism, and one that is frequently forgotten. We have previously pointed out that no one would punish or admonish, if he did not believe that the person concerned was capable of improvement ; in other words, he gives expression to the conviction that the person is, in his inner and real nature, better than he appears from his action.

I know that I am in conflict with current opinion when I infer from the foregoing that *all humiliating punishments are reprehensible*. It may well be that in certain cases, humiliation acts as an effective deterrent ; but in many instances, in addition to the desired result, the consequence is an entirely undesirable undermining or destruction of self-respect. This leads us naturally to the second aspect of the practice of severity.

(ii.) *The attitude of general disapproval.*—This is as likely as not to hinder the development of that healthy self-respect which forms the basis of all real efficiency in life. If a constant mistrust supplants that confidence which the child unreflectively expects as a matter of course, then in his world of chaos the little soul, robbed of his sense of security, fails to acquire any feeling of his own value, his own vocation and his own ability to achieve anything. The knowledge of counting for something with his parents and teachers, the knowledge that they believe in him and his worth, is a vital necessity for the child, whatever his age.

The mistrust in children that so often lies like a maggot in the minds of adults, definitely derives from a quite un-Catholic belief in the "inherent wickedness" of man. This belief is altogether alien to the Catholic view of life and the universe ; it springs from a mode of thought that knows nothing of " the miraculous restoration of the dignity of human nature." and is unwilling to recognize the transforming power of grace. Whoever believes, in the Catholic sense, that the baptismal grace and the kinship with God given us thereby not only " cover " but in virtue of Christ's atonement truly remove all trace of original sin, cannot and may not accept this heretical doctrine of inherent wickedness. And where shall this miraculously restored human nature, where shall its dignity, be more perfectly encountered than in the little child, who as yet has not had occasion to incur the loss of his baptismal grace, and imperil his soul by mortal sin ?

A true understanding of the natural and supernatural conditions in which man moves and lives and has his being should incline us to repose more trust in children than in adults.

This *trust in children* is the only means that enables the parent or teacher to realize when he is in the wrong, as frequently happens. But vanity, the assertion of one's dignity, a belief in one's infallibility, the determination, arising from a lack of self-confidence, not to step off one's pedestal, and the justification of one's actions by the assertion of the child's innate wickedness : all these things give rise to distrust, dislike, reserve, obstinacy and lying in the child, who knows perfectly well when he is in the right and when he is in the wrong.

(iii.) *The withholding of praise.*—Corresponding to the attitude of general disapproval, the parent or teacher may refrain from according due praise and recognition ; this negative attitude is even more keenly felt by the child than the more positive disapprobation. In order to foster the self-respect of the small growing human, it is not sufficient to refrain from persistent nagging or the even more reprehensible general antagonism ; the child's self-respect, which, as we have seen, is constantly imperilled by general situational factors, must be positively promoted and nourished by recognition whenever it is justified.

Against this plea for the child's due of praise and recognition, it is frequently argued that it encourages self-satisfaction, conceit, vanity and the like. But the risks of such undesirable consequences of sensible, well-justified recognition are usually grossly exaggerated ; and they are negligible as compared to the dangers of the opposite attitude. It is true that children and young people are inclined to think too highly of themselves, but in normal development—the conditions of which we still have to learn, for up to now we have only considered the negative, destructive, as opposed to the positive, constructive factors— this tendency is balanced by being brought up against the realities of life. *Der Most, der sich absurd gebärdet, giebt doch zum Schluss 'nen Wein :* " Sweet, fizzy must settles down into a drinkable vintage in the course of time." Paradoxical as it may seem at first, conceit, vanity and similar qualities arise much more readily from a lack of recognition than from its excess.

(iv.) *Tenderness and affection.*—It is necessary to distinguish between the affection shown to the child and that received by us ; both are important, the latter perhaps even more so than the former. The child expects affection, for in the absence of achievements of his own to which he can point, he relies on that knowledge of being loved and treasured for his own sake, in order to be able to sustain his own sense of personal value, which is always a matter of inward doubt. That is why, to repeat ourselves briefly, praise is of such importance, for it makes the child conscious of having somehow accomplished something, even though the sphere of his accomplishment is restricted. The affection that the child experiences is to him the symbol and guarantee of that safety which he needs in the face of the difficulties of life.

It is quite mistaken to suppose that in the affection shown to children there is the somewhat alarming risk of a premature awakening of sexuality. If anything, it is the opposite attitude that involves that risk, because there is a close and physiologically determined connection between fear and sexual excitement. Everyday experience and scientific research show that the emotion of fear is associated with a contraction of the peripheral blood-vessels—skin and muscles—and a congestion of blood in the internal organs, especially in those of the abdominal cavity. As the physiological basis of sexual excitement is a strong determination of blood to and through the organs concerned, and as the vascular supply of the genital organs is from the abdomen and pelvis, the connection between fear and sexual excitement is physiologically intelligible. In fact, it is reported with extraordinary frequency that sexual excitement occurs for the first time in situations coloured by fear—anticipation of punishment, examinations, danger, and so on. The question whether there exists an inner (psychological) connection between sexual affect proper and anxiety will not be further investigated here. It is only necessary to remark that the idea formerly put forward by the psychoanalysts, that anxiety is somehow brought about by a transformation of sexual excitement—that it is, in fact, a product of the *libido*— has been recently discarded by the author of the theory.

We have implied above that the greater importance attaches to the rejection of those demonstrations of affection which the child feels to be the natural and necessary approach to adults. It is not only that it is thoroughly harmful to repress the obvious expression of a tendency which is of positive value—" out of the fullness of the heart the mouth speaketh "—but a positive wrong is thereby done to the child, the effects of which are frequently permanent. For the young child—and it is to him that our observations chiefly apply—cannot, as we have said, point to any achievement ; he has no possessions, he can give nothing save his naive and trusting love. The rejection of this spontaneous and therefore so much the more attractive gift, offered " *ex plenitudine cordis*," is tantamount to telling the little child that he has nothing whatsoever that he can give. We imply that he is poor, poor in the worst sense of the word ; the child is then, following the failure of his first attempt to give, to give himself, forced by his sensitive nature to the conclusion—which is not always the product of conscious thought, though its results are none the less serious—that he is nothing and of no account. He has nothing to give except himself and his love, and these are clearly valueless.

The evil consequences of such mistakes in our dealings with children can indeed in many cases be made good later ; but what can *never* be remedied is the irretrievable loss sustained by a man by reason of a misdirected childhood. The past can never be restored to a man, even though he can be taught to regard it with other eyes, and to accord it a different place and a different meaning in the whole continuum of his life.

It must, however, be noted that most people concerned with the upbringing of children fall into errors of the kind we have been considering, not because of some definite conviction that, however mistaken, can yet from the subjective point of view always be assigned some positive value, but because they entertain an insufficiently serious conception of their task and an inadequate respect for the child. Very often it is just bad temper ; still oftener, probably, the person maintains that he has something more important on hand at the moment than to attend to the child. Sometimes that is the case, but usually the matters that in the parents' imagination compel them to reject the child's affection or desire for affection are trivial and postponable till later. In the various preoccupations of housekeeping " good housewives " are especially liable to forget the claims of their children. Admittedly one reservation must be stressed. Many children—the type to which they belong will be discussed later—make use of both active and passive affection in order to tyrannize over the people in their environment, especially their parents. They express their desires in various ways the moment they see that their mother has something else to do, just as if they had deliberately said : " You are in my power, you can only work when I let you." It is easy to understand that " only " children, especially those who associate exclusively with their parents, can easily adopt such an attitude ; but other children are also guilty in this respect. This leads us on naturally to a discussion of " *spoiling*."

One preliminary observation must be made. Although spoiling is a bad preparation for the realities and responsibilities of life, and can undoubtedly sometimes lead to far-reaching and serious distortions of character, yet, generally speaking, these consequences are less serious and more easily corrected than the results of excessive severity or a loveless childhood. This can be realized without our having to adduce practical examples in confirmation. Severity breaks a man's spirit ; pampering, although it fails to train him for the difficulties of reality, gives him the impression that success is easily achieved. It is far more difficult to revive the crushed and withered self-respect than by subsequent discipline to recover the opportunities lost for the preparation for life in the years of childhood.

Mistaken attitudes in education of the kind we have been considering fall, then, into two main groups. In one group, the excessive strictness is not infrequently the result of a falsely exaggerated consciousness of or fear of responsibility, which allows of no possible slip ; another factor governing the strict attitude is an immoderate opinion of one's own importance and perfection, which is often so exaggerated as to be grotesque. Such people are unable to conceive of a proper development being possible except along exactly the same lines along which they themselves were brought up. Excessive leniency, on the other hand, has its roots in a deficient sense of responsibility, an indolence that, as we find in the case of so many nursemaids, prefers to yield rather than be disturbed by entreaties and tears—a sentimental flabbiness that masquerades as sympathy and good nature, a form of vanity that does not bel eve in the possibility of going far wrong so far as one's own children are concerned.

In extenuation of many cases of unreasonable severity or weakness, and of many other varieties of educational error, it can indeed be said that there are two powers at work to which men are delivered up. For the one—stupidity—there is hardly a possibility of remedy. Against the other—family, caste, and cultural tradition—there are indeed some remedies, but those who can apply them are as yet too few and too much lacking in influence. It is not only that " law and order are inherited like some eternal disease," but also that the mistakes made in the upbringing of the parents revenge themselves on the children. So much the greater, then, is the responsibility of those to whom the upbringing of children is entrusted.

10. THE WILL TO COMMUNITY

Before proceeding to investigate the effects of educational errors and blunders on the further development of character, we must pay some attention to that second inhibitory, and at the same time correctional, factor in human nature opposed to immoderate exercise and development of the will to power. We have termed this second primal tendency " *the will to community*."

Adler and the individual-psychologists employ the term *Gemeinschaftsgefühl*, " community-feeling " ; we do not favour this term, because we are dealing here with a direction of life that has a definite goal, and in principle, therefore, with active conduct, which, as such, must clearly be " structurally " analogous to actively adopted attitudes, and so volitional. The will to power and the " feeling or sense of power " are quite distinct ; and the sense of community or herd-feeling is, strictly speaking, different from the will to community, which we can logically place in the group of primitive tendencies. The sense of power somehow enables a man to enjoy in consciousness the attainment of the goals striven for by the will to power ; in the same way, the feeling or sense of community implies an experiencing of community attained and realized as a goal set by the will to community. This " feeling " can be more nearly described as a sense of " belonging to," " being a member of," " being at home with," one's fellow-men ; negatively, it is a feeling of strangeness, distance, or separation by an airtight compartment or glass wall, as it were, from our fellow-men. Apart from this terminological indefiniteness, which admittedly involves the risk of some confusion of ideas, the tireless insistence on the fundamental importance of the communal factor and of the corresponding development of a will directed towards the community is a service rendered by Alfred Adler and his school, which can never adequately be recognized.[1]

It would have been unnecessary to rediscover this fundamental fact and to emphasize anew its all-powerful influence on character-formation, had not the intellectual tendencies of recent decades, and even centuries, so completely estranged us from the age-old views which in the last instance depended on revelation. Just as in the abstract and philosophical

[1] The significance of this constant insistence on the necessity for communal ties—experienced and realized as such—for the mental and moral development of the individual, and for his psychic well-being, is not confined to the matters under present consideration in the text. Its recognition renders impossible the " absolutizing " and the interpretation of human nature solely in terms of the individual. Many representatives of the individual-psychology school make this idea serve as a justification for pragmatic tendencies ; this shows a grave misunderstanding, for they fail to realize that the logical consequence of their principle is the establishment of an ontology of the worlds to which man belongs and which shape him. Expressions such as " the immanent logic of human communal life" and "absolute truth," used by Adler in this connection, conflict with the pragmatism of some of his later teaching ; this fact is only noted in passing.

thought of our own day we notice more and more the re-emergence of *motifs* that were already current in the hey-day of Catholic scholastic and mediæval philosophy, but were almost entirely rejected with the advent of the Renaissance and the Age of Enlightenment, so also do we find that in the empirical and applied sciences, such as education, sociology, psychology, and the study of human nature in general, the re-awakening of old knowledge and modes of thought to a new life. This in no way detracts from the credit due to those who rediscovered this knowledge and placed it once more at our disposal. It does, however, teach us to understand the new doctrines as a partial manifestation of a great historical intellectual movement, and gives us criteria for distinguishing things of greater from those of lesser value. We cannot here attempt to sketch the main lines of this historical movement, which Joel has brilliantly described as a fivefold renaissance.[1] We need only point out that much of what today many people regard as new-fangled and revolutionary in reality rests upon the firm foundations secured by the laborious mental toil of bygone generations.

To return to the subject of the will to community : we regard it, like the will to power, as a primal tendency of human nature ; but here, in contrast to the case of the latter, it is not possible to point to a biological analogy applying to the whole living order of creation, as provided by the tendency towards self-preservation. Of course, there are certain well-known forms of association among animals—state-forming insects, gregarious animals—but these are only isolated occurrences. One would therefore have to fall back on the analogy of a community of cells, a " cell-state "—a procedure, which, in my opinion, would be altogether reckless and irrelevant—and even then there remains the fact that there are unicellular organisms that also display a

[1] *Kantstudien*, 1928,

tendency to self-preservation. We must therefore assume that socialization or the tendency to it is not only a fundamental feature of human nature, but peculiar to it ; man not only exhibits a will to community, but is distinguished by that will. Aristotle thought that he could not describe man better than as ζῶον πολιτικόν, a " political animal," a term taken over by scholastic philosophy and rendered as *ens sociale*, or better still, *sociabile*, that is, " capable of forming a community, and regulating existence in accordance with it." [1]

All restriction, crippling, and check to the development of this primal tendency limits man, as we shall show, in the expression of the most representative traits of his character ; it renders his participation in the conditions governing natural and supernatural life difficult or even impossible, to a large extent robbing him of his ability to discharge his tasks in either respect. " It is not good for man to be alone " : the creation of woman was coincidently the foundation of the community, the first and original form of which was the family.

As the moral goal of the will to power, when rightly directed, is self-preservation, the development of the sense of personal value, and the complete realization of himself by the individual, so the moral goal of the will to community is love, love of one's neighbour and every other kind of love ; for, without presupposing this, love, sacrifice, and openheartedness cannot exist. The close reciprocal interconnection and interaction of these two primal or fundamental tendencies of human nature are obvious. Neither can develop properly independently of the other. If a man were

---

[1] It might be pointed out, if space and strict relevance allowed, that the faculty of speech and its extreme importance for the attainment of psychical maturity render relations with one's fellow-men inevitable. (Cf. P. Honigswald, *Grundlagen der Denkpsychologie*, Leipzig, 1925.) Corresponding to this idea, there is a second classification applied to man by the ancient philosophers : ζῶον λόγον ἔχον.

wholly absorbed into the community he would lose himself, his individual value and his identity ; finally, he would no longer be able to expend himself for the community, because in fact he would cease to exist. In thus losing his value as an individual, he would become incapable of loving his neighbour : for " thou shalt love thy neighbour as thyself." On the other hand, equally, a movement of the will to power in the direction of moral and cultural goals is rendered impossible—likewise any possible achievement—unless a person's will to community is given full scope.

One observation of a general nature must be here interpolated. The above-mentioned interdependence of these two " wills," all the implications of which cannot be pursued in this place, demonstrates the error of the view that man exists and subsists in virtue of these two, or some other, tendencies alone—to say nothing of " impulses." Man is not compounded of " parts," although he expresses himself on various levels and manifests various aspects. Such " watertight-compartmenting " and views that maintain that man is a summation of his parts result from limited and discursive thinking and from the practical necessity of considering the aspects of man one by one and one after the other. In reality the human person is a collocation of contradictory factors and antagonistic forces under great tension from all sides. That which in the Divine Being, God's *ipsum esse*, may be regarded as a tensionless unity, appears in His creation man, as a unity of tensions. Man lives only in, and in virtue of, this field of tension. Guardini[1] states that a one-sided concentration on, or preoccupation with, one of these opposed factors or forces to the exclusion of the others is incompatible with life. " Unity of tensions," to borrow a phrase of E. Przywara's,[2] is in fact the essential structure of

[1] *Der Gegensatz : eine Philosophie des Lebendig-Konkreten* (Mainz, 1926).
[2] *Religionsphilosophie katholischer Theologie*, in the *Handbuch der Philosophie* (Munich, 1927).

human personal existence both in relation to its earthly and natural limitations and to its associations with the supernatural life.

It must not be supposed that we believe that man in general or any particular individual can be explained in terms of the stronger development of the will to power on the one hand or the will to community on the other. We do, however, certainly maintain that these two primal tendencies and their equilibrium or disequilibrium play a decisive rôle in character-formation ; and, further, we maintain the importance of a thorough knowledge of these factors for the theory of characterology and for its practical application as a guide to moral conduct and its maxim, character.

L. Feuerbach has written : " An entirely isolated man would perish as an undiscriminated object in the chaos of nature." This thinker, the consideration of whose other theories we must unfortunately leave aside, propounds in that statement an unconditional truth ; his remarks on the problem of the " thou " and the " I " are well worth reading even today. It is only in virtue of its relation to the " thou " that the " I " comes into being, or at least becomes conscious of itself (cf. also Fichte). At any rate, we may say that this applies to human nature in its present state, *i.e.*, since the Fall. How it was in *in statu innocentiae* we need not inquire. However, in the light of the saying quoted above, " it is not good for man to be alone," it is conceivable that in that state also a " thou " was a necessity of man's nature.

It is unnecessary to demonstrate at any length that the whole physical existence of man is bound up with that of his fellow-men. That principle applies from the moment that one can speak of a culture of any kind, however primitive, and we know of no state of mankind in which that is not the case. It is still more applicable in the case of the more advanced stages of culture. Even a Robinson Crusoe, cast

up naked on the shore of his island, would have been unable
to maintain himself had he not brought with him the knowledge he derived from others.

It is equally clear that the development of the intellect, the
acquisition of knowledge, and the understanding of how to
apply it are only rendered possible through the existence and
co-operation of one's fellow-men. The development of the
" moral personality " also only takes place through and by
means of vital contact with the " thou," a living, sentient
human being. Man takes his commandments not from himself, but out of the mouths of others ; he is only able to
recognize their cogency and observe them. (If we were to
pursue this argument still further, we should arrive at the
conclusion that a belief in the first giving of the law to men
is forced upon us quite apart from revelation. It is an
inevitable consequence of man's nature ; God, as the original
source of all morality, must have spoken and revealed Himself
to man ; and our moral nature must derive not from
the human spirit, but from Him " Who spoke by the
prophets.")

It is the will to community that makes it at all possible for
man to enter into contact with his kind, and to become
conscious of the presence of a " thou " and of its nature.
This will to community, this mutual dependence of man on
man, is so fundamental an element of human nature that it
is correct to say that man perceives his fellow-men sooner
than his own self. " The perception of self is secondary to the
perception of an ego outside the self," says M. Scheler [1]
Is not the first manifestation of spiritual life that which we
see in a baby's face—a gleam in its eyes in answer to its
mother's loving gaze, the smile in answer to the love lavished
on it ? And is it not true that a little child grasps the emotions,
moods and affects of others long before it is made reflexly

[1] *Wesen und Formen*, etc. See note 1, p. 58.

aware of its own ? If we observe carefully, we find that children guess, or in some way get to know with intuitive certainty, people's natures and dispositions—who is well and who ill disposed towards them—long before there can be any question even of the most confused thought or reasoning in such matters.

The more the will to community expands, or the more the development of the individual life perfects itself in virtue of that will—the more, that is, man feels himself to be a member of a community, which embraces him together with all other individuals—the less does he suffer under the limitations of the will to power inherent in his personal make-up, and the less will he be driven to regard as evidence of personal inefficiency or inferiority the impossibility of achieving his most cherished aims owing to force of circumstances, as, by means of his membership of the community and the living association of his kind involved in it, he becomes aware that such limitations of personal ambition are not confined to himself, but are the common lot of humanity. There is thus created in him the *psychological prerequisite for that internal attitude* which as a virtue is called *humility*. True, every virtue, like everything positive, is in some way a gift and a grace ; but " grace presupposes nature," and " grace does not dispense with nature, but completes it."

As such knowledge helps to convince man of his complete dependence on, and his obligations to, his neighbour, and of the truth that men collectively form a unity, the soil is prepared in which that virtue—the love of one's neighbour, which is imposed upon us as a duty—can flourish and reach maturity.

We shall further see how it is that the breakdown or the faulty development of the will to community renders impossible not only humility and love of one's neighbour, but also another series of dispositions, upon which the whole of morality is based. For the moment we are content with having emphasized the general importance of the theory here presented, and its special importance for the development of the religious outlook on life.

Two critical observations must be made on certain opinions that are current in individual-psychology circles. Many individual-psychologists are disposed to place man's attitude to the community and his communally directed aims —all the things summed up under the idea of the will to community—on a " utilitarian " level. If the idea of the " useful " is understood in a sufficiently wide sense, the most that can be said against the employment of the term " utilitarian " is that it is very unsuitable ; for utility is, strictly speaking, only one particular kind of value amongst other values, and can hardly be conceived of as one enjoying sovereignty over all other values. Obviously, every realization of true values proves in the long run to be " useful," but this stretching of the utilitarian point of view is illegitimate special pleading. Another objection : individual-psychologists regard the community as something ultimate and self-sufficient. No one, unless he be blind to metaphysical and ontological problems—and such blindness does not prevent those problems from existing any more than colour-blindness robs the spectrum of red, green and blue— no one, that is to say, who pays any attention to the final and supreme problems that engage human thought, can approve of this " absolutizing " of the community ; he will always be questioning the basis for the belief in it. More especially will he be unable in the last resort to grasp the fact of human solidarity in all matters affecting the common weal for good or ill, which is in some respects a consequence of the individual's subordination to the community and of its obligation to him, whereby he has his part in the communal good and shares communal guilt. Finally, he will be faced with the following decisive questions : Why is it that man, even if he is " by nature " dependent on the community, is unable without suffering ill-effects to act contrary to this natural " disposition," as he can in the case of others ; what is it that binds man to fulfil his communal obligations ? In order that this primal deep-rooted tendency, the will to community, which, as we have already seen and shall see even more clearly, is the natural antecedent to morality, may be recognized as being above all directional, the community, and also morality, must be founded on something other than the idea of service to the natural community. If this is not the case, then the whole argument moves round in a vicious circle. The supporters of this doctrine, who fancy that they can dispense with and reject its foundation by recourse to a powerful and non-naturalistic metaphysic—of the person, the *ethos*, and its justification—are also thereby involved in many inconsistencies and obscurities. One must be careful not to confuse the main content of the teaching of individual-psychology with the philosophical assumptions and conclusions of many of its adherents. Their so-called " conclusions " are, moreover, nothing of the sort ; they are merely repetitions of subjectively formed conceptions of the universe with which such investigators approach experience in a " pre-scientific " kind of way. The wish to develop a philosophy of the universe out of a single realm of facts (and these facts, too, regarded from a single standpoint), however comprehensive the facts may be, may be likened to a naive attempt to balance a pyramid on its point. A philosophy of the universe assumes a knowledge of the universe, and not only of particular aspects of human character, and of its normal and abnormal development. It is as foolish to call individual-psychology a universal philosophy as to attempt to make one out of it. A critical examination of such an attempt reveals how many assumptions of a totally different order, of which the author in question had no inkling, are involved implicitly, even if not explicitly, in the whole edifice.[1]

In order now to understand the part played by the will to community in the normal development of character—and by normal development I mean one that does not give rise to some insoluble conflict with reality, but allows of a conduct of life in harmony with the objective standards of value—we must revert to the conceptions (set out earlier, *vide* p. 93) of *compensation* and *over-compensation*. The little child finds himself, as we have shown, objectively in a position of natural subordination, which is subjectively reckoned as one of inferiority. A compensation realizable within his direct environment is only possible to a very limited extent. The attempt is seen in all those forms of behaviour in which the child aims at making himself the centre of attraction. This kind of behaviour is harmless enough within certain limits, and intelligible in the case of every child, and therefore to be tolerated up to a point. Beyond a certain point, however, and especially if the child's conduct in other respects shows signs that he is developing in a direction away from life, reality, and the community, such " showing-off " must be regarded as a threatened anomaly of character. We shall return to this matter later.

Seeing that the actual environment gives the child so little scope in his attempts at compensation, his effort to balance his subjectively experienced inferiority is forced to take another channel, that of fantasy.

11. FANTASY AND THE NECESSITY FOR COMPENSATION

Even *play* is important in this way as imaginary compensation. Even if we admit the undoubted fact that children's play is an active expression of the tendencies directed towards " pleasure of right function," and that it is also of great

[1] Cf. my observations : *Zur Frage nach einer Psychopathologie der Weltanschauungen*, in the *Zeitschr. für die ges. Neurol. und Psychol.*, Bd. 100 (1926).

importance as a gradual preparation for the serious activities of life, it must also be acknowledged that most games represent an imaginary compensation for the child's position ; for the *motif* of almost all games is " being grown-up." Whether the girl plays mother to her dolls, or the boy plays the part of an engine-driver or chauffeur, or children play at being shopkeepers, teachers, Indians, bandits or anything else, in the game they are always grown-ups. Further, when a number of them play at school together, they consent to take the part of school-children only because, in consequence of their generally very democratic relations amongst themselves, each in turn plays the part of the teacher.

This feature is even more apparent in the fantasies or dreams of children. Very frequently their content may be described in the words in which a twelve-year-old girl described her own dreams collectively : " It always comes to the same thing, that I am somebody very important."

We have now to inquire into the meaning of *fantasy* in general—so far, that is, as it is not a preparation for real activities, a consideration that we shall waive for the moment. Obviously, as has often been pointed out, fantasy broadly speaking provides an imaginary world for the day-dreamer, in which all those factors which trouble him in the world of reality are either eliminated or converted into their opposites ; where he fails in actuality, he triumphs in imagination ; the poor man is rich ; the prisoner is free ; the oppressed rules ; the unsuccessful man is envied ; and so on. Apart from this, the fantasy or day-dream has one noteworthy peculiarity. As this imaginary world exists only at the pleasure of the dreamer, and the events of that world are what he chooses to make them, he is in truth the creator, protector, and law-giver of that world. Man's helplessness and impotence are transformed into unlimited power ; the restrictions to creative achievement give way to actual omnipotence.

As with adults, the only realm in which all their unsatisfied desires for power, authority and greatness can be satisfied—artificial as that satisfaction admittedly is—is that of fantasy, so we find the same thing applying to children and young people. Oppressed and weighed down by their inferiority or their belief in it, they take refuge in fantasy, which, in addition to correcting the unsatisfactory realities of the moment and providing a better world in their place, also enables them to picture a happier future in the stead of the present that has proved so incomplete. In the case of the child, fantasy and reality are indeed not so very much divorced ; children try to " realize " many " fantastic " ideas and dreams. Only as they become increasingly conscious of the impossibility of giving their wishes and dreams substance in the world surrounding them do they defer their fulfilment to the future, a future that is to provide complete compensation for all the shortcomings of the present. These fantasies of the future can to a certain extent be summed up thus : " You wait till my day comes ; then you will see." This explains much of the excessive exuberance and lack of restraint that often characterizes the conduct of young people.

Now, it is not as a rule natural to man to be content with a simple correction of the conditions of life that weigh on him so heavily ; he covets something further ; he strives not for mere compensation, but for over-compensation. Simple compensation has its place only in ideology, on the programme, so to speak ; the secret wishes of men, revealed by their conduct, cover totally different desires. A social-revolutionary party may inscribe on its banners " Equality for the Under-dog," or " Justice " ; by its actions it shows that revenge is what it desires. This was the case with the Servile Wars of ancient Rome, with the great Revolution of 1789, and with many other revolutionary movements. The same applies in the lives of individual adults and of children. Not only to be grown up, but to be great grown-ups, is the content of the childish imagination. We shall see that this mechanism of over-compensation in the sphere of unreality, which plunges a man in the depths in direct proportion to the height of his aims for the future, plays a decisive rôle in abnormal development.

If the child experiences situations that he interprets in terms of prejudice, oppression and inferiority, the mechanism of over-compensation proportionately raises his future aims to inordinate heights—but these aims are hardly ever confided to adults by children and young people. The formula is : " The lower to-day, the higher later on, when my day comes."

" Thoughts dwell easily in harmony together, but facts press hardly one against the other." The laws of reality are stronger than the desires of man. It is reality that decides whether the goals a man sets before himself are attainable ; it determines the pace at which he may advance, and prescribes the limits beyond which he may not step. The golden apples do not drop into our idly outstretched hands ; we must struggle for the gifts that life seems to dangle before our gaze. We must wrest from life the fulfilment of its promises.

It is not that it is unlawful to wish, and to seek to realize our wishes. What is unlawful is to demand, which can only lead to conflict and finally to disaster. A *demand* differs from a wish in that it strikes a bargain, so to speak, in payment for achievement. It takes the following form : " If I cannot obtain this one thing, I will not do what is bidden, or I will do what is forbidden." It is, however, required of man that he freely decide to do the right and the good because it *is* right and good, indifferent whether wish-fulfilment is involved.

As with everything else, this attitude must be acquired ; it does indeed lie latent in man, but needs to be given actuality. It is more in accordance with the plain nature of man—his more superficial nature, so to speak—to regard his own wishes as directional even in world affairs occurring outside the sphere of his personal influence. That this is so is demonstrated by a kind of reaction that is widely spread, although very various in its forms : " being disappointed." *Disappointment* simply means surprise, affliction and anger because the world of men and things ventures to be and to behave otherwise than the man concerned had imagined. Behind disappointment there lies a demand, which on formulation admittedly seems unreasonable, but springs from secret tendencies, especially from an inadequately corrected will to power. This demand is, " If things were as they should be, then the world would have to obey my thoughts and wishes " ; in its extreme form it is simply, " I must be omnipotent " : the words of deceit and temptation of the serpent of old sound anew.

Now, in order that man may win his way through and raise himself up to this attitude of subordination to the laws of reality governing natural and supernatural life, he must take his place in the community and bring a good will with him. Only in living connection with others will he find succour in his isolation and abandonment in this great and terrible world ; only in the consciousness of being one amongst others can he free himself from the oppression created by his individual impotence, which impedes his will to self-assertion, and so become capable of a voluntary subordination to that which simply is and prevails. Centred in the life of the community and at one with it, man finds himself for the first time in a position to readjust, in accordance with the dictates of reality, the fantasies and aims that have grown up with him from his childhood. It is only when man recognizes such-and-such a situation, which gives rise to a feeling of inferiority, as something that does not arise out of his own personal nature or guilt but is part of the very nature of man, that he can preserve his own sense of personal value and at the same time eschew " hope's mirage-pictures, painted on grey and distant mists," and that he can cease to strive to be a god, to bid " the clouds and winds to sport with him." Then only can he find content within his " mortal coils " ; then Goethe's words come true :

> " If he is standing
> Sturdily, steadfast
> On the years-defying
> Firmness of earth,
> He stretches not upwards
> Himself but to liken
> With the great oak-tree
> Or tendrillar wine-stock."

We repeat that from the foregoing we can deduce the importance for the development of the supernatural in man of a proper relation to the community ; for if his inward attitude must be one of humility as a psychological ante-cedent of the will to community, clearly a right attitude towards the supernatural also demands the same premises.

While we propose to devote attention in the subsequent chapters of this work to particular varieties of character-development, we must here consider the problem of how the will to community can in the child be—not indeed awakened, for as a primal tendency it is already there—but fostered and developed ; and what are the endogenous or exogenous factors that disturb or impede its development.

The community as an existent factor cannot be eliminated from human life. No man can secede from the community, since his very nature binds him to it, as we have already said. Even the " unsocial " man remains under an obliga-tion to the community. Only the man who is totally indifferent to the community can be regarded as free from such obligation ; and such a man does not exist. So long as a man denies the legitimacy of the claims upon him of something other than himself, and his consequent obligations either by word or deed, he has actually established relations with that something ; the very fact of a passionate denial of anything is a recognition of its existence. Hate is a tie, just as love is ; only indifference can dissolve the bonds. Hate can always change into love ; but love seldom springs from dull indifference. " I would thou wert cold, or hot. But because thou art lukewarm, and neither cold nor hot, I will begin to vomit thee out of my mouth." It is not the business of education to enrol man as a member of the community ; he is already a life-member from the moment of his birth. It *is* its task to cause him to realize this membership through his own experience, and to make his subjective acceptance of this objective fact possible. In order that an active membership with the community and participation in its life may be made possible for the growing man, it must somehow be brought home to him. He must experience it, learn to know it, not as one learns to know a scientific fact, but in the way the whole reality is brought near to and made one with the child—by living contact with it. To this extent, the will to community is in some way something peripheral and secondary—or, if one likes, antagonistic—to the will to power and the tendency to self-assertion, because the latter is more directly bound up with the individual person ; and to this extent, then, the will to community requires more direct and positive fostering, whereas in the case of the will to power, all that is necessary is, on the one hand, the prevention of anomalies and, on the other, the avoidance of its destruction.

From the historical point of view, the essential and primal communal formation is the family. No other educational environment, however skilfully constructed, can equal a rightly directed family upbringing in effectiveness. Unfortunately, it is only too often directed along the wrong lines. Consequently it is frequently desirable to remove children from their home environment ; but it must always be borne in mind that all institutional upbringing is in itself only a makeshift.

12. EDUCATING THE WILL TO COMMUNITY

It must be understood that in this chapter we are dealing primarily with the small child. It must be strongly emphasized that the very early years of life preceding the school age are the most decisive for a man's development, his behaviour in after-life, and the moulding of his character.[1] The study of both normal and abnormal psychology confirms this beyond a shadow of doubt. On persons concerned with the upbringing of children during their first six years of life devolves the greatest—probably the entire—responsibility for their spiritual and moral development. School, later life, and the efforts of priests and physicians can do much by way of improvement ; but the product that has to be improved comes from the hands of those who had the fashioning of it up to school age. It is true that in the later years an unconscionable amount of harm can be done, and consequently the responsibility of teachers is no small one ; but the developmental foundations are laid in the years of early childhood, which as a rule are spent in the home circle.

There, in his own family, the little child must acquire his communal experience. The bond of community is love ; only where that prevails can community exist ; it is only in an atmosphere of love that the child can experience community.

---

[1] The emphasis laid upon this point by Freud redounds to his enduring credit ; although in my opinion the conclusions drawn by him from his observations are largely erroneous.

Community is the living relationship of others to the
" thou." The " thou " is represented in four forms, and
there are four variants of this relation : parents and children,
husband and wife, the individual and his fellow-men, myself
and God. In all four dimensions, so to speak, the communal
life within the family must be ordered according to objective
principles, if the child's will to community is to develop
along normal lines.

We have already seen that mutual confidence must govern
the relations between children and parents ; and this may
be shattered by the adults' show of infallibility, their vanity,
their domineering, and their exaggerated importance.
Admittedly parenthood confers a certain dignity, but the
parent must show himself worthy of that dignity.

The relation between husband and wife takes the particular
form of mutual devotion. It is endangered by any idea of
prestige, by the domination of one over the other, by selfish
demands and the incorrect assumption of either party that
the other exists " for " him or her in place of the acceptance
of the truth that every marriage is a problem requiring an
ever-fresh solution.

Exaggerated reserve, self-isolation, anxious safeguarding
of one's own personal sphere, failure to appreciate the
essential and ultimate equality of all men as human beings,
above the level of which none may dare to seek to raise
himself—these are the factors that undermine the relationship of man to his fellow-men, a relationship that takes the
form of love for one's neighbour in the fullest sense. " If
thou dost not desire for the man whom thou hast never seen
the same good as for thyself, thou art utterly perverse,"
says Meister Eckhardt.

The form taken by the relation of myself to God is
humility, and it is the root and source of everything else.
It is pride that dissolves the relationship, pride which is the

original source of disturbance in the other relations of life. "Pride is the root of all diseases, because it is the root of all sins," says St. Augustine, who may be right in supposing that the effects of pride have repercussions even in the purely organic realm. As pride was the original sin, so that same pride is the final cause of all the sins of the past and the present. It is also—even though it be hidden and denied access to consciousness—the primary cause of many, and indeed probably of all, characterological anomalies and perversions. The way in which this pride, this legacy of Adam, "in whom we have all sinned," this ominous attribute of fallen human nature, operates more disturbingly in some cases than in others will be discussed later. At the moment we are primarily concerned with the development of the will to community.

Things present themselves to the person whose experience is still in an undifferentiated, naive stage in such a way as to correspond to man's original nature, enabling him to master and incorporate them ; he not only experiences things, but, so to speak, lives himself into them. Love is an obvious thing to anyone who has experienced love, and community to anyone who has had experience of community. The man who has experienced community as it should be—in accordance with the ideal of it—becomes capable of leading the communal life, and his will to community develops if his environment satisfies the four conditions formulated above.

Now, there is a series of factors that raise obstacles to active membership of the community and to the whole-hearted affirmation of that membership. It is important to know them—though it is often difficult enough to neutralize their operation.

(i.) *Weakening of the experience of personal value makes it increasingly difficult for a person to take his place in the community, every time it occurs.* We are seemingly faced with another

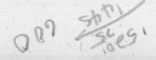

vicious circle ; only by establishing a correct relationship with the community is it possible to overcome the sense of inferiority arising out of actual and "metaphysical" loneliness and childhood conditions, and to maintain the sense of individual personal value ; whilst, on the other hand, that experience of counting for something is a necessary antecedent to "finding one's feet" in the community. This vicious circle is only apparent, and need not surprise us ; for these discrete, isolated factors and features, which we use for descriptive and classificatory purposes in relation to primal tendencies and human nature in general, are only abstractions ; in actual reality all of them—contradictory as this may appear—are different aspects of one and the same thing.

All those conditions, then, which we previously described as endangering one's experience of incorporating a value, impede one's communal progress and weaken one's will to community. The educational misconceptions and errors already listed give rise to two trains of serious consequences, which reciprocally strengthen each other. *Ergo, caveant consules.*

(ii.) The correct development of the will to community is hampered *if the communal form offered to the child is allowed to appear in an unfavourable light.* Where inconsistency prevails, where hate and enmity show their horrid forms, where tyranny and oppression rule, the genuine will to community cannot reach maturity.

(iii.) The will to community fails to develop properly even when the narrowest community—that of the family and possibly a few other people—is satisfactorily constituted if the wider community is left out of account. A deficient extension of the communal relationship can express itself in a carping, belittling or hostile representation of people outside the little home circle. One cannot expect the child to develop a genuine feeling for the community if he is constantly hearing how bad and untrustworthy all men are —the speaker, of course, always excepted—and how one must be always on one's guard against them. Such talk saps the natural courage of the child, to whom outside life in the world of men is thus made to appear as a path set amid ever-threatening dangers, which he cannot trust himself to face.

Thus we find that excessive exclusiveness is a drag on the developing feeling for the community. Most important of all, every expression of hatred towards individuals, social grades and classes, nations and races, poisons the community idea. To detest evil and to hate mankind are two totally different things. The saint detests sin, but loves the sinner.

A true sense of community enables one to see in every man without exception a brother, and an actual or potential, visible or invisible, member of the " mystical body of Christ." The true community feeling, as the Apostle knew full well, is identical with the love for one's neighbour : " He that saith he is in the light, and hateth his brother, is in the darkness even until now." [1]

(iv.) All occasions that give rise to the belief that a person is incapable of community living, or unworthy to take part in communal life, block the channels to it. These occasions fall into two groups. First of all there are those conditions which we have already considered as damaging to the sense of personal value, amongst which must be especially mentioned all those situations which lead to an actual slighting of the person concerned ; these may arise from physical or even mental injury, lack of affection, favouritism shown to one's equals—brothers and sisters, for example— or from social disadvantages. Secondly, there is deficient preparation or training for the community life.

[1] 1 *Jn.* ii. 9.

Membership of the community, life in and with it, has to be learnt ; and as is the case with all the other important vital functions, such as walking, talking and the like, this training must be begun early. Consequently, all artificial isolation is undesirable. Parents who, in their excessive anxiety, keep their child from contact with others to avoid the risk of infection—" only " children are especially liable to be treated in this way—or who, from a kind of jealousy, wish to keep their child wholly to themselves, ignorantly inflict the most severe injury on the object of their tender but unreasonable love. All isolation, no matter what its motive, is harmful.

Stress is frequently laid on the importance of a child's associating with his equals in order that he may learn from an early age to " find his feet " in a community of his peers. We must admit that this demand contains a grain of sound sense ; in fact, this early acquaintance of children with others of their own age and kind is a good training for after-life, and is especially indicated in the case of only children, who are denied the common life with brothers and sisters. Yet I do not believe this demand to be a *sine qua non ;* it seems to me to have been extravagantly made in many quarters, and not so much for reasons arising out of the actual content of the demand as from a philosophical outlook of the kind which has led to attacks on the family as an institution, and to the really absurd and Utopian idea that children should be removed from their homes at a very early age. Such an idea is justified only by the fact that education in the family circle is unfortunately very often seriously defective. However, we learn from experience that even only children can be excellently well prepared in the family for communal life. Such a family training prevents the otherwise frequent occurrence of " catastrophic re-actions " (K. Goldstein) and the development of childish failings and irregularities or even serious " nervous " disorders, in response to such situations as going to school or association with strange children for the first time. Moreover, it is the necessary preliminary for the child to be able to live in real communion with his parents, so that the distance between parents and child is not exaggerated into something terrifying, and the child is assured of the respect that is his due, and does not feel himself to be merely " an object for upbringing " or the subordinate and slave of adults.

It is a mistake to address children only by way of issuing orders ; one can also explain to them what is required of them and the reasons. Further, one can and should request children to do things as a favour or a kindness, and thank them for their compliance. Membership of the community involves other obligations than those operating directly within the community—by the latter we mean the establishing of desirable relations with one's fellow-men ; in other words, love for one's neighbour. The obligations imposed by the true community ideal are not identical for everyone ; first, they vary according to sex, and, secondly, they transcend the simple communal relation inasmuch as they also include the idea of work.

On the first point more will be said in the chapter dealing with the characterology of the sexes ; on the second, some observations must be made here.

These obligations operating outside the communal relationship proper, and which sooner or later every man must fulfil, may be considered under four main heads : humanity, family, work and faith. Although the first three are in the last resort grounded in the supernatural, they constitute the realm in which man fulfils his natural obligations. Two of these require to be positively discharged in all possible circumstances ; humaneness and industry are demanded from everyone. The third obligation, which includes such things as love and community in wedlock, and the foundation of a family of one's own, must equally be discharged by everyone ; but in this case it may be met positively or negatively. The negative discharge, however, is not necessarily the same as a denial of marriage and the family, in the sense of treating them as of no value. Virginity, the monastic life, the celibacy of the priest, the renunciation of family life by a man who chooses to " live his ideal " and fulfil the obligations imposed by it in retirement : all these lose their meaning and value if that which is renounced is regarded as worthless. The renunciation of marriage because it appears distasteful is not consistent with morality, and implies cowardice and flight. Because the " world " is an abomination and unsatisfying, there is no justification for beating a retreat and devoting oneself to the monastic life ; for then where and what is the sacrifice ? One can sacrifice only what one values. Only he who looks upon this world and all its gifts as unutterably beautiful and precious is entitled to renounce them because he sees something even finer and more splendid before him. Thus a negative discharge of the marital obligation, to be of any value, must involve an uncompromising approval of the institution of marriage and the family. How mistaken and indeed illogical it would be to deny their worth, when God himself has set his sacramental seal on their value !

Everyone must be a fellow-man and a fellow-worker. Of course, the conception of work must not be one-sided or narrow. To be a fellow-worker means that one must take one's place in the fighting-line of mankind in its struggle for cultural progress ; whether one's co-operation is intellectual, economic, social or anything else—this is a matter of indifference. It is perhaps not superfluous to say that a man who has devoted his life entirely to prayer and contemplation may equally well be considered to have taken his place in that fighting-line ; for in consequence of the principle of human solidarity in the acquisition of collective merit, and the sharing of collective guilt—a principle which, as we have previously seen, is not a matter of revelation, but the result of speculative thought—such a life not only benefits the individual but the whole community. Moreover, a completely contemplative life is impossible ; even the contemplative monk is under obedience to perform certain manual tasks.

To work always means to collaborate. Work may be defined as the creation of values that endure beyond the period of activity. In every piece of work values are made concrete and visible ; therefore work is subject to the moral law, which is also one of its premises. This twofold nexus with the moral law extends, therefore, on the one side into the realm of the supernatural, and, on the other, as joint work, into that of the community. Herein lies the ethical and educational value of work. No one who has the determination to work can escape from an ultimate " acceptance " of the community. (This enables us to grasp the importance and scope of the so-called " occupational therapy.") Although work often gives pleasure and lasting satisfaction, it is in the last instance toil, and, as we learn from Holy Scripture, also in some way a punishment, or at least a consequence of the Fall.[1] For if one of the objects of earthly punishment, ordained by man, is to serve as a means and act as a stimulus for the mastery over conduct of a kind involving punishment, and is at the same time a demonstration of confidence in the inner man, who is deemed better than his external actions, this must be even more the case with divine punishment, which is an expression not only of absolute justice but also of supreme love.

[1] *Genesis* iii. 17–19.

Moreover, death came into man's world as a punishment ; and yet it has become a way, and indeed the only possible way, of atonement ; once through the redeeming death of Christ, but also by reason of the fact that by his knowledge of the inevitableness of death man is made aware of his responsibility. Thus work is endowed with a twofold nature ; it is an oppressive burden and at the same time an exhilarating pleasure. To seek to deny its oppressive features, to degrade it to a game or a sport, is to do violence to the nature of work ; any attempt—it would be a Utopian attempt—to establish an order of society in which work would altogether lose its character as toil would be founded on a failure to understand its true meaning. On the other hand, work should never be so arranged and so represented as only to be burdensome. Graver grounds of complaint against the prevailing attitude and the industrial system scarcely exist than those shattering accounts which inform us how overwhelmingly large a proportion of our industrial workers feel their work to be only a burden and an oppressive and unjust infliction.

Thus education is saddled with a task and a duty transcending the formation of the individual. The so urgently needed reconstruction of the ethics of work can only be made from below, through individuals, and involves the education of the individual's thought and character.

It is obvious that, to compass this end, educationalists must rightly understand the deeper meaning of work. We will leave the question at this point ; but it should be borne in mind that even in the presence of such understanding, principles must be observed and mistakes avoided in the method of conveying this knowledge and implanting it in the minds of the pupils.

Firstly, work must not be represented to the young child as a curse ; the years in which he will have to learn and work must not be pictured to him as a banishment from a happier state of being. It is understandable that even parents rejoice in the small child's freedom from cares and duties—although that freedom is only relative—and regret to see their playful, innocent little one forced into contact with compulsion and restraint ; but they should take care to conceal this feeling from the child, and should paint for him the acquisition of knowledge, the enrichment of his nature, and effort and achievement, in glowing colours. Above all, they should make the child early acquainted with the nature of work ; that is, they should make him familiar with the idea that every man has his active rôle to play in life—an idea that children grasp far better than is commonly supposed. The quite small child can put away his toys and tidy up the disorder he has made, and can easily be taught that these little duties are the equivalent of work. This sort of training also helps to lessen the distance between the child and adults which, as we have already learned, reacts unfavourably on the child's stock of courage and self-confidence ; he no longer regards himself as the useless parasite he is (regrettably often) foolishly represented to be by his parents and teachers ; he knows himself already to be a fellow-worker, and grows up in an atmosphere of willing industry.

Working in common leads to common feeling ; but the one also presupposes the other. We are again faced with the inner reciprocal interdependence of all sides and aspects of human existence. Since work itself creates enduring values, it extends unconditionally beyond the sphere of the ego into that of the non-ego—that is, once more, into that of the community. A man whose development was in a direction away from the community would take unkindly to work. We see that it is possible to regard a dislike for and an unwillingness to do work as something other than a constitutional defect or a fault involving blame ; it may be the secondary result of an ill-developed will to community. However, if a man is to believe that he is under an obligation to create values, he must believe in his own ability to fulfil it. It seems obvious to the naive intelligence that values cannot be generated from or created by that which is worthless. Therefore, if a man, as a worker and a fellow-worker, is to be equal to his task and fill his place in life, his maintenance of his sense of personal value is an absolute necessity.

Thus one thing is interwoven with the other thing. The effects of errors and blunders in upbringing are never limited to any one aspect of human life and existence ; for as man always acts and expresses himself as an undivided unity, so he must always suffer as an indivisible whole. The special consequences of an error or a misunderstanding depend on the situation of the moment, on the previous history, on the most recent psychological influences, and finally on those operating at a later period of his life ; it is always possible that these consequences may be unusually far-reaching or even disastrous. Now, we can never avoid blunders entirely, just as we cannot " without especial privilege of divine grace " steer clear of all venial sins ; but the more clearly we recognize the danger, and the more vividly we are alive to the possible consequences, the more easily shall we be able to avoid mistakes.

It was not our intention in this section to construct a system of character-training ; these remarks were intended rather as a justification of our insistence on the paramount importance of environmental influences. Before proceeding to deal with separate problems in detail, we must draw attention to one possible misunderstanding. It would be mistaken to interpret the opinions here set out simply as a statement or modification of the doctrine which has become unenviably known as the "milieu theory." That theory, which is the child of naturalism and positivism, maintains that in some way or other a man's nature is determined simply and solely by environment ; it is fundamentally an extremely primitive theory, and extremely foreign to our own. The sharp distinction between person and character, and the way in which the latter is defined, would be enough to prevent our acceptance of it. If we regard character as the guiding principle of conduct, constituting a relation between the ego and the non-ego, we assert thereby that the person plays just as decisive a part in its ultimate make-up as the environment ; but the general make-up of the person is something definite, and the environment is fluid. The depths of the former remain unplumbable by rational, analytical thought ; the latter can in some degree be resolved into its elements, and its mode of operation can be detected. Every effort must be made to effect the development of character favourably through the environment, for we are ignorant of the possible extent of the influence of that factor ; certainly, it extends further than we commonly imagine.

Theoretical characterology, as a pure science, may content itself with the description of types and the estimation of genetic factors ; practical characterology must act, and there are problems that it alone can tackle. Therefore, the more boldly hopeful and the less passively resigned the applied science shows itself to be, the greater will be its success.

It goes without saying that every human being can develop only in certain definite directions ; and, speaking metaphorically, in each direction there is only one path that seems there for the person to take. Certainly, however, more than one path does exist, and what is important is that for each individual there is at least *one* path that leads to favourable development. How far one can go, and in which directions, cannot be foreseen, but only experienced. Woe to us, if we do not make every effort to guide every human being entrusted to our care along the road that leads to his fullest development !

A detailed description of this road and the special features distinguishing various " normal " and " anomalous " characters will, with certain other matters, form the content of the following chapters of this book. We shall there in many respects be able to work out our theoretical principles and practical conclusions in greater elaboration.

CHAPTER III

CHARACTER IN CHILDHOOD AND DIFFICULTIES IN UPBRINGING

I. THE REACTIVE ORIGIN OF CHARACTER-TRAITS

IT is extraordinarily difficult, as we have already said, to decide whether any particular feature distinguishing the principle governing a man's conduct (*i.e.*, his character) that we may happen to notice, is to be regarded as a reactive response to environmental influences, or as something inherent in his final make-up, his very person. Even when we are totally unable to put our finger on the origin of such a reaction or to discover an intelligible derivation of the feature in question from the man's life or experience, it is always open to doubt whether our failure may not be due to our short-sightedness or insufficient knowledge of the man's past history and the laws governing suggestibility. It would almost seem as if there were no quality, no character-trait, that might not be considered to originate reactively. We know that a certain laziness, intellectual torpor and thick-headedness, combined with a cheerful obtuseness, may result from hypo-function of the thyroid gland, and that these qualities can be made to disappear on treating the condition : there are, then, characteristics that must be regarded as symptomatic of a certain organic state and also, therefore— since this is only one aspect of the psycho-physical unity of man's nature—as indications of a certain state of his nature as a whole. We know, on the other hand, that the same traits—or traits that in appearance are quite indistinguishable from those observable in cases of hypo-thyroidism—may be generated reactively. Torpor, for example, has no especial peculiarity about it to enable one from its presence alone to diagnose the mechanism of its origin ; there are always other factors, especially physical, contributing to a diagnosis, if their presence has made us suspicious of a disturbance of thyroid secretion. Only in very few cases are we able to recognize clear connections between the physical condition and subtle variations of conduct, enabling us with justification to speak of direct determination by organic factors. There is much we can guess, but we cannot prove it. Much less, then, are we able to maintain that this or that trait depends on the congenital constitution peculiar to a person whose real nature remains concealed and beyond the reach of investigation either by the experimental method or by clinical observation.

It might be supposed that the study of conduct in children would supply the most satisfactory information about the person's original state—what his make-up was before it was overlaid with reactive concretions whose origin depends on experience and external influences, factors that are, quantitatively speaking, minimal in early childhood.

But even this hope proves deceptive. In the first place, as we have said, a person's physical and congenital make-up is to be considered not only as the cause or expression of a certain kind of predisposition, but also as the vessel of experience, in fact of that primal experience which from the first breath—or indeed earlier—enters into all our life-experience, however dim. Even if this experience be regarded as unconscious, it exists nevertheless ; and it must have left behind some traces to form a foundation upon which all subsequently realized experience will build. The strength and form of the foundation determine the height and structure of the edifice that can be erected. Secondly, we know remarkably little about the time when environmental impressions begin to exercise an influence on the infant ; it is more than likely that such influences make themselves felt from the first moment of the child's life. Perhaps even the popular belief is not so foolish—that the mood, manner of living, and surroundings, of the mother during pregnancy influence the make-up of the still unborn child ; after all, the maternal organism is the environment of the growing embryo.

Moreover, it is often the case that the stories told by parents of their child's showing some special peculiarity from the very first are untrue and based on a kind of self-deception. Even if these stories were founded on correct observation, and even if a careful record of conduct established certain character-factors, it could never be maintained with certainty that they were of unconditionally spontaneous, idiopathic and personal, and not of reactive, origin.

We must emphasize this again : we have no doubt whatever that there are, and must be, primary natural features dependent on the person's most " intimate " make-up ; we very much doubt, however, if we are in a position—at least in the present state of our knowledge—to recognize these features as such, and to distinguish them from those of reactive origin. Consequently, it must always be made clear that we should accept personal characteristics as constitutional and inherent only if an explanation in terms of reaction to environment and external circumstances is found to be insufficient. We regard this principle of method as essential for all characterological observation and research. It is one of the services of the individual-psychology school that it has laid the greatest stress upon this. It is, admittedly, on the other hand, an unwarranted exaggeration of a simple principle of method to assert the absolute equality of all persons and to ascribe all differences to environmental influences. This opinion, which sometimes takes grotesque forms, arises, in my view, in two ways—from a philosophy, with which we need not here concern ourselves, and from a therapeutic technique, in the practice of which it is maintained that the unwarrantableness of the inferiority-feeling can only be insisted on by assuming the fundamental equality of all men. This is a mistaken view, and rests for its part on quite insufficient ontological and metaphysical foundations—but this is not the place to demonstrate the error.

Against the view that character-features are for the most part reactive as opposed to constitutional, the objection may be raised that many people who enjoy " the same " environment yet show markedly diverse characteristics. This objection may be met as follows : We recognize the existence of certain features common to vastly different persons who happen to live and grow up in the same condition of life ; as one example we may cite all those types which can be grouped together as occupational and class types, the officer, the civil servant, the peasant, the teacher, the doctor, and so on ; the " manner " associated with certain occupations is so " characteristic " that even the most ignorant can easily recognize those who are connected with them. But it still remains to be investigated how many of these " characteristic " peculiarities are mere " externals " and how many are actually character-traits ; in the former case the character-trait would simply be ability for self-adaptation to such externals. However, over and above these externals, there are undoubtedly genuine character-traits which are determined by occupation or class. If we see that truly " like " conditions associated with a particular occupation, especially one involving membership of a class (*e.g.*, officer, priest, peasant), invariably give rise to traits which to a greater or lesser extent are repeated in all those engaged in that occupation, the obvious conclusion is that when " like " conditions fail to bring out such uniformity, then the

" likeness " of the conditions is not true but only apparent.
As a matter of fact, it would be very difficult to find any two
men whose conditions in life have been truly " alike." So
we must adhere to the *non liquet* that we felt ourselves
bound to express : as things are today, it is impossible to
assert with any final conviction that a particular character-
trait is inherent in a man, causing him to be as he is and not
otherwise in accordance with an inner " law of individuality."

We can only make suppositions ; what directions these
may take will be considered in another section. Bearing in
mind the limitations already pointed out, we shall now turn
our attention to the peculiarities of character at the various
periods of life. As we are concerned mainly with practical
problems, it will be understood that we shall pay most
attention to the peculiarities of the periods of life preceding
maturity. Character, as we showed in detail in our preliminary observations, is both in principle and in fact
susceptible of change at all the periods of life ; but the
possibilities of successful intervention to bring about a real
change of mind and character in the later years are naturally
smaller, and, so far as they exist, belong more to the sphere
of " soul-therapy," a subject hardly suitable for treatment in
these pages.   We are entitled to deal with these matters only
up to a point, in a special section.

We have already said much on the general characterology
of childhood, and only in certain respects need we elaborate
those remarks. On the other hand, it seems useful to describe
with more precision certain well-distinguishable types of
childish behaviour and character, and to investigate certain
isolated traits found with greater or lesser regularity amongst
children. As previously, we shall frequently direct attention
to " abnormal " phenomena, and by " abnormal " we mean
here phenomena, occurring in the course of, or as the result
of, upbringing, that are undesired, although by no means

unconditionally pathological. The reason for this is that it is much easier to describe developmental errors and to trace them to their source than to point out the " royal road " to development ; it is always less difficult to indicate what should be avoided than to prescribe what ought to be done. This applies equally outside our particular theme. Hygiene occupies itself far more with naming the dangers to be avoided, and prophylactic measures, than with positive pronouncements ; and, finally, the commandments of faith and morals are to a large extent negatively uttered.

It is necessary to distinguish carefully between the inevitable necessity of couching one's teaching to a large extent in terms of negation and prohibition, and the attitude in practice towards those to whom the commandments are to be brought home. A mistake frequently made with children and even with adults is to stress the negative rather than the positive. Certainly, no one should be blind to the dangers of the material and the moral life ; but to limit description to these dangers, or to overstress them without at the same time indicating that they can be overcome and avoided, is to sap the child's courage. It would be a good thing to replace the everlasting " You cannot, may not, shall not " by " You can, you may, you are." It is my impression that all our educational methods neglect far too much the positive factors of natural ability and supernatural aid.

2. FEAR IN CHILDHOOD

We must now consider a factor of great characterological importance : fear.[1] Fear, as such, is an emotion ; as a character-trait, the tendency to be afraid in every possible situation is termed " timidity." But timidity is not our real

[1] The extremely interesting problem of fear cannot be pursued here along general and metaphysical lines. Of great importance is M. Heidegger's recent work, *Sein und Zeit* (Halle, 1927) ; noteworthy also is H. Liebeck's small study, produced under the influence of Heidegger, *Das Unbekannte und die Angst* (Leipzig, 1928).

concern here. Fundamentally, the mental attitude of the timid man is such that the most various events, situations and happenings appear to him to fall into the category of " danger." Ultimately one might be tempted to say that this attitude covers a lack of understanding and an error of judgment ; for what else can it be termed, if one man sees danger where others fail to see it ? For the moment we will leave the deeper sources of timidity on one side, and concern ourselves rather with a description of how it arises.

First of all it should be explained why we have given priority to a discussion of fear. There is no case of characterological anomaly either in children or in adults, no case of dissociation, as in neurosis, no case of difficult upbringing or of childish shortcomings, in which open or variously disguised fear does not lurk ; it is a never-failing symptom of all faulty adaptation to the actual conditions of life. But only in part is fear a consequence of this lack of adaptation ; it is to a far greater extent a cause of it. Here, again, we are faced with a vicious circle, whose nature we must grasp if a way out is to be found.

It is not too much to maintain that in innumerable cases of difficult upbringing involving such features as stubbornness, excessive reserve, lying, rebellion against school, self-neglect and childish " criminality "—if this term is really applicable to the misdeeds of children—are at bottom all founded on fear.[1]

We have seen that a feeling of insecurity is an essential feature of life in childhood ; its correlative is fear. An individual experiences fear whenever the general situation is either actually, objectively or only subjectively insecure or threatening to his physical or moral existence. In the absence of true qualification, the higher a person's position, the more

[1] With reference to this and the following remarks, cf. R. Allers and E. Freund, *Ueber einige Fälle von Schwererziehbarkeit und kindlicher Kriminalität*, in *Zeitschr. f. d. ges. Neurol. u. Psychiat*, Bd. 103 (1926).

does fear enter his life. The tyrant surrounded by his guards, who could not trust himself to sleep two nights in succession in the same bed, may serve as an example. Moreover, visible externalized position or power is not a necessary premise ; internal exaggeration of one's value and importance suffices to produce fear. St. John Climacus was right when he stated in his *Scala Paradisi* that fear is the sign of a haughty spirit.

We have made it sufficiently clear why it is inevitable that the child, owing to his natural position or the conflict between it and the limitations imposed upon his tendency to self-assertion, must experience insecurity. Education must seek to convince him of his security, and foster his confidence in himself and the world, despite these conditions.

The child, then, is, strictly speaking, justified in feeling afraid. To rebuke him or scoff at him for his timidity is wholly perverse. It is still more perverse to strengthen his natural timidity either by the narration of tales of horror or by making him the victim of one of those entirely stupid unscrupulous " jokes " whose only object is to arouse fear ; yet there are actually people who believe that one can " harden " or " ginger up " a child by frightening him. If a child is afraid, it is because he feels he is not equal to the world. One will never be able to convince him that he is as well qualified as others for the struggle of life by chiding him for being a coward or a weakling, or, as did the father of one of my small patients, by calling him an " old woman." The natural feeling of insecurity is also increased by an exaggerated description of dangers. I knew a girl of twenty-seven, suffering from anxiety-neurosis, who as a child never went to school without her father's saying as she set out : " Be careful in the street ; death is to the right and left of you." Is it surprising that all her life she was never free from fear ? The father was, of course, himself a prey to it. The daughter had not inherited her fear from him, but had acquired it—a contribution of some interest to the problem of the inheritance of psychical qualities.

All those factors can create fear which we described earlier as being calculated to increase the sense of insecurity, lessen the sense of personal value, and restrict the will to community. It can therefore be maintained with great probability that the *timidity* of children, so far as it is not the product of physical weakness, *results from upbringing*. If the child is timid for physical reasons, he obviously requires the most careful and sensitive guidance, so that he may learn to overcome his fear, or, it would be better to say, to win his way through to an inner standpoint from which fear is no longer justified.

We shall return later to the subject of fear in the life of adults. We must show here that fear is at the bottom of most cases of difficult upbringing. To grasp this, it must first of all be understood that this early fear of insufficiency and inferiority cannot be clearly experienced in its pure form ; for to acknowledge such a fear would be to admit the possibility of such inferiority and personal worthlessness ; but such an admission would be intolerable. To possess a personal value, and to have certainty of it—these are from the point of view of experience one and the same thing ; doubting it at once implies its absence. Thus this primal fear finds expression in many forms, partly by being linked to other objects that happen to be occasions for fear, and partly by taking shelter under various disguises.

It is quite easy to fathom the kind of fear occurring in situations in which it is possible for others to concur with or confirm one's own self-judgment. Such forms of fear are shyness, embarrassment, fear of strangers or of unusual situations. To laugh at a child for such behaviour, to scoff at him or to punish him, is to show a complete misunderstanding of the whole position. It can no doubt occasionally happen that a child is forced by such treatment to "overcome" his shyness, because his fear of the forces behind his upbringing is stronger than his fear of strangers. The primal fear, however, is not thereby removed, and will quite probably manifest itself in a still more alarming way either in childhood or in later years in the form of a neurosis of greater or lesser severity. The shy or otherwise nervous child needs encouragement, and not punishment.

The secret fear that to give expression to the inmost self may discover a total worthlessness keeps a man's mouth closed. Aloofness and reserve are not always signs of contempt for another who is not deemed worthy of the precious gift of confidence ; they are frequently signs, specially in the case of children and adolescents, of a constant, gnawing doubt, which resists every fresh attempt to save the threatened sense of self-esteem. The more frequently a man who, like the child, cannot measure himself by the test of achievement, meets with misunderstanding, scorn and lack of appreciation of his attempts at self-expression, the more readily does he fall into such a state. How often do not educationalists, in their ignorance and lack of sympathy for the children who are still so helpless in the world's confusion, show a disposition to make a cheap jest of the talk of the little ones, which sometimes seems futile and ridiculous, but is meant in all seriousness ?

How rich is the experience of children, and how deep, even though often imperfectly expressed, their thoughts may be, can be realized only by one who is ready to devote his love and patience to tracing out their connection and significance, and does not irritably grudge the trouble of requesting (but never demanding) explanations of what he does not understand. Somehow the soul of the child is closer to the ultimate core of existence than those of adults, who are deflected from their original life-course by the culture, wisdom and cleverness of this world. We have always, I believe, paid too little heed to our Lord's saying : " Unless ye become as little children. . . ." Even in these times which we ostentatiously presume to name the " child's century," we still have made but a slight approach to the nature of children. We have taken care of them, and in fact a very great deal has actually been done ; infant mortality has decreased, and we have learnt much about physical culture—it is unnecessary to enumerate all our achievements. Only one thing is lacking now, as ever. Nor need that surprise us, for it would indeed be surprising if a generation that has lost all sense of reverence should have retained it for the child. A little is still there ; and it says something for the inalienable goodness of human nature that a gleam of reverence still illumines the faces of men when they gaze upon a child, and that if anything can touch them it is the suffering of a child, and if aught can move them it is a child's request.

Fear, however, often attaches to conditions whose immediate significance escapes the child's inexperienced mind. Intelligible enough are the fears evoked by the unusual, the uncanny and the like, which by themselves are calculated to increase an already existent sense of insecurity. Even if the average adult is not afraid of being alone in a dark room, he yet has many a qualm when he is compelled to walk at night in a lonely lane, in unfamiliar parts of the town, or in a wood. The child is afraid in the dark room, or if he has to stay in the house alone ; he is afraid of motor-cars, dogs and people. This is no justification for scorn or severity ; punishment and mockery do not encourage the child, they only add to his discouragement.

Sometimes, however, this childish fear is not apparent as such. A special kind of mechanism, which we shall frequently be coming across, comes into play. The timid child is seeking for protection, and always wants to be assuring himself that the succour of his parents is ever at hand. That he will not enter or remain in a dark room alone is no longer an expression of fear, but already an effort to rid himself of this fear by requesting—and, if the fear-reactions are sufficiently strong, enforcing—the presence and companionship of others. We must not forget that at the basis of this timid conduct lurks the actual fear itself, the fear that the individual's total worthlessness may be discovered to others as it is to the ego whose self-esteem is threatened. Inferiority is gauged, as we have seen, above all in accordance with the distance from the adults. What could be more calculated to overpower this consciousness of inferiority, and to allay this secret fear of being nothing, than conduct that while dispensing with the need of putting oneself to the test, yet guarantees the certainty of strength ? It is a demonstration of power, if the child—or, in similar divagations, the adult neurotic—compels his fellows to serve him by parading his helplessness and weakness.

This conversion of the fear-reaction into an instrument of power is still clearer in other forms of disguised fear. These include, for example, all those displays of fear which apparently occur independently of the intervention of consciousness, such as terrifying dreams or crying out in sleep (*pavor nocturnus*). A great number of cases, if not all, of that unpleasant childish weakness, bed-wetting (*enuresis nocturna*), fall into the same category. Both forms of behaviour compel the adults to pay the children attention at night-time. We will not for the moment consider the factors that determine the particular type of fear-reaction ; we must content ourselves for the moment with having drawn attention to their symptomatology and general ætiology.

3. LYING, WILFULNESS, OBSTINACY

Closely connected with the foregoing are lying, wilfulness and obstinacy. It must be strongly emphasized that one can talk of lying [1] only in cases where untruth is uttered with intent to deceive, and for reasons that exclusively concern the person of the speaker. It is recognized that neither the *bona fide* repetition of an untruth nor a mistake of recollection are lies. (It is beyond doubt, however, that the latter is often associated with a definite mendaciousness ; of this, more later.) Now in very early childhood the distinction, as experienced, between the recollection of an actual perception and the memory of a fantasy or a dream is undoubtedly very faint. This can be explained in terms of physiology or, if one prefers the term, sensory psychology ; E. R. Jaensch [2] was able to demonstrate that the so-called " eidetic " faculty—the ability to experience exogenously or endogenously generated subjective images of a more or less strongly perceptive kind—is very strongly developed in childhood. To this may be added the lack of worldly experience, in consequence of which the small child is unable to apply the test of conformity to law that enables us to distinguish fantasy from reality. In short, it is a normal phase of development for the small child to narrate as reality things that are only the product of his imagination. To brand such stories as lies, and to treat the child harshly or punish him on that account, is a great mistake, the result of which is only seriously to shake his confidence in the justice of adults. At a somewhat later age, we find the transparent lie told in joke. This originates in various ways.

[1] See for example, Fr. Baumgarten, *Die Lüge bei Kindern und Jugendlichen* (Leipzig, 1926).
[2] *Der Aufbau der Wahrnehmungswelt* (Leipzig, 1927). It should, however, be mentioned that the general validity of the author's conclusions on the eidetic faculty is greatly doubted in many quarters. See the recent work of Bonte-Liefmann-Roessler, *Zeitschr. für angew. Psychol.* (Leipzig, 1928), B. 43.

One is the naive joy taken in romancing, in the newly-acquired ability to create something in words—a faculty that is stimulated by the child's own reading. How often does one not hear the question, " Is the story true or not ? " and how easily does the child himself invent " untrue " stories, which are at first naturally quite primitive untruths ! A second source is to be found in the attempt of the child in this way to begin to test the omniscience and infallibility of his upbringers. If he succeeds in deceiving them, this immediately involves a naive feeling of triumph—which throws much light on the whole situation—and his striving after power and greatness is appreciably satisfied. Although this tendency is more questionable, punishment is not always indicated, but rather explanation of the folly and bad taste of such conduct.

The first real lie is born of fear, and is almost without exception a lie to escape punishment. As a rule, the child will resort to this means of escape only if his natural attitude towards punishment has already been spoilt, which almost always implies previous mistaken treatment. An innate mendacity, or a disposition to it, does not exist ; or, alternatively, one may say that it exists in every human being without exception. Whether the small child resorts to lying as a means of escape or not depends entirely on the way he is treated. I have come across many mendacious children, but none in whose case it was not possible to trace the grossest blunders in upbringing.

In the true lie, the power-factor becomes even more obvious. By a successful piece of deception, the child not only attempts to demonstrate to his own satisfaction that he is somehow superior to the adults he fears and envies, but at the same time makes use of the lie to protect his own will from the encroachment of others. Since the lie is, in the first instance, an attempt to escape punishment, it seeks to conceal the commission of a forbidden act. The child does what is forbidden first, as it were, by accident, because in the excitement of play his relatively small power of concentration makes him forget, and secondly because it *is* forbidden.

Now, it is a characteristic not only of children but of people in general *to be attracted by what is forbidden.* Children, young people and adults not infrequently find pleasure in things that in themselves would by no means be so enjoyable unless they were prohibited. This applies largely to school-children, who smoke, for example, not because they like it, but because smoking is forbidden.

What is the attraction in doing what is forbidden? There is no need for any very searching analysis to arrive at an answer. We recall the fairy-tales : " You may open all the doors save the one whose lock is fitted by the little golden key." That is a constantly recurring theme in German as well as in Arabian fairy-tales. Each of these stories relates how the little golden key exercised a secret power, and how the fateful door was unlocked. Why ? The answer is given by the form of the prohibition. " You may open everything except the one " ; and the person entrusted with the key—generally a woman ; this is clearly an echo of the Fall—says to herself, " But why not this particular one ? Why am I not allowed to open this one door ? Why should I permit of such a restriction to the complete exercise of my power ? "

In fact, every prohibition involves a restriction of the power of the person on whom the prohibition is enjoined. In the second book of the *Confessions*, St. Augustine, in a passage to which too much attention cannot be paid, relates how as a boy he stole pears from other people's gardens, not on account of the fruit, which was bad and which he threw away, but just for the sake of stealing. In stealing, as in the case of all contravention of commands and prohibitions, the inducement is, as the Saint rightly points out, that at the time of the action we imagine ourselves to be greater and more powerful than the person issuing the order.

Did we need confirmation of this illuminating explanation, it could readily be found in the fact that it is often sufficient to forbid a thing to assure oneself of its performance ; conversely, the lifting of a prohibition removes the temptation to commit a prohibited act. I remember the case of a maid-servant who had an obsessive and irresistible impulse to steal. She believed she had an unconquerable longing for sweets, and used to take them secretly from her employers. The idea occurred to one of them to make sugar, chocolate and the like always available for her ; after this, she lost all enjoyment in her act. A mother who complained that her eight-year-old son, despite all prohibitions, would step into every puddle, was advised by me to encourage the boy to do so ; he did not care to do it any longer, from the moment that it was not only not forbidden, but permitted and even encouraged.

The doing of what is forbidden, then, always means a secret, if fictitious, triumph—a victory over the law-giver, a sign of one's own greatness and power. So indeed all sin, says St. Augustine, is an effort by man to raise himself above God. " *Eritis sicut dii* " ; the old saying still works much evil, and it almost seems as if man, not satisfied with being as God, seeks to be even greater.

We find, then, that the lie enters into the service of the perverted will to power, to protect it and its operations. However deeply rooted this inclination may be in man, as a sign and *modus operandi* of his fallen nature, yet insight and knowledge can free him from it. " The truth shall make us free from sin," says St. Augustine in a passage already quoted. What is the truth that must be known by us ? Assuredly it is the reprehensibility of sin, the majesty of God

Whom we dishonour, the sublimity of His commandments and of His love which we disdain ; further, the incredible folly of attempting to place oneself on an equality with God, and the utter hopelessness of seeking to outwit or surpass Him. Would one risk the qualms of conscience, the dread of discovery and punishment, all the evil consequences and accompaniments of wrongdoing if one fully realized the hopelessness of attaining one's purpose ? That is why it is necessary for man to attain to the knowledge of the real nature of his goal ; he must realize that he is not really aiming at stealing pears, not even at theft as such—however much false glamour and heroism may attach to the act— but at imitating the greatness of God, and even aspiring to super-divine greatness.

The fact that man fails to realize the true nature of his goal cannot abolish or diminish his responsibility. It is important for the psychology of disobedience and punishable actions, and consequently also for the technique of education and the guidance of souls, that probably the best means of exerting the desired influence is to convince the person in question of the ultimate goal behind his conduct. Every healthy child, everyone whose *amour propre* has not been too greatly weakened and who has not been compelled to resort to every kind of dodge to bolster it up, is in a position to realize that the driving motive behind the commission of forbidden acts is a struggle for greatness and power, which is as unintelligent as it is futile. Wrongdoing involves punishment, and the child is sensible of this, as we have said ; therefore it is mistaken to substitute instruction and explanation for punishment. But one should not be satisfied with punishment alone. The child should be addressed with affection and seriousness, especially at times when recent wrongdoing is not in question ; and he should be encouraged to ask questions and by the method of a Socratic dialogue,

as it were, to arrive at understanding. It is simpler merely
to punish without bothering about the motives behind the
child's actions ; it is certainly easier ; but it is also more
dangerous, and generally less successful.

In the secret commission of forbidden acts and their
subsequent concealment by means of falsehood, it is directly
implied that the person lacks the courage necessary for open
defiance. To this extent the indignant educationalist is
justified when he says to the delinquent whose misdeeds
have been found out : " It would have been better if you
had done these things openly ; what makes me most angry
is the deceit," and so on. Such people, however, fail to
realize that discouragement is an important motive and
conditioning factor of the form of the misdeed. To the
coward who really suffers under his cowardice, the statement
that he ought not to be cowardly sounds like telling him
that his eyes ought to be of a different colour. Thus that
kind of " moral lecture " is justified to a certain extent, but
it is bad pedagogy and ineffectual. Its justification is of the
same order as that of the current opinion that the neurotic
person can behave differently, that he can learn to control
himself and not to give way, and so on. That opinion is
again objectively right, and that the demands are not outside
the range of the neurotic's possibilities is shown by the many
cases of cure ; but from the point of view of the neurotic,
such talk is not only untrue but absurd, and hence extremely
mortifying. If the child who had been treated in the way
described above were in a position to express his own feelings
with clarity and courage, his answer would be something
like this : " I know it too, and the fact that I cannot bring
myself to make my defiance open and above-board is my
misfortune and my sorrow, since it shows my inefficiency,
my worthlessness and my ' nothingness.' "

When he resorts to the negative methods of defiance and

anti-social conduct to maintain his position and to confirm his self-esteem, he must already have lost confidence of arriving at his goal by the positive way of achievement. Hence all educational homilies containing prophetic references to the child's probable future as a spur to improvement —" If you are like this now, you will never make good ! " and the like—are altogether mistaken and objectionable.

If discouragement and the defiance so closely related to it are combined with a kind of courage, the product is *obstinacy*, which is nothing more than a passive resistance to orders. So far as it comes out into the open and is levelled against authority, it shows a certain order of courage. Obstinate children are generally very unhappy, and their unhappiness colours other periods than those of definite obstinacy-reaction. They are bound to their obstinacy by threats to their self-esteem ; if they " give in," they admit their own inferiority to themselves and others. As a rule, obstinacy can be overcome by affectionate treatment combined with intelligent investigation of the child's endopsychic conflicts. It is a well-known fact that obstinate children are very easily handled after a change of environment. A twelve-year-old girl who at home showed herself altogether intractable and obstinate, and had made her people's lives impossible with her nightly scenes of screaming and terror, behaved completely differently when by a fortunate chance she left the parental home to enter a convent school in a distant town. The first nun to whose charge the little girl had been entrusted spoke to her with affection and understanding, and there was an end of her obstinacy. I have seen diaries of such children, which are full of complaints of loneliness, unfulfilled longings for affection, thoughts of running away, and of death. In one of them there is a constant recurrence of the following alarming cry : " It's too late ; I can't—and they don't help me ! " " They "—

the grown-ups—and " it is too late " : the poor child cannot get away from this frame of mind.

We are too readily aware of the vexation and sorrow that children cause us, and too little of that which we cause them. We say to them : " How could you do that to me ! " and do not see in their eyes the reproachful answer : " And you, how could you do that to me—you, a grown-up person, who must have known ! "

Surely there is need in this " century of the child " not only, as P. Lippert, S.J., once wrote, " secretly to side with the children," but to speak up for them openly and with full publicity. Of all the people who do not find their own level in life and are failures, who see that they are in danger of breaking down completely in the struggle, and invoke the aid of the doctor as a last resort, of all those whom I have seen in my consulting-room, fully ninety per cent. owe their lot to their childhood impressions and the mistakes and misunderstandings occurring in the course of their up-bringing.

Wilfulness is another means by which a will deflected from its proper goals seeks to attain its own ends. This needs no further elucidation, in view of what has already been said.

As we have repeatedly said, we aim not at the destruction of the individual will and a man's tendency to self-assertion, but at its guidance. Incidentally, we may add that the destruction of the primal tendency to self-assertion is impossible, and attempts only lead to perversions of it. Further, since it is one of the most fundamental tendencies of human nature, it needs to be indulged to a certain extent in the years of relative ignorance and inexperience, which are at the same time the years of greatest vulnerability ; and this means that one must not insist too much on prohibitions. If one forbids too much, one gains nothing at all ; for children have a very delicate sense of the reason or unreason of the orders given by adults. Much that they do not immediately understand is intelligible if one takes the trouble to explain. In many cases their secret criticism is warranted. To issue prohibitions simply in order that a child may learn to observe them is quite unnecessary ; there is a sufficient wealth of inevitable prohibitions. The up-bringing of children is not like the training of a dog, with a whip, to sit motionless with a piece of sugar on his nose without snapping at it.

The outsider—doctor, teacher or whoever it may be—who has to sit in judgment on cases of difficulty in up-bringing, and relies on a sketchy account of the circum-stances, must always bear in mind that there are cases of justifiable rebellion and disobedience—justifiable at least from the point of view of the child, who is the only person to be taken into consideration in passing judgment. In consultation, we often find it necessary emphatically and earnestly to insist on a mitigation of prohibitions which restrict the child's freedom unduly, threaten his sense of security, and undermine his courage.

This is also the place to mention various conditions that can be grouped together as those *preparatory for independent life*. We have already said that every one of man's inherent faculties needs exercising for its development ; it needs training so that the man may acquire the appropriate technique of giving active expression to it. If one does not give children the opportunities for the training of the vital and necessary mental attitudes and forms of conduct appropriate to their age, they will, as adults, be helpless to cope with the demands of reality. They will shrink from and turn themselves away from reality, in proportion as they find that the efforts they made, in spite of their inefficient preparation for life, are not crowned with success.

4. SPECIALLY SITUATED CHILDREN

As games provide a preparation for more serious things in life, and children's play prepares them for work and the overcoming of difficulties, so do we find that team-games and association with other children are, as we have already mentioned, a preparation and a training of the will to community, which is indispensable for the realities of life. For that reason, we find that those children whose social position is ambiguous or appears in a false light are sooner or later wrecked on the shoals of reality. We are thus entitled to speak of " danger-points " in development ; they occur especially at those times when a child is about to enter into a new phase of his life. If he is insufficiently prepared for such situations, he will develop, either before the particular situation to be met or when it occurs, certain unpleasant traits, whose strength will vary proportionately with the degree of insecurity experienced ; if he is possessed of some courage, his development will suffer a regression when he finds that his efforts to get the better of the situation have been unsuccessful. Such danger-points are, for example, the arrival of a little brother or sister ; going to school ; change of school ; promotion to a higher educational establishment ; sometimes mere change of surroundings, like going to live in another town ; and finally puberty, to which we shall pay special attention.

Fear of going to school must be regarded as pathognomonic of inadequate preparation for communal life. The child is afraid of the other children ; he fears that he will be unable to win a place among them, that he will be lost in the crowd, that no one will care for him ; that is, that he will receive confirmation of his own secret and terrifying belief in his own worthlessness.

The experienced person should be able to detect certain

other pathognomonic features in the make-up of such children, even before the state of the child's will to community is put to the test on his going to school. Children who cling to their mother and hide behind her, who are shy in the presence of strangers, who support themselves against a wall or a cupboard on being called upon to make a reply, take refuge behind a chair, avert their eyes, and so on, should be suspected of an insufficiently developed will to community. The child who is well prepared for communal life stands at his ease with head erect, adopting an attitude that several over-strict schoolmasters, inclined to emphasize their own authority, find displeasing, although in its natural and naive self-assurance, both æsthetically and humanly speaking, it is charming.

We have reserved for another section the fuller description of the mechanisms of the attitudes and varieties of conduct that come to light as difficulties in upbringing, the so-called childish faults of character, nervousness and what is called "child-criminality." We must now turn, after discussing some important individual features, to the description of *particular types of children*.

We must keep the following points in mind. The descriptions that we shall give are of necessity somewhat exaggerated; they are representations of extreme cases embodying a strong combination of all the phenomena observed in connection with the particular type. These extreme cases are by no means inventions; they exist in quite sufficiently large numbers; but there are also, naturally, countless children of the same type and living in the same situations who answer to the description only approximately. No representative of a particular type is altogether free from the traits about to be enumerated; but in most cases they are not so strongly marked, nor all to the same degree. It is therefore not a fair objection to our description of the only child, for instance, to cite such and such a child, in whom these traits seem to be wholly or for the most part absent. For, first, the detection and recognition of these features requires sharp and well-trained observational powers, and secondly the type is not always perfectly clear-cut : not every quartz crystal is a beautiful hexagonal pyramid, although that is the characteristic formation. And, further, even if it happens that all the features that distinguish particularly situated children are encountered in all the representatives of the group in question, it does not necessarily follow that all such children must develop along the same lines. As in the case of the physical make-up, the nature of the environment cannot be said to stand for inexorable destiny. There is no call for educational pessimism if it is shown, for instance, that an only child runs special risks and encounters particular dangers ; for all these dangers are essentially avoidable, and the more so as they become better known.

We will now proceed to describe these typical " situations " one after the other, in such a way as to establish their characteristic features, how they effect character-formation, and how they influence the attitude and reaction-patterns of the child subject to them.

(i.) *The only child.*—The situation of the only child is characterized by the concentration of all the care, affection and educational effort on him, and the absence of companions and competitors. The situation may be viewed in two ways : firstly, from the outside in the direction of environmental influence on the child, and, secondly, from the inside, from the child outwards in the direction of his reaction on his environment.

Because the only child is the sole object of parental care, the consequences are apparent in their most sharply defined form ; excessive strictness as well as undue leniency have especially noticeable results in the upbringing of such children. Further, the absence of companions whose own tendency to self-assertion would be opposed to and set limits to that of the child, and whose needs and rights would make an appeal to his will to community, affects the development of that will to community adversely.

Moreover, the more external factor of the readier satis-faction of desires, and especially the better economic situa-tion, must be taken into account ; for parents with only one child can naturally provide him with more pleasures and greater amenities than fall to the lot of children belonging to a large family in the same social position.

The—quite understandably—greater care lavished on the only child easily results in his becoming timid and depen-dent. The parental anxiety, the conscientious watch and ward over the child's health and factors that might threaten it, the desire to save him any unpleasantness and the increased opportunities of helping him in all his occupations or compelling him to withdraw from them—all these operate in the same way. Impressed with remarks such as : " Take care, or you'll hurt yourself," or " Let me do it ; you can't ! " the child soon gives up his own attempts to train himself and relies more and more on the support of the grown-ups. Such children grow up into helplessly dependent people, in constant need of their mothers, from whom they are never in a position to break away. If they marry, they either force the married partner to play the rôle of the careful mother—a part which can be played as well by the husband as by the wife—or else never cease to feel the need of the actual mother ; in the lives of such people, even after a long period of marriage, the death of the mother may cause a very severe breakdown. Of course another person may fill the same place, if he or she has in the child's early years been a constant refuge and a never-failing source of comfort and help. I remember a girl whose childhood, owing to maternal neglect, was entirely coloured by her relations with an old nurse ; the latter's death, when the girl was seventeen, caused a severe nervous breakdown ; life seemed to the girl entirely empty and without a haven.

Only children, it has often been observed and recorded in workaday psychology, in legends and fairy tales, are often inclined to be selfish, gullible, unenterprising and inert ; they flag quickly, because they are brought up to expect assistance, easy appreciation and admiration, constant guidance, encouragement and support, none of which are offered to them in " real " life. They often grow up to be people who make unusual and quite impracticable demands on others, especially in the matter of the warmth of human relationships, friendliness and sympathy ; but they them-selves are incapable of any real relationships with their fellow-men, because they have learnt to look on these merely as a means and not as an end in itself. That type of person (it can usually be "spotted" by even a moderately acute observer) who demands constant love, but gives none in return, or if he does, only conditionally—" the other person must behave in such-and-such a way, and then I too . . . " —is often to be found amongst only children ; and it is easily understood how this special childhood-situation can give rise to such a development.

Only children pampered and treated with excessive care, as well as those who are too severely brought up, suffer much more than children exposed to similar influences, but along with brothers and sisters ; for the only child lacks that powerful corrective to threatened self-esteem, the experience of community and the common lot.

In addition to the factors already mentioned, there is another that affects the developing character of the only child, although not so regularly : *the claims that the parents make on the child*, quite apart from those involved in their educational duties. This is a question deserving special attention, and, as it is closely connected with the present subject, we will deal with it at once.

The love of parents for their children is by no means entirely unselfish. That they " seek not their own " can only rarely be asserted of them. Starting with the highly unpleasant, and to my mind almost impermissible, idea of children as a sort of capital investment, down to quite attenuated forms of the same idea, there are all possible shades of parental egotism. The term " capital investment " must not be understood only in the narrow sense, that the parents desire and expect a return on the material, money and time that they have laid out ; many parents would like to know that their love, care and even the performance of their duty have been capitalized and that they can draw an income from them later. Parents quite frequently point out deliberately to the full-grown child that they gave him so much care and attention when he was ill at the age of five years ; and this seems quite intelligible and " natural " not only to these people, but also to others. Natural it may be, but it need not on that account be right.

They appeal to the Fourth Commandment ; [1] but that commandment lays down an obligation of the children, and is silent on the rights of parents ; there are many such unilateral obligations enjoined upon men, without others having a right to demand their fulfilment and, as it were, " to cash them in." There is, then, an obligation of gratitude, but no right to it. So long as emphasis is laid on this commandment for educational purposes, well and good ; but if parents seek its support in order to compel services that are due, but have not been rendered by their already grown-up children, then, in my opinion, they commit a wrong.

[1] According to the Catholic enumeration.

The grown-up person has to settle with his own conscience and with himself about his observation of this commandment ; the parents may, if they will, put to him the question whether he can justify his conduct to himself and to God ; but they cannot presume upon a right that is at the best questionable.

This error is by no means limited to the relationship between grown-up children and parents and the question of the observation of the Fourth Commandment. The underlying idea may be described as the " balance-sheet standpoint " in life, according to which everything done, whether under obligation or otherwise, is entered into a sort of ledger in which the credit column must equal the debit column, if the account is to balance. So many kindnesses, benefits, good works, right actions on my side : for these there are due to me so many benefits, good works and so forth— or at least an equivalent return. Even if it does not go as far as this, people who run their lives on these lines are guilty of a perverted and harmful attitude. Behind this attitude lurks a lack of all generosity ; it implies an absence of the true " freedom of Christian men," and the disposition that gives freely ; our ideas and sentiments in these matters are weakened and corroded by the commercial spirit of our time.

It is strange that people expect and demand reward for their simple duty. Is it not quite obviously and undeniably the duty of parents to tend their child when he is sick, and generally to do their best to bring him up and care for him ? To demand an especial return for this, beyond the consciousness of having fulfilled a natural moral obligation, seems to me wholly mistaken and inadmissible.

It should be quite clearly impressed on the mind that education involves unselfishness, and that the special task of the educationalist—including the parents and all those concerned with the bringing up of children—must be, to borrow the phrase of a famous man, " to educate the children away from themselves." *Education means education to independence and responsibility.* This object is difficult to attain in the case of only children. In a family where there are a number of children it is not taken so much to heart when, first, the eldest releases himself from his intimate bonds, makes his own way in the world, takes up a profession or marries. The others are still there, and in the case of the next one, there are still others, down to the youngest. It is different in the case of the only child, who as a little one was the first to fill the home with shouts and laughter, whose development was followed with joy and anxiety, and who formed the very fulcrum of his parents' lives. The parents have made it possible for him to arrive at occupational, human and moral completeness ; but as the time for his entry into independent life approaches they are filled with gloom and apprehension, and when he takes his departure, the home is almost as cold and gloomy as after a death ; then it is that the parents live more in memory than in the present. This is the reason why parents fail to understand the grown-up child properly, and expect from him the kind of behaviour that was appropriate to earlier childhood. " What an affectionate child he used to be," they say, " and look at him now ! " " How seldom he comes to see us, and how he is changed ! " He must be different, for he lives in another age ; and he must break away, for he has his own life to live. It must be recognized that the position of parents always contains an element of tragedy, and that this is intensified when there is only one child. However much, here as always, we feel bound to " take the side of the children," who are the coming generation and the future members of the Church, we must also be able to take the side of the parents a little and to understand them and their standpoint. Further, it is desirable (and often very successful) to make the children—not only the older ones, but also the quite young ones—obtain psychological insight into their parents' point of view and way of thinking ; in this way, a strained relationship between parents and child is not infrequently smoothed over much more readily than if the parents had attempted to presume on their right and insist on a particular line of conduct.

For all these reasons, in the case of the only child all these trying situations, involving self-assertion under difficult circumstances and the taking and maintenance of a place in the community, are especially difficult. It may be looked upon as a test whether the child, in spite of being an only child, has been properly prepared for the community, if he makes a success of it on first entering school. Schooltime will probably never pass so smoothly with such a child as with others ; his adaptation to the community of his classmates and to the school system always takes a longer time. If no catastrophes occur, if he shows no fear and takes no strong dislike to the school, if his progress in work is not below the average, then it can be said that the dangers connected with his isolated position have probably been overcome, and that further undesirable consequences need not be anticipated.

(ii.) *The eldest child* finds himself, until the birth of the next brother or sister, in the position of an only child. If this favoured position has lasted for several years—three, four or five—the arrival of a second child means the *dethronement* of the first. If the difference of age is greater, the situation is more favourable, because the start of the eldest child is so great that he has no need to worry about his position's being menaced. If, on the other hand, the difference in age is small—say, one or two years—the positions of the two children are so much alike that any disadvantage to the elder will pass unnoticed by him. Admittedly, with unskilful behaviour on the part of the parents, there may be as much danger with an age-difference of one and a half to two years as with one of seven years. A girl who for seven years had been the apple of her parents' eye was dethroned by the arrival of a little brother on whom, as the son, all the attention was lavished. The little girl felt herself, as it were, despised and rejected ; she doubted and finally began to disbelieve in the possibility of ever winning back her position and the loving care of her parents. We find evidence of this in an entry in her diary, when she was already seventeen or eighteen years old : " If only Fred would come a cropper ! "—which simply meant that she hoped to regain her importance, if only her brother would do something to disqualify himself in the eyes of his parents, but believed herself incapable of reaching her goal by her own efforts. Conversely, I have seen a child who at two and a half years could not bear to see her mother take the baby to her breast without herself being held at the same time.

As eldest children see in their younger brothers and sisters more or less dangerous rivals for the parental love and attention, they fall into diverse reaction-type groups. One of the most usual forms of reaction is encouraged by a certain type of parental mode of address : " You are the eldest ; you must be sensible ! " and so on. The child, as it were, makes a deal with the parental authority and sides with it in order to strut before the younger children in its reflected light. It is noteworthy that the eldest children often display a tendency to conservatism and the observance of tradition, whereas the younger incline to reform and revolutionary ideas. Younger sons have always been a somewhat uncertain company ; one has only to recall the *Cadets de Gascogne* in Rostand's *Cyrano*. The fact that in bygone centuries younger sons were earmarked for the Church by no means entirely depended on economic considerations and entail. We are thus provided with a more satisfying explanation than any provided by biology of the striking approximation of the character of eldest children to that of the parents (usually to the more dominant of the pair), whereas the younger and youngest children are more out of the picture.

When there is a sufficient difference of age, eldest children are to a certain extent compensated for their dethronement not only by their approximation to the parents by their own efforts, but by their being placed by them in a position of authority over the younger children, and encouraged to assist in their education. Such an arrangement may benefit the eldest children, but it is for the most part disadvantageous to the younger brothers and sisters. In numerous cases we have seen attitudes of obstinacy, disobedience, defiance and even childish criminality and degradation immediately disappear upon the withdrawal of the children concerned from the oppressive authority of the eldest child.

Let us not, however, forget that in a very large number of cases eldest children have actually taken over the parental rôle with conspicuous success. This happens if the children are orphaned, or if the parents neglect their educational duties or show their offspring no affection. The exercise of authority by elder children in bringing up their younger brothers and sisters requires infinite tact and love ; for the younger ones are fully aware that the elder are by the natural order of things on an equality with and not superior to themselves. Such a usurpation of authority—for so it must appear to the naive sensibilities of the younger ones— must, if it is to be brooked, be exercised with great discretion, a discretion not born of knowledge or precept, but of love and real insight into the moral obligations of authority. This is generally lacking, but one can hardly regard this as blameworthy, for it is only natural, psychologically speaking that these elder children, clothed with an authority that is not their own from the start, and not being entirely sure of their position, privileges and powers, incline to " lord it " and thereby arouse strong opposition. The result is generally lamentable for both sides. Whenever possible, it should be a matter of principle for parents to avoid any delegation, even partial, of their authority to their elder children. If the younger children are particularly lively, the eldest child will usually develop a tendency to sedateness ; if they are untidy, he or she will incline to fussiness, and so on.

In particular, if the eldest child or children are held up to the younger as examples—this the latter detest, and it usually fails in its object—it may happen that they are confirmed in their conceit and model themselves entirely on their parents. The danger in this is that in life outside the home circle, such recognition is hardly come by, and in many positions in real life no privileges are accorded to mere seniority. These considerations might help to throw some light on the psychology of occupational choice. It would be interesting, for example, to investigate statistically what proportion of eldest children incline towards official careers in which seniority plays a part. As far as I know, no one as yet has worked on these lines.

On the other hand, it must not be forgotten that many difficulties are involved in the position of the eldest child, even when the dethronement-mechanism has not played an important part. In some circumstances it is an almost intolerable burden for the eldest child to be made too early aware of, and thereby made to participate in, the parents' trouble. In the case of girls, this may lead to a premature gravity of outlook, a tendency to take everything too much to heart, a degree of pessimism and mistrust of their own lot and " luck." There are some cases in which it is unavoidable that the child should share these burdens, as the result, for example, of various tragic circumstances ; unfortunately it is none the less true that such children are robbed of their childhood.

The particular formation of the family also exerts an influence on the development of the eldest child ; it is not a matter of indifference to which sex it belongs, or whether the second child or the others belong to the same or the opposite sex. In order to avoid repetition, we will postpone discussing these questions until we come to consider the characterology of the sexes more comprehensively in a later section.

(iii.) *The youngest child.*—There is a certain dichotomy in the situation of the youngest child ; he finds himself in many respects at a disadvantage compared with the older children, but he also enjoys many advantages. He can and may do less than the others ; this would not in itself be of importance if his sense of personal value were not thereby threatened. The child knows, however, that he is actually on an equality with his brothers and sisters, especially in respect of the parental relationship. The fact that his brothers and sisters, to his mind unjustifiably, lay claims to and obtain privileges over himself, rankles in his childish soul. The result varies with the general situation as a whole. Either the presence of the elder children stimulates him to achievement of some kind, in games, in the home, or at school, or he will give up the competition, which he feels to be hopeless unless carried on by unfair means. If the youngest child sees that the achievements of the elder win parental approval and recognition, and that he himself has nothing of the same order to offer, he will attempt to bind the parents to him and compel their regard by other means. It is comparatively harmless if this competition for parental recognition is conducted by means of affectionateness and exemplary behaviour, although the latter is in a sense

" unnatural " and generally associated with a strong inclination to project all independence and responsibility from himself to the parents. It is already an unhealthy sign if the child begins to exploit the usual tendency of the parents to coddle and pamper him as the youngest. Similar manifestations are, if he overstresses his helplessness and exhibits fear, not permitting his mother to leave his side ; or he may exhibit every kind of petty ailment, and, finally, as a last resort, attempt by means of the heavy artillery of various " nervous " symptoms to strengthen his position by becoming a constant source of anxiety and the chief, if not the only, object of parental care.

Even these methods, much as they undermine the vital potentialities of the child concerned and mar his preparation for the realities of life, and much as they obtrude themselves as disturbing factors in the home community, are not the worst. Worse are those forms of conduct which, if the child is not content with using any weapons, even unlawful ones, in the struggle for his privileged position, *secure their object by belittling others*. This applies to adults as well as to children, and therefore the point deserves to be treated somewhat more fully.

There are two methods at people's disposal whereby they can attain to a superior position, or at least enjoy the subjective experience of such attainment. This position of superiority looms so large in their eyes because their lack of self-assurance compels. them to be in constant need of external confirmation that they are something, mean something, represent something. The two methods are, of course, first, the exaltation of oneself over others, and, secondly, the degradation or depreciation of others. The depreciation of one's fellow-men is only a special instance of a general belittling or depreciatory tendency, with which we shall proceed to deal next.

5. DEPRECIATION

The simplest, and at the same time least aggressive, kind of depreciation is the belittling *criticism*, or at any rate, an exclusively mental disposition to criticize. That such criticism contains strongly depreciatory elements can readily be seen. I once asked a youth of fifteen, under treatment for stammering, his motive for his frankly admitted tendency to criticize everybody. After a little thought he answered with a laugh indicative of complete insight : " If I run other people down, I put myself in a better position." Depreciatory criticism can disguise itself in many ways ; many people say and do things in which this attitude is clearly manifest, without themselves being aware of it. It is already abnormal when a woman official says : " Then I felt as if the soul of my colleague had entered into me, and I knew I was in a state of mortal sin." This was indeed a highly ingenious way of expressing her opinion of her colleague's complete moral degeneracy. To this class belong all those who are unwilling to shake hands with people, or must at least wash their hands immediately afterwards—to these, everybody else is " unclean," is " a pig "— or those who " can never understand how so-and-so could have done such-and-such " ; and, above all, the many pharisees who say now as of old, " Lord, I thank Thee that I am not as other men are ! "

These last-mentioned forms of conduct—the avoidance of any personal contact, and the like—exceed mere criticism, as does the attitude of those who " cannot get on with " their fellows, do not know " what they ought to say to them," and so on.

In the same way, all that kind of talk which in its extreme form is called *calumny*, exceeds mere criticism. In the strictest sense, this term covers only actions that have as their intent the deliberate spreading of unfavourable reports of a third person, with the intent to do him harm ; but on the road to this extreme there are many stages. The knowledge that the meaning of " calumny "—apart from certain none the less objectionable complicated cases in which it serves as the instrument for other purposes, such as revenge, or political or economic rivalry—is " the depreciation of another person," enables us to interpret many otherwise unintelligible varieties of conduct. One recalls anonymous letters, rumours and the like, which can disturb the peace of a whole township, and drive people to suicide. The will to power here involved and operating secretly like a conspirator is as clearly to be seen as the depreciatory tendency, which is also a constituent.

Similar is the type of behaviour which seeks to camouflage disagreeable views of one's fellow-men with kindness, by means of some modifying phrase. " I don't want to say anything nasty about him, but. . . ." " I will have nothing said about him, but for your own sake I ought to warn you. . . ." " One simply can't imagine why so-and-so does this ; I could never do it myself." Who does not know this sort of talk, and who indeed does not indulge in it himself ?

To return to the children. Those children who feel their position threatened, and employ the weapon of depreciation in its defence, are seldom able to remain content with a merely mentally critical attitude. Either they feel themselves compelled, as it were, to carry out their depreciation into the open, or, lacking sufficient power of their own, they enlist those possessed of power and authority in their cause ; but the only weapons at their disposal are *tale-bearing*, *treachery* and *slander*.

I use the strong expression " treachery " intentionally. From the standpoint of the child, it is treachery and breach of faith for one who is privy to some misdeed, which need not necessarily be heinous, to "sneak" about it to parents, guardians or teachers. From the standpoint of objective law and justice, action of this kind may have a positive value ; we are faced with a problem that cuts both ways. We must bear in mind the fact that we all feel uncomfortable on hearing, for instance, that a member of some gang has betrayed his leader and his fellows. Admittedly, the arrest of the gang and the prevention of further crime is desired, and we congratulate ourselves and society on its occurrence ; but we are nevertheless disposed to withhold our approval from the "traitor." This is not the result of romantic sentiments about robbery ; it is the outcome of the value we attach to loyalty, and the realization that the betrayal was not inspired by any understanding of an objective system of law and community, but by the most selfish motives. This applies to childish "treachery." Children, who are unable, or hardly able, to conceive of abstract law and order, and who are aware of the chasm separating their lives from those of the "mighty ones," immediately regard the tale-bearer as a traitor. They all feel that children should stand together, and that any "deal" between one of themselves and those in authority is in the nature of treachery. Nevertheless, we are bound to maintain that children must be brought up to recognize discipline ; and this is rendered difficult if they learn in the course of their upbringing that such conduct as tale-bearing is treacherous. It would be more satisfactory to teach children that moral standards and justice are of higher value than the idea of childish solidarity. What is one to do ?

I should say that these somewhat disturbing and difficult situations occur with less frequency when fewer regulations are imposed upon children. This provides further confirmation for our earlier statement that the number of prohibitions should be reduced to a minimum.

Children should also be taught the importance of law and

order and their striking similarity to their own unwritten social code ; but one must not encourage or put a premium on tale-bearing, otherwise one runs the risk of seriously impairing the child's experience of solidarity, on which is built the adult's experience of community. Especially must children be made to understand that one of the express duties of parents and teachers is to supervise and judge their conduct. If, for instance, a child stands up in class and says, " Please, Teacher, Smith is reading a book under the desk," the teacher is naturally bound to take notice of the information, and to reprimand Smith ; but at the same time he should let the self-appointed supervisor know in no uncertain terms that Smith's behaviour is the concern of the teacher, and not that of another pupil. On closer examination it will be found that in a number of cases the motive for tale-bearing does not lie in any special " uprightness " or regard for discipline, but in the child's own aims and desires, whether it is to show off, to attract the attention of the teacher— often these " righteous " children are poor scholars—or to satisfy a private grudge.

We have already drawn attention to the fact that the delegation of authority or punitive power to elder children is likely to harm the spirit of the younger children, who are thus subordinated contrary to their own sense of justice. This applies equally to school-children in the same class. To give children a kind of police authority over others is in my opinion dangerous ; it is also quite unnecessary from the point of view of the teacher or parent. The danger is a twofold one. The tale-bearers turn into pharisees ; the others, disillusioned by these examples, lose their confidence both in the community and in their upbringer.

Such conduct seems to come naturally to those children who see in other children—brothers and sisters, for example —invincible rivals for parental regard, and seek to win such regard for themselves by ejecting the others from their favoured positions. Some children in these circumstances even have recourse to the weapon of real calumny.

Herein we find yet another motive for childish mendacity, a subject we have already discussed. In this case the object of the falsehood is to win a position for oneself or to strengthen it when won ; the more one depreciates one's competitors by means of lies, the more one gains in personal importance. From this form of lying, the transition to boasting, swaggering and imposture is easy.

I believe that the indications already given, although capable of development in all directions, are sufficient to demonstrate the importance of the constitution of the family for the formation of character both in childhood and in later years, and to signal out the dangers to be avoided and the precautions necessary for a satisfactory education. The subject will come in for further attention in subsequent sections of this book. In particular, we shall have much to say on the importance of sex as a factor in character-formation, and also on the problems of delinquency, degradation and neurosis in childhood.

Before, however, proceeding to treat further of the conditions affecting character-development, we must interpose a digression on another matter.

CHAPTER IV

THE IDEAL OF CHARACTER AND THE OPERATION OF EXAMPLE

I. PRELIMINARY REMARKS

As perhaps might be gathered from the above heading, the ideals we are about to treat of are not " ideal characters " in the sense in which that phrase is often used—as, for example, when one speaks of anyone as an " ideal " priest, officer or doctor, or as " the ideal " of goodness, amiability or equanimity. We are going to consider not ideal types, but personal ideals, those pictures fashioned by man of what he should be and how he ought to act ; nor are we concerned with the idea which a person has of his own actual make-up. It would seem more correct to give priority to this problem of self-knowledge and self-evaluation, since the ideal, regarded as a directional force and as a goal, is somehow experienced through the difference that is felt to exist between it (the ideal) and the person as he really is. For convenience of method, however, we shall defer this problem for the present, and conduct an inquiry into the nature and origin of these ideals.

Quite apart from their genesis, there are two points of view with regard to ideals. According to the one, an ideal, if not an attainable goal, is at any rate one towards which it is possible to progress ; a man may suffer from the slow progress he makes and his inevitable relapses, from the fact that he regards the complete realization of his imagined ideal as an impossibility ; but still he has the consciousness of movement in the direction of his ideal—not a continuous movement perhaps, nor one free from periods of arrest, but yet, on the whole, movement. The man who regards the ideals from the other point of view sees in the ideal that floats before him something that is quite unattainable—indeed, so far beyond all possible approximation, even, that it is felt to be wholly useless and impracticable to take steps in its direction. Ideals regarded in this way may be thought of as falling into two groups. The first group is characterized by the formula : " According to my inner and real value, I should and could be so-and-so ; but I cannot follow that path because I [and then follow various reasons] am too weak or too evil, because it is too late, because others have made it impossible for me, because I was badly brought up, because this or that condition must first be fulfilled and cannot be fulfilled." The other formula is : " One [not " I, as I am "] ought to be or can be so-and-so, but I am not like that." To this group belongs, for example, the ideal of the man who is weak and puny and says to himself : " Really, one ought to be big and strong ", the ideal of the woman who thinks she really ought to have been a man, and so on.

2. THE SOURCES OF IDEALS

Those ideals which in the course of life can undergo many changes, arise, as far as I can see, from various main sources. In the first place they may be said to arise from emulation and imitation. These two concepts have not quite the same meaning ; but they shade one into the other without any sharply defined boundaries, and the behaviour-patterns appropriate to each are easily blended. True emulation, which presupposes the inward approval of the person taken as exemplar, very readily passes on to imitation. Conversely, mere imitation can become emulation, or the latter can substitute itself for the former. But even the negative aspects of these attitudes can be responsible for an ideal of character ; it is obvious that the radical dislike of someone can colour the picture of the person " whom one would like to be " as strongly as unqualified admiration.

The importance of the character-ideal, both for the life of the individual and for the form taken by the actually realized character—the principles forming the basis of action —vary with the nature of the ideal and its primary origin. A further difference arises from the fact, already mentioned, that there are people for whom the ideal is an important determining factor for their conduct and practical experience and others on whom it exerts no practical influence whatever. There is also an intermediate type ; for the individuals belonging to each group vary with the extent to which their point of view is allowed really to impinge upon their concrete selves.

If, on the one hand, these distinctions affect the position of the character-ideal from the point of view of the experience of the individual ego, on the other hand these ideals must be considered in respect of their content. Between the latter and the functions attaching to the character-ideal in actual experience there are, naturally, close relations. It is clear that all those ideals whose content is such as to preclude their realization from the outset exercise no decisive influence in practice, and are pre-eminently such as to give occasion to an experiencing of the ideal in pure fantasy or to a consciousness that it is absolutely unattainable.

Further, there are two forces at work in the genesis of the character-ideal and its sources. There are, in the first place, recognition of the operation of the laws of value and the gradation of values, and, secondly, the mechanisms o compensation and over-compensation, which have been fully dealt with in a previous section. Of course, we do not desire to interpret the formation of ideals exclusively in terms of the operation of these latter mechanisms ; such an attempt would involve a failure to appreciate the reciproca deter-mination of all human conduct and experience by the ego and the non-ego ; further, it would involve an extreme naturalistic psychology in our conception of things, and as such must be rejected. Yet there is urgent need for careful investigation of these subjective factors, for they play an important part in the development of ideals, and the neglect of this aspect of the question ruins the most conscientious efforts on the part of a teacher to impress on the pupil's mind the claims of ideals of any kind.

3. THE SIGNIFICANCE OF THE IDEAL

A detailed description of the individual varieties of the character-ideal, and the way in which they are experienced, is outside the scope of our present work. We shall limit ourselves to some points of practical importance, amongst which particular significance is attached to the character-ideal that is in itself unattainable and is experienced by the individual concerned as essentially unattainable or un-attainable by himself.

That which is by its nature unattainable can neither be " willed " nor striven after. With such goals, which are really unworthy of that designation, one can deal only as if they were in fact striven for. The development of a character-ideal of this kind results only in a completely fruitless dissipation of energy and a general demeanour and behaviour that bear the stamp of " artificiality." (Artifi-ciality will be fully dealt with in a later section.)

We have seen that the stimulus to compensatory and over-compensatory fantasy-formation and the holding of exaggerated character-ideals is the experience of actual or imagined inferiority. Once more we are brought up against the great practical importance of the inferiority-experience and the necessity of guarding against it as much as possible. Anyone who has had much experience of people in whose lives exaggerated ideals have figured considerably is aware that these attitudes, which are so prejudicial to his internal and external life, originated in childhood, and, in fact, in experiences of inferiority.

In the genesis of the personal ideal, the character-ideal, decisive importance attaches to the *figures of the parents*. The child knows, to some extent, as we have seen, that he will grow up and will one day be called upon to take his place as a fully-grown adult. By observing his parents, the child seeks to learn and experience how this place in life is conditioned, and how he ought to behave when he has attained it. Consequently, the ideas given by the parents to the small child of the conditions, obligations, rights and duties of man's estate, indicate the direction he himself must take to assume this position.

There are possibilities of deviation from the proper lines in various directions, amongst which is the sex of the person concerned.

The first danger arises from *the one-sided predominance of one of the parents*. Children in such families are in a position to see one of the parents, who as a rule has retained some measure of authority over themselves, unable to " stand up to " the other, the dominant parent ; these children, in accordance with their natural disposition, desiring power and expecting by its possession to rid themselves of their feelings of inferiority and subordination, are easily discouraged by the spectacle of the parental situation, and tend to regard the attainment of their own personal full adulthood with all its implications as almost impossibly remote. They have no confidence of ever reaching such heights of power and importance as they see wielded by the domestic dictator. Greatness of any kind, fame, positions of authority and the like, are interpreted by children solely in terms of power ; they therefore run the same risk, although usually not so immediately, as that resulting from one-sided domestic hegemony, by being brought up against these factors in relation to the parents. Let us not forget the tragic element, and only too often the real tragedy, in the lives of " children of great men."

The effect of such impressions on the development of the childish character is frequently that the child becomes unwilling to relinquish his childish attitude or to sacrifice the situations of childhood at all.[1] Burdened with the knowledge—in fact deceptive, and naturally not admitted—that they are incapable of adulthood, which to their imagination towers above them as something immeasurably grand, some people cling permanently to the child's attitude. Often it is simply a case of the small children who " don't want to grow up," but sometimes a more or less childish attitude persists well beyond the years of puberty. Obviously the result is a series of conflicts ; internal because this obstinately preserved attitude is not in correspondence with the realities of adulthood ; and external because the person's contemporaries are unwilling to concede to him the privileges of childhood.

We may select this opportunity to note that a close investigation of many cases of so-called " psychic infantil- ism " reveals their reactive genesis. One is apt to assume that all those cases of " arrested development " which resist our therapeutic efforts are organically determined ; but such a pessimistic diagnosis should be resorted to only after a process of elimination involving a most exhaustive investigation of the whole make-up and life-history of the person concerned.

[1] Crichton Millar employs the useful and picturesque phrase " the Peter Pan complex " to describe this attitude. The more correct phrase would be " Peter Pan attitude."—TRANS.

This clinging to childhood is only one of the means by which a person who despairs of attaining a goal that seems necessary for him but yet beyond him seeks escape from the demands this goal makes upon him. A large variety of developments, which in their extreme form are obviously pathological, can be traced to such childhood impressions. We shall later become acquainted with some of these under the heading of " the nervous character."

In any case, the presence of a dominating figure in the small child's environment is liable to increase his discouragement. If the father is the wielder of power and greatness, it reacts more ominously, as a rule, on the girls than on the boys, especially if the position of the mother in the family is unfavourable. Under such circumstances the girl tends to grow up with the impression that importance, greatness and power are masculine perquisites, and that woman—even the mother, who is so infinitely superior to the small child— melts into nothingness, as it were, in the presence of the male, or at the most, can only play a subsidiary and subordinate part. If in addition, as unfortunately only too often happens, the little girl observes the father showing scant respect for the mother, belittling her before the children, she can only form the worst possible conceptions of woman's place in the world. The consequence of this is, on the one hand rebellion, provided she has sufficient courage, and on the other a deep sense of dissatisfaction with the position of her sex. This rebellion sometimes results in an active alliance of the daughters with the mother to form a front against the father, but as the opposition party is generally the weaker, it is usually forced to have recourse to the weapons of the weak—cunning, lying and deception —and an atmosphere is generated that can certainly hardly be considered suitable for the development of the moral character.

The presence of a dominant female figure acts in the same way on the boys, though not as a rule so strongly or so frequently as in the opposite case. If the father is " henpecked " and the mother is seen as the person in undisputed authority, there can be implanted in the boys a more or less strongly reacting dislike and fear of women, which may give rise later to all kind of aberrations, the most extreme of which is homosexuality. This twofold attitude—the desire to comport oneself as a man while one is yet possessed of a secret dread of women—shows itself most clearly in the case of those men who strive after a pronounced, or even exaggerated, masculine form of life, except on the erotic side, which they reject completely.

We will not go further into other questions connected with those on which we have just touched. That the personal disposition of the parents—and the whole complex of education—must be of paramount importance in view of the part it plays in the formation of childish ideals is obvious without further elaboration. It is not talks, lessons or homilies that decisively impress the child with the nature, position and obligations of adults, but the general make-up, deportment and conduct of the latter.

In discussing the problem of character-ideals we must, of course, be quite clear that here also a person's professions of his ideal cannot be accepted at their face value ; once again the rule applies that the purpose that a person has really set himself and that truly colours his life can be deduced only from his actions and conduct regarded as a whole. There may be conflict not only between " ideal and reality," but also between two ideals, of which the one may be in harmony with the deeper make-up, or at least the outcome of the life-experience, of the person concerned, and the other can be merely " wished on " him, suggested to him or implanted in him.

The latter type of ideal, which is often foreign or even antagonistic to the person's true nature, is often modelled on some definite figure, either living or historical, who in the course of the child's education is set before him as an eminently desirable example for emulation and imitation.

Such well-meant attempts to present the child with a definite figure as an ideal, and to encourage him to model his life on it, are sometimes questionable. It must be borne in mind that this ideal is presented by a person wrapped in the robes of authority, that the presentation is made persistently with energy and emphasis, and that consequently the child, with his lack of discrimination and self-criticism, submits to this kind of suggestion, even though he may be unable to establish any true inward relationship with the ideal figure. In this way an entirely unnecessary and undesirable conflict is set up in the child's soul. Often the enthusiasm of their delineators deprives these ideal figures of all human features, so that they emerge as mere bloodless abstractions, no longer able to represent the incarnation of virtues in a man who, in spite of these virtues, still wore all the trappings of humanity. The realization of such an ideal is impossible, because the image is outside all reality ; an entirely artificial situation is thus created, which is exceedingly harmful for the individual, who is made to cherish an essentially unattainable ideal, impossible to live up to, and the source of unwholesome conflict.

For these reasons, amongst others, it is unwise to set as examples before children ideal figures that belong to quite different conditions of life to those in which the children are placed. A young mechanic should not choose Julius Cæsar, nor a tax-collector Napoleon, as his ideal figure ; St. Catherine of Siena is not a suitable example for girls of our time, and the life of a solitary is not an ideal for the realities of modern social and economic conditions. We may add to this that the lives of most of the saints, as they are described for us, are quite remote from all actuality, not only from ours but also from that of the saint ; compare, for example, the more modern, historically accurate biographies of St. Aloysius Gonzaga with the older ones. In particular, there seems to be danger in presenting people who have to pass their lives in secular pursuits, under active conditions, with the ideals of monastic existence.

4. AMBITION

Since we are dealing with ideals and aims, it seems appropriate at this point to introduce the discussion of a concept that, although unspecified, has been more or less continuously in the background of our speculations : ambition.

Often parents and teachers complain that a child is totally lacking in ambition, stating frankly that it is essential for him to display this quality, and try to incite him to it. They do this, for instance, by holding up someone else as an example, a fellow-scholar or one of his brothers or sisters ; or else the unambitious little creature is assured that unless he changes in this respect, there is no prospect of his ever doing anything. (We have already seen that this kind of talk is, to say the least, unskilful and calculated to cause discouragement.)

The word " ambition," in German *Ehrgeiz*, has a dual meaning. According to its etymology, it means, of course, like its synonyms in other languages, a desire for honour from outside, for recognition and acknowledgement—in fact, a desire directed towards all those ends which we have learnt to associate with the primitive will to power. But the word is also used in another sense. Both meanings share in common the sense of efforts directed towards certain higher goals. However different these two meanings may be, they become entangled on account of an extremely widespread confusion of two other concepts. It is rare to come across people who can clearly differentiate between *achievement* and *success*, or at least act in such a way that the distinction is made apparent as not merely conceptual, but also actual. Everyone concedes in theory that not every achievement is necessarily bound up with success, that many a great intellectual achievement will often be honoured only in later centuries, that many an achievement passes altogether unnoticed. It will also be willingly acknowledged that the reward of achievement lies primarily in the consciousness of achievement, that it is sufficient to be able to say to oneself, " I have done this as well as I possibly could." Such admissions, however, are too exclusively on the theoretical, the purely intellectual, conceptual level ; it is rare for them really to become part and parcel of the person concerned, so that they are alchemized into truly " experienced " knowledge. The inner uncertainty that is inherent in every human being prevents such self-confidence, and yearns for confirmation by outside approval of that self-esteem which is always doubted ; and it cannot be maintained that such a wish is in itself objectionable. Man's yearning for the recognition of himself and of his deeds by others is part of his nature, and derived to some extent from the primitive tendency of the will to community. For many a man it is sufficient if a few persons, or possibly only one, approve what he does or is ; not everyone desires universal admiration. Here, as in all the attitudes and directions taken by human life, the inner antithesis finds expression. The desire for recognition derives not only from the will to community, but also from the will to power. The contribution made by the will to community to the desire to count for something amongst others and to win their recognition is some such thing as the wish to feel oneself on an equality with the

rest, to see oneself welcome to them and not a burden, or the
desire for frictionless inclusion within the community that is
demanded by the objective laws of being. The same wish,
in so far as it manifests the will to power, means the desire
to be more than others, the desire for a position above them
so that they are compelled to look up to one. The more this
second aspect predominates in a person's general conduct,
the more is the desire for achievement converted into the
desire for success, for mere success, for success at any price,
and finally for the mere illusion of success.

This mistaken attitude, which, if adopted to excess, is quite
fatal, is encouraged by an indisputable fact, consciousness
of which seems to act like a sort of inner necessity : the fact
that quantitatively speaking, as a general rule, achievement
varies in direct ratio to success. Finally, even those men
who were ignored by their contemporaries, and whose
achievements first came to be admired by later generations,
have almost without exception had a small circle of followers
and admirers. It is true that one does not know how many
human achievements are lost owing to unfavourable
circumstances, or prevented from completion by lack of
recognition by a few or even one of one's fellow-creatures ;
but so far as we can see into things, all real achievements
seem to have enjoyed some measure of success. It follows
that people have come to see in success a criterion for
achievement, and doubt its authenticity in the absence of
success. It depends, however, on a person's opinion of his
need of success, with how much he can content himself. It
is given only to the few to accomplish great deeds ; and only
great deeds have any claim to great success. Those people
who crave for great success (and in accordance with the
law of over-compensation their craving will vary inversely
with the certainty of their own value) and who are not in a
position to produce great achievements—for these depend

on their innermost personal disposition, and this, again, on their sense of personal value, and hence also on their courage—those people, I say, who crave for a success in excess of their achievements are the victims of a false and unhealthy ambition, an ambition that cannot lead to real achievement, and whose cultivation must therefore be condemned.

The great difficulty is that practical life is generally (at least in theory) so constituted that success and objective achievements run in some measure parallel to each other. We added the proviso, " at least in theory," because we naturally cannot ignore the fact that outward success not infrequently comes the way of those who can point to no achievements whatever, or only to small ones, and who owe their success to a thousand and one factors, none of which is related to achievement. Not everyone is called upon for objectively great achievements. It may be that the circumstances of life do not permit of the full realization of all the possibilities of achievement inherent in a person, or it may be that the scope of their potentialities is restricted ; in any case not everyone can claim to achieve greatness.

If a person grows up in an atmosphere of competition, with incessant references to the achievements of others as a standard and as a goal, and if by reason of external or internal considerations he is unable to attain such a standard, his self-confidence and self-esteem are seriously threatened ; not only therefore is he unlikely to scale the heights of achievement which tower before his mind's eye, and for which he is objectively unsuited, but he will also achieve less, and often very considerably less, than his real possibilities allow.

We have already pointed out that, strictly speaking, achievement should be measured by individual and not by objective standards. If a small child, by expending all his

strength, carries a pack that for us would be quite negligible,
it corresponds in terms of achievement to our dragging along
a hundredweight sack ; but in the workaday world and
above all, in economic life, the objectively greater achievement is the thing that counts. From ethical and other
standards, the subjective expenditure and not the objective
result should constitute the criterion of value. Let me refer
again to the parable of the talents.[1] The servant who had
received only two talents and rendered four was received
with the same words and the same reward as the one who
had received five and rendered ten. This demonstrates that
it is not the objective amount of achievement that counts,
but the degree to which a man converts his potentialities
into actualities. Assuredly, the third servant, to whom only
one talent had been entrusted, would have received the
same reward if he had appeared before his master with two
talents ; and who knows if he might not perhaps have been
able to render two and a half talents ?

The difficulty lies in the discrepancy between ethical and
" practical " standards.[2] It is not our business to inquire
how this unsatisfactory position, which, moreover, makes
itself felt in many economic and industrial problems, is
to be remedied ; education must take the world as it
finds it.

Recognition, however, of the fact that only achievements
that are relative to a person's potentialities should furnish
the basis of judgment is not without its hidden dangers.
One is, that the individual, especially in a state of discouragement, will too readily content himself with objectively
small achievements, consoling himself with the thought that
he is not called on for anything further, nor capable of

[1] *Mat.* xxv. 14.
[2] This difficulty extends in many other directions, affecting, for example, the
problem of the dismissal of employees, and similar industrial problems. Cf.
my observations on the subject in *Arbeit, Ermüdung, Ruhe*, in the *Handbuch der
socialen Hygiene* (Berlin, 1927).

anything greater. In other words, the recognition of this truth, as of every other truth, can be misused to support a cowardly attitude, an attitude ill-adapted for life.

The second danger is perhaps even more significant and perilous. It consists in people's inclination to measure the greatness of their achievement against the factor of subjective effort and self-mastery involved. Such people, whose name is legion, regard some objectively trivial or even futile achievement as valuable and great, because it involved a victory over inward resistance. This point demands some consideration.

In the first place, it is not right that self-mastery should serve as the measure of the moral value of an action, or at least the sole or most preferred standard of measurement. The decisive factor in the value of an action is first and foremost the value actually realized in and by it. The opinion we here reject derives from a one-sided over-emphasis of the *subject* in action, which is always to be conceived of as a relation between subject and object, ego and non-ego. Just as a murder is neither to be more nor less abhorred and condemned because the murderer had to master himself— to overcome his inhibitions against murder—so an action of positive value does not acquire greater value from the element of self-mastery. We find, in the cases of the greatest saints, people whose every action impresses us with the quality of unattainable goodness and inestimable value, that their deeds seem to them easy, obvious, " natural." Not that there is any doubt that self-mastery is necessary, and must be fostered in education ; but self-mastery as such, regarded by itself, is of no value, and becomes valuable only in proportion to the value for whose sake it is acquired. Behind the idea of self-mastery as a value in itself there is a mistaken heroic ideal and in the last resort a subjectivist individualism that assigns the value of an action to itself alone without regard for the dependence of man on others, and on all the inter-related hierarchies of being of which he is a part.

This last consideration leads us directly to the second point. It should be clearly understood that it is an easy matter for a person to conjure up internal resistances and obstacles, the overcoming of which, by reason of that mistaken subjective conception of self-mastery, gives him the illusion of an action of ethical value, but in reality only feeds his vanity and serves as an escape from actions that are difficult, but actually demanded of him. We shall see that the symptomatology of many of the so-called functional nervous diseases derives largely from efforts of this kind, which serve as the subjective exaggeration of achievement. When a woman patient, prevented by agoraphobia from going about the streets, tells me triumphantly over and over again for weeks on end that she has been to a shop perhaps a hundred yards from home, she really means that this achievement, which for anyone else would be trivial, has been for her a deed of heroism. It is certainly more difficult to climb a hill 600 feet high with peas in one's shoes than a mountain 6,000 feet high with proper climbing equipment; nevertheless, 6,000 feet is ten times as high as 600.

Now, if people crave for outward success and believe that they are unable to secure it through achievement, and if the consciousness of having done their best—of having doubled their talents—fails to satisfy them, then they resort to these (admittedly unconscious) artifices to exaggerate the subjective experience of achievement. In this way, although this is not the only way, neurosis may arise from mistaken ambition; but of this more later.

Parallel with the confusion of the concepts of " achieve-ment " and " success," which we have just criticized, there is a twin confusion of " failure " and " defeat." Failure does not always imply defeat or disgrace ; is it not often due to the impracticability of the enterprise, and even more often to inadequate experience ? The more ambitious a person is, the more will he crave for success, which becomes more and more essential as a means of bolstering up his self-esteem and silencing the ever-nagging voice of secret doubt, reminding him incessantly of his own inadequacy ; the more he comes to depend on immediate success, the more inclined is he to regard failure as defeat and defeat as dishonour, and the more will he shrink from putting himself to the test on any occasion, because every test involves the possibility of defeat.

Consequently it seems ill-advised to imbue children and young people at too early a stage with that kind of ambition which views success as its goal ; and, above all, it appears expedient to avoid holding up before them overmuch any individual figure as an example, since it is difficult to determine whether such a figure corresponds with the particular nature of the person concerned. It is much better to point out from the outset that no one can do more than his best, and that no more can be asked of him. I know full well that there are great difficulties in the way, one of which is the fact that evaluation according to the objective measure of achievement begins at school with the system of " marks." It is obvious that a pupil who has not attained the requisite standard of knowledge cannot be recommended for promotion to a higher form, even though one is convinced that he has done his best. We need not, however, pursue these matters further at this point, as we shall have another opportunity to speak of them.

5. TRUE AND FALSE IDEALS

After this necessary digression, we shall now return to the subject of this chapter, namely, ideals of character. From what has been said above, it follows that the universal form of the " right " ideal of character is to be defined as the complete realization of all the positive potentialities inherent in the person. Before we can discuss the nature, origin, and mode of operation of particular forms of character-ideals, we must elaborate a little this concept of inherent potentialities and their realization.

It is impossible to determine the kind and number of these potentialities in advance ; only the effort to realize this or that potentiality can inform us of the position with regard to it, and even then the issue of such an effort may lead us into error—rarely, when the issue is positive, but very frequently when the result is negative. The negative outcome may be due quite as much to internal inhibitions and lack of courage as to the actual lack of the assumed abilities ; but this will be more exhaustively dealt with later. For the moment, we may make one deduction from such experiences, namely that it is extremely difficult to diagnose the presence, and still more the absence, of particular potentialities, and that hasty diagnoses of this kind are therefore very often erroneous. It may be added that this applies to positive as well as negative potentialities (with a reversal, in the case of the latter, of the terms of the statement) for one is far too readily inclined to assume hastily the presence of " evil dispositions."

This difficulty of determining the presence or absence of potentialities applies not only to external observation, but also, and indeed to a higher degree, to introspection. As a matter of fact, we can learn from everyday experience that people possess unimagined possibilities which unexpectedly come to light under certain conditions. What changes have been brought about in people by true love, what achievements have been accomplished by quite ordinary people in fits of enthusiasm, how many people have surprised us by performing some deed of which we should " never have believed them capable " ! During the war a Polish reservist in our field-hospital, who was generally considered a ne'er-do-well, and who had certainly never shown any particular qualities of self-sacrifice, was the first to rush into a burning house in the village to rescue a small child who was entrapped in the flames.

Many people believe that they have, so to speak, " got everything out of themselves " that happens to be in them, that they have " touched their limits "—I am speaking in the moral sense—and that they could not be better, more lovable, and generally different from what they are ; they are simply what they are. They believe it, and others believe it of them, because they see that the person has remained the same and unchanging for years : he is quite a good fellow, he does no harm to anyone, he fills his place quite well, though he is nothing special ; one does not demand more from one-self, and certainly one has not the right to demand more from one's fellow-men. Such an attitude is extraordinarily common and widespread, and yet it is fundamentally false. It is so false that it is actually disproved every day ; and yet people persist in it. It is difficult to understand why they cling to it so firmly when, as we have said, and shall demon-strate more clearly, it is quite mistaken. One reason is undoubtedly that the belief in the stagnation and immuta-bility of one's fellow-men, and indeed of one's own individual ego, appears to provide a certain security. Confidence in cosmic law and regularity is necessary for the orderliness of our life and the making of plans, and we also need, or imagine that we need, a belief in the stability of our fellow-men and a certain calculability in their actions. Life would seem to us far too difficult if we regarded it as a continuous adventure, a series of not wholly foreseeable events, causing us continually to be on the *qui vive* for what might happen. (In reality life *is* an adventure. and must be so lived and endured : " Be ready, that is everything.") A second motive for persisting in this mistaken attitude is that people gladly deceive themselves, through a kind of conceit that they know something of the inner working of the world and its laws. As in the case of disappointment, there is a secret revolt against the fact that the world and people choose to be and act differently from what we had imagined ; underlying which is a demand that the laws of cause and effect, as they are apprehended by us, should remain inviolable. It is a reversion, perhaps, to the age-old mistaken effort to be like God, of which we have already spoken.

A man's potentialities—the values inherent in him but not yet realized—are not to be thought of as all laid down in some " surface stratum," but must be sought in the uttermost depths of the person, in the most individual and ultimate core of his being. From this region, whose depths are not to be plumbed by introspection and are only just perceptible to outside observation, they emerge on their mission of realization. That we ourselves know even less of our latent possibilities than the outside observer is shown by a not uncommon experience. Often our own actions come more as a surprise to us than they do to other people ; frequently someone else is able to persuade us that we could do something of which we believed ourselves incapable, and he proves to be right. The wise admonition of educationalists : " Only try it, and you will be able to do it ; I know you will ! " is often justified. If the educator enjoys the child's confidence and understands him—that is, perceives his latent possibilities—there is hardly anything more likely to encourage him than such a remark.

I declare that it is fundamentally false to maintain that the potentialities of anyone, including our own, are exhausted. Such an attitude leaves out of account the fact that by the influence of grace something unexpected may emerge from a human being. It is true that it is likely that grace works on something that is already there—" *gratia non tollit naturam, sed perficit* "—but it is also conceivable that it creates something new. Therefore, this argument in itself cannot be of very considerable weight.

Individual life, like the historical life of mankind—but this begins, be it well understood, with the Fall !—is nothing more than the *successive realization of all values inherent as potentialities*. The transformation of potentiality into act, to employ the terminology of scholasticism, is the essence and meaning of human life. I am convinced that the tension between what has been realized and what remains to be realized—granting the possibility of a storehouse of values in the core of the person—that this " gradient of values," as I call it, provides the real motor power, the actual driving-force, by which the movement of life is maintained. When a man has ceaselessly realized all that there was of value-potentialities in the depths of his being, his life must come to a standstill ; he must die. That is, I think, why so many saints die young. If we consider the life of a St. Aloysius Gonzaga, a St. John Berchmans, a St. Theresa of the Child Jesus, or her uncanonized but very saintly companion in the same Order, Maria of the Most Holy Trinity, or Angelica of Jesus, or many others, do we not get the strong impression that for these people there was nothing left over for them to do on earth, that they had realized everything that it had been in any way possible for them to realize ? And further, that so many of these young saints had died in such grievous suffering because the endurance of pain and sickness was the last task for them to accomplish ? In German common parlance one says of such people that they were *früh vollendet*, " completed early," a delicate and penetrating phrase. They have completed what was in them to complete ; they are complete, because all the value-potentialities they housed have become value-actualities. It is true that we cannot reverse the formula and say that when a man's life comes to an end, he *has* realized all his value-potentialities. Most people's lives decline without their having done so ; but as long as a man lives, so long does he incorporate realizable values. So long as he lives, therefore, a man cannot say of himself—and no one can say of him—that there is no possibility of emergence from him of something different, something new and unheard-of. It is not only an unusual *commotio*, such as inspiration, an emergency, or deep and genuine love, but even quite trivial occurrences that may awaken something unexpected in a person ; sometimes illness, or a passing word spoken by anyone, or an experience in no way unusual in itself, may for some unknown reason act catalytically.

Since no one himself really knows, nor can another determine definitely, the content of his inmost being, it is extraordinarily difficult to select an ideal appropriate to the true person, to " the dweller in the innermost." The difficulty would not be so great if one could expect a man to modify his ideal in accordance with his own development and experience ; but that happens either not at all or only to a very small extent. Men cling to their conscious or unconscious ideal images ; for their fantasies are rooted in earliest childhood, reaching back to a period in their lives when criticism was not yet functioning and receptivity was at its highest. Thus people cling to their ideals, the ideal images of themselves, because their modification involves a great undertaking, often no less than a complete reorientation, in the compassing of which not only inertia, innate conservatism and servitude to habit, but also external obstacles must be overcome. For this reason, also, it is at the least imprudent to set before a child too early in life a definite, clear-cut ideal figure which he is encouraged to imitate and emulate ;

there is too grave a danger of forcing his life into channels for which it is not created. Not only are the values incorporated in the ideal figure not re-realized, because the person's potentialities lie in other directions, but other values are smothered.

An easy way out of the difficulty may occur to people, and attention may be redirected to an idea that was greatly in vogue in the recent past and regarded as an educational panacea. In view of one's inevitable ignorance of a mans' potentialities, it seemed logical to bring him up in such a way that the " development of his own personality " was set before him as his own business. If no obstacle were placed in the way of this development and every encouragement were given on the first indication that the developmental process had started, then, automatically as it were, a character-ideal would form, appropriate to the person's special needs.

Plausible as this may sound to many ears, it is wrong from beginning to end.

The general idea represented by this theory can be described as the product of that brand of individualism which since the Renaissance—it actually began in the late mediæval period—has been steadily gaining ground and giving rise to a series of by no means desirable by-products. Since no one is so foolish as to believe that the good of the community, regarded as a whole, can be simply set aside— if only for the reason that the individual cannot assure his own well-being if that of the community is not equally assured—such a view can only be held on the assumption that the most complete development of each separate individual coincidently secures communal progress. One must also suppose that in some way or other the selfish interests of the individuals will balance each other or cancel each other out, engendering a kind of physical equilibrium of

forces favourable to collective interests. We are unable to
criticize these views here ; we desire only to indicate that the
above-mentioned educational principle was grounded on
a quite definite philosophical position and on economic
theories arising from it.

We have already seen that every person is from the beginning informed by the will to power ; so much so, that unless
the will to community effects the necessary adjustment, it
will show a disproportionate development. If, then, all
restrictions that might serve to check " the free development
of the personality " were raised, the primitive urge of the
will to power would obtain the upper hand ; true development of a person's latent potentialities would thereby be
rendered impossible ; for even a single one of them, in the
absence of obstacles, would by hypertrophy choke the
remainder. The idea of a free, unrestrained education with
the object of developing an all-round, complete personality
is thus shown to be self-contradictory and to nullify its
object by its own procedure. We shall have further opportunity of showing how little such an ideal of autarchy,
whether designed by the educators or by the person concerned, is calculated to provide a satisfactory solution of the
problems of life and a frictionless existence. Experience
teaches us, on the contrary, that the regulation of his life in
accordance with such an ideal sooner or later brings the
person into conflict with the laws and powers of reality, and
ultimately renders him more or less incapable of facing life.

On the other hand, the development of a person's positive
potentialities is indubitably one of the duties of education,
the more so in that, in a certain sense, it is also a moral
obligation imposed upon the person himself. But it is not the
primary duty, since neither from the standpoint of natural
science nor from that of religion should the individual be
regarded as the main objective. A moral autonomy of this

kind is wrong, philosophically unjustifiable, and leads in practice to bad results. How little such an idea can assure a peaceful and successful development, and what a disturbing factor it proves to be, is shown by the countless religious difficulties of people who see in their own completion the most important object of the religious life. Very rightly has Fr. Bichlmaier, S.J.,[1] argued that individual perfection can never stand as the primary goal of the religious life, which should always be God and the keeping of His commandments ; for man may in no wise be set up as something absolute, or be regarded as an end in himself, as St. Ignatius teaches us in the Foundation of his little book of *Exercises*. We will therefore turn aside from the ideal of the autarchic and autonomous personality, and investigate other character-ideals, their justification, their operation in the life of the individual, and their origin.

6. GREATNESS AND HEROISM

We will first consider a group of ideals—greatness, strength and heroism—that show a close relationship with those we have just rejected, and are in fact, one may say, derived from them by a series of gradual transitions. These ideals are in no way calculated to make life subjectively pleasant or objectively productive ; but, in order that there may be no misunderstandings on this point, which I believe to be a very important one, we must give it a somewhat fuller discussion.

Here also, lack of definition in the meaning of the words used in current speech is painfully apparent. The words that are our present concern are, like many others, so blunted and worn out, and their real meaning is so often diverted and obscured, that their use always involves a certain risk. Everyone may understand them in a different sense ; and

[1] *Zeitschrift für Aszesis und Mystik*, Vol. I, Part 1.

even if the various meanings differ only slightly from each other, the conclusions reached with the help of such words may show a very wide divergence. We may remark at this point that for this reason it is mistaken to wish to eliminate—particularly from scientific expositions—words deriving directly from a foreign language or a special terminology. Such words, just because they are less hackneyed than those in everyday use, tend better to preserve their original or special meaning. The history of intellectual development shows clearly that newly coined and newly introduced words are often quickly absorbed into the vernacular and then speedily lose their sharpness and definition. Apart from the blurring of the well-defined conceptual contours by everyday speech, this obscuring of the original meaning is partly due to the fact that many words were first used metaphorically. Such metaphors are evidently related to something that serves as a common link between the true and the metaphorical meaning of the word. This link, however, which was clear to the mind of the original designer of the metaphor, is not perceived in the same way or so distinctly by those who subsequently make use of it. Thus it comes about that the metaphor is no longer understood in the sense originally intended, and therefore the idea intended to be conveyed by it as a whole is also seen in a different light. Further, the deductions based on this diverted interpretation are also thrown out of their course, often with results entirely inappropriate to the matter in hand. This shows the great danger inherent in the use of all metaphor and simile ; and yet their use is unavoidable, because there is much, especially in psychic matters, that is incapable of direct designation. One must bear in mind this ambiguity in metaphorical phraseology and be prepared to revise it, as it were, from time to time.

In respect of the two concepts, " greatness " and " strength," as applied to characterological peculiarities, the position is such that there appears to be a real need of a revision and a return to the original meanings. It is clear that strength, originally, is an attitude of bodily power. By transference, the word next comes to denote things that are opposed to the expenditure of bodily power so that there is need of strength to overcome the resistance. Thus we speak of a " strong " stick, whereas, on the other hand, phrases such as a " strong " wind are rather a personification of the wind or some such power of nature. It is true that the two sources of the metaphor can combine, as is exemplified in the term a " strong current." As a personal quality applied to character, " strength " seems to have two meanings ; first strength in the sense of the ability to overcome resistances, and, secondly, strength itself regarded as a constant resistance in opposition to outside forces.[1]

From what we said in the first section, the primary resistance to be overcome is clearly that of one's fellow-men. This is shown in the expression " a strong man," applied to the type of man who is needed to restore order in an organization like a state or a factory. Strength therefore has as its first connotation an idea or an ideal of character that corresponds closely with that of the " man of power." We have had to admit that this is a false ideal, seeing that it is founded on only one of the two chief fundamental tendencies of man, and that it is self-contradictory and must lead to conflicts with reality ; moreover, it runs directly counter to the commandment of love, in that it degrades one's fellow-man to the mere instrument of an egotistical purpose. But as the second meaning of strength—the capacity of resistance to external influence—blends with the first meaning, and can claim to embody a commendable

[1] In other words, strength may be regarded statically as well as dynamically.—TRANS.

ideal, it follows that strength in the first sense, which we have seen to be objectionable, can clothe itself with a mantle of moral value. This is the more apparent in our age, which on the whole is individualist, and in which the idea of self-development with which we have already dealt plays an important part.

The second meaning of strength, however, is also not unexceptionable, for here, as in many analogous cases, it is easy to lay weight on resistance as a purely formal factor, whereas it can be of value only in relation to that against which it is offered. Clearly if a man can resist temptation, that is a morally valuable attitude ; but it is the antithesis of a moral value if resistance is made merely for the sake of resistance, as when a man resists every external effort to change his course of life, even though this change involves the turning towards a higher value, which is recognized as such by the man himself, as sometimes happens.

This is the fundamental error of subjectivism, which adversely influences so many different kinds of attitudes, a subjectivism that over-concentrates on the undoubted value of the individual whilst overlooking the values that are operative outside the person. We must here mention the concept of " loyalty to oneself." Even this loyalty has a value only so far as it is directed towards positive values ; as an isolated function, without regard to the values that are to be striven for or preserved, it is as nothing. Incidentally, we may remark that this ideal of loyalty to oneself often reveals itself on minute examination as a mask covering a disinclination for change, a distrust of one's ability to meet higher demands, dread of those demands, and, finally, an attitude of discouragement ; thus paradoxically enough, this attitude of " to thine own self be true " can conceal an insufficient sense of one's own value.

Regarded by themselves, strength and this kind of loyalty

to one's own person are by no means commendable character-ideals ; they first win meaning and value by reference to other values. The development of strength is therefore a mistaken educational purpose, and it is equally wrong to set up " the strong man " as an ideal figure for emulation and imitation. I should be inclined to put the situation in this way : if a man possesses a sufficient depth of insight in the objective orders of value, which he has made his own in a vital sense, then " strength," in the sense of an effort to realize these values and to reject their opposites, will develop more or less automatically.

Similar considerations obtain in the case of the ideal of greatness, which is even more dangerous than that of strength. Strength can be a personal experience, and is associated with active conduct on the part of the individual ; it contains an incitement to action, a call for personal courage and self-assertion. Further, the consciousness of strength is very largely independent of purely external success, for it measures itself against the height of the obstacles to be overcome. Greatness, on the contrary, is hardly connected with individual experience, depending as it does on the opinion of other people. We cannot, generally speaking, assign the attribute of greatness to ourselves ; it is awarded us by our contemporaries or by posterity. We must be perfectly clear in our own mind that " greatness " as a character-ideal never means greatness of achievement, but always greatness of success in the eyes of other people. In this sense, greatness and fame are interchangeable concepts.

Greatness, therefore, is something that cannot be striven for as a primary goal. It is the same as in the case of satisfaction, happiness and self-perfection ; they come to man in the nature of a reward for adequately meeting the definite objective conditions and demands of life.

It is possible, indeed justifiable, to regard oneself as a
" great man " even without the recognition of the crowd.
History provides us with instances of important persons
who prophesied with no uncertain voice that they would be
held in honour by posterity, but who did not enjoy success
during their lifetime. With these people it was not a question
of greatness, but of accomplishment, of the endowment of
humanity with their achievements ; in essence they were
servants, fulfillers of a mission and not aspirants to the
pantheon. There is no place in the ranks of the immortals
for the man who strives to place himself on an equality with
them, but only for him who is the servant of a cause or of a
task awaiting accomplishment.

If we represent the great figures of history in their true
light, as servants and the humble accomplishers of the task
devolving on them—and in reality the greatest amongst
them were that—no objection could be raised against the
setting-up of such ideals ; but the stressing of the factor of
" greatness " awakens a false ambition which, if not satisfied,
as is the inevitable case in the great majority, bears strange
fruit. Herostratus undoubtedly achieved his purpose ; even
today, after so many centuries, one knows the name of the
man who set fire to the temple of Diana ; but he survives
only as a dreadful example.

Very much the same considerations apply with the *ideal
of heroism*. Heroic conduct first gains its essential value from
the idea for whose sake it is displayed. In my opinion, our
judgment of heroes is coloured by the introduction of
fragments of past cultural epochs ; we do not understand
that today they have lost their meaning. It must not be
forgotten that even ideals are in part conditioned by time ;
at least this is true of the forms of life in which men try to
realize them. In comparing the present-day connotation of
the term " chivalry " with its eleventh- and twelfth-century

meaning, many people are inclined to complain that the lustre has departed from the ideal ; but it can truly be said that it has undergone a process of refinement, so that today it more clearly reveals its ethical nature and meaning as an inner attitude, having been stripped of what were merely unessential trappings.

Our conception of heroism is still largely influenced by the ideas of antiquity. Possibly our justifiable reverence for the glorious eras and masterpieces of Greek and Roman classicism still permeates the whole of our culture—even that of those whose knowledge of humanism is small—and the reappearance of the ancient heroes in the art of later centuries is partly responsible. Perhaps also the heroic ideals of bygone civilizations respond to something primitive in human nature. Be that as it may, common expressions like " passive heroism," " heroes of science," " heroes of faith," and so on, strike us immediately as being merely metaphors and even as doing violence to the concept of heroism.

The hero is one who is prepared to stake his all for his ideal, even if it leads to his own destruction ; but, as we have said, it is only the ideal that makes his action heroic. The fact that in some circumstances a criminal may seem to us to be a hero is only made possible by the fact that we are inclined to regard his conduct purely " formally," and that we credit him, as it were, with good faith. An instance of this is the figure of the " noble robber " which is constantly occurring in literature, and the tendency in popular legends to cover criminal figures with the whitewash of ethical value. (There are doubtless other motives, but this one is unquestionably very important.)

The hero, then, is an extremely unsuitable ideal of personal development, because it does not lie in a person's power to play the part of a hero, for which quite definite environmental conditions are demanded, outside the person's control. To use a somewhat trite expression, heroism is not a career ; one cannot take a course in it. During the great theatre-fire in Madrid, which claimed many hundreds of victims, a theatre-attendant made repeated journeys in and out of the burning building, saving many lives but finally losing his own. A hero ! I do not suppose that this simple man had ever thought or dreamed of heroism ; he did what he believed to be his duty, and the idea of doing what was right directed his action even in such a situation, making him a hero. One might almost go so far as to assert that a man automatically becomes a hero, as circumstances require it, if only he has come to regard the ideal as something greater than his person, achievement as more important than success, and service as more moral than self-glorification. Did we not learn from the war that persons whose thoughts and sentiments had hardly touched upon heroism turned out to be heroes ? Possibly amongst those who had cherished heroism as an ideal there were relatively fewer heroes than amongst the majority, who were not so minded. For the moulding of one's life, the heroic ideal is attended by much that is questionable. It burrows deep into the soul, because it is well adapted to the primitive tendency of the will to power, and can make constant demands, which are often only vaguely comprehended, upon a man's whole life and destiny. It can become so obsessive that a man may come to believe that only in heroic conduct can he find the fulfilment of his life-purpose and the final confirmation of his own value. But in real life only the few are granted the opportunity of becoming heroes in the sense in which such people understand it. The heroism of every day—patience and love—finds little favour in their eyes ; and driven by the need to prove the heroism denied them by fate, they resort to fantasy or to all kinds of tricks and dodges in their search for a fictitious heroism. To this type belongs the man who seeks to gratify a craving for heroism by a martyrdom that is not objectively demanded. Martyrdom is, as we learn from Indian stories, the heroism of the weak ; the Indian hero who has been captured by his enemies and cannot display his heroism by further victory maintains it at the martyr's stake. Here again an entirely subjective attitude comes into play, an attitude previously mentioned with reference to the ideal of strength ; it consists of regarding martyrdom as a value in itself apart from the idea for which it is suffered. Another example of the craving for heroism at all costs is furnished by those persons who are continually championing " lost causes." We have a tendency to admire people who defend a hopeless position, but in this we are, I think, misled by the metaphor deriving from a military situation, where such an attitude is right and proper. We forget that the lost position is almost the only one in which defeat brings as much, if not more, fame than victory. Thus people who cannot rely on themselves to conquer, but yet crave for the fame of the hero, willingly take up such positions—especially if, as in the cases thus metaphorically designated, defeat involves only a modest or illusory sacrifice, certainly not that of one's life. Many people also take to a form of life that overtaxes their strength ; this provides an interpretation for many cases in which sport is carried to excess.

Since, as we have said, the moral value of heroism resides only to a small extent in itself and mainly in the value of that for the sake of which it is displayed, over-emphasis in education of the heroic ideal is hazardous rather than unconditionally commendable. It is not the death of the hero but the motive for his death that should rivet the attention of young people. Nobler blood soaked into the sands of the Roman Colosseum than was ever shed in the adventures of the Knights of the Round Table.

Therefore it is not a question of strength but of the will to a higher value, not of greatness but of " doing one's job in life," not of heroism but of disregard of one's person. In themselves, fame, importance and recognition are goals not worth the seeking. Men should learn not ambition but reverence ; they must learn that the reverence and admiration that is worth while is that which emanates from themselves and is objectively directed, rather than that which they might desire to be paid to themselves.

7. HUMILITY

It is not, however, to be thought that the desire for recognition from others is inadmissible or false. The desire is a proper one, if recognition is sought as a sign and a proof of association with one's fellow-men, and as an index of a living communion. To only a few can it be granted genuinely to seek after scorn and humiliation. Even the adoption of this ideal that seems to be advocated in many ascetic writings—they are, it is true, for the most part entirely misunderstood—is not without considerable risk.

In the Foundation, which we have already mentioned, in the *Exercises* of St. Ignatius, we are told to be indifferent— " *indifferenter se faciat* "—to fortune and to misfortune, to crave no more for wealth than for poverty, for honour than for shame, for health than for sickness. We are not told to desire poverty, shame or sickness. What that great saint really means is that we should desire nothing at all—that is, nothing at all for ourselves. I believe St. Ignatius demanded this " indifference " because he realized the danger involved in the setting up of the goals we have in mind. Benjamin Franklin once wrote in his diary that even were he to succeed in completely conquering his pride, he would probably become proud again—of his humility !

In a little book called *Formation à l'humilité,* published

anonymously many years ago, the clerical author states that
a certain amount of self-love is not only permitted but even
commanded, and that even the wish for recognition must be
deemed natural and admissible. To be completely lacking
in self-regard is not the true course ; one must seek the
mean between necessary self-respect and exaggerated self-
approbation, between the lawful desire for recognition and
mistaken vanity. To maintain this middle course is difficult
and impossible without a constant effort ; it is much easier
simply to avoid the struggle by complete self-abasement. In
fact the clear-sighted priest was quite right ; only too often
the attitude of self-contempt and condemnation is merely a
form of flight, a flight not only from the particular struggle
just mentioned, but also from the other obligations of life.
People who adopt that attitude behave as though they were
saying : " How can anyone demand anything of me ? I
am such a worthless and pitiful object ! " And their acts
say : " You, my fellow-men, must make allowances for me,
take the will for the deed and be kind to me, because I am
a mere nothing ! " When Socrates saw one of these world-
contemning philosophers in a ragged cloak approaching
him in the market-place at Athens, he said to him :
" Through the holes in your cloak, Cleanthes, your vanity
peeps out."

Yes, if a man who declares he has no opinion of himself
and craves nothing for himself were to go about the world
with cheerful courage, fully equal to the obligations of life,
and accomplishing more and better work than the rest, then
his attitude would represent truth and value ; then indeed
would he have attained to that " withdrawal " from things
and from himself which the mystical and ascetic writings of
the German middle ages describe so beautifully. But how
many people are like that ? Are not the majority of those
who talk and act in that way depressed, narrow-minded and

unemancipated ? Are they not a burden and an annoyance rather than a source of joy to their fellow-men ? I have known a number of such men, who were anything rather than well adapted to their life-conditions, who were by no means examples of the " freedom of the children of God," and who, above all, were sadly lacking in true love. On the contrary, such persons are often pharisaical and harsh in judgment—in a word, lacking in charity. They behave, says the anonymous author already quoted, in a laboured and unnatural way which causes piety to appear to outsiders as repulsive rather than attractive.

Such an ideal, right as it may be in itself, can lead a person wholly astray, force him into a course unsuited to his inner nature and hence also to his proper functioning in that system-complex to which he belongs, and so give occasion for the development of various and often far-reaching aberrations of character. The danger lies not so much in the nature of the ideal itself as in the way in which the ideal is regarded, taken up and incorporated into the system of their lives by the persons concerned. That absorption in " the job in hand " and service to objective validities can determine both the conduct and the innermost attitude of a person, is a thought that seems to be accepted with difficulty by the childish intelligence ; further, there are many adults who cannot readily comprehend it. Even children realize that work for the sake of others, work as service to the community, work as a return, as it were, for what has been done for me by my fellows, involves for the individual definite and inevitable obligations ; but much deeper reflexion is required in order to realize that the like applies to the religious and ethical attitude. If children, even elder children, are too strongly impressed by the ideal of self-denial, self-abasement and so forth, they are liable to see in it a personal advantage to be gained, a goal for their ambition.

The temptation to accept such a perversion of the ideal is very great, and may be strengthened by the fact that people who showed the real and genuine virtues of humility and the like are now honoured as saints and set up as examples. It must be borne in mind that it is by no means easy to grasp the paradox of " the chosen," seeing that man does not " choose " himself, and of the exaltation of one who abases himself. A ten-year-old girl answered my reference to the humility of the Mother of God—" *ecce ancilla Domini* "—by saying : " Yes, but she is the Queen of Heaven ! "

All these things can be genuinely realized (as in the case of ideals of the order of greatness, already discussed) if they are understood somewhat impersonally. It comes to something like this : what is of importance is not that I am humble, but that humility can be realized in the world ; similarly, it is important that such-and-such a thing " gets done," and not that it is I that do it. It might almost be said that the individual is there only accidentally as the instrument of some purpose which happens to come his way.

It will be readily understood that it is without any sort of intention of disputing the ethical importance of the formation of such ideals, or of seeking to deny the necessity of imparting them to children, that I have ventured to point out how questionable is the manner in which they are imparted.

8. AN OBJECTION

It seems possible to raise a fundamental objection to our observations, an objection that cannot be passed over if misunderstandings are to be avoided ; it is as follows : It is clear that morally valuable actions can emanate only from a corresponding disposition ; but such a disposition is a quality of the person, or at least a *habitus*. If, then, the action is secondary to the disposition—*operari sequitur esse*— and the disposition is bound up with the person, then the shaping of the person must be the chief concern of the individual and the main object of education. We are thus placed in the following dilemma : either the attention of the individual must be directed to his own person, to its complete development or whatever one likes to call it, and character-training is possible only in this way, in contradiction to all that we have said up to now ; or, if our propositions are sound, then education cannot possibly attain its object, namely the forming of the person as the antecedent for the direction of his actions. If education, then, is not directed towards the person, it has lost sight of its purpose ; if it is directed towards the person, the attainment of that purpose is thereby rendered impossible.

The solution of this difficulty, which at first sight seems serious, is as follows : The person as such is not an object to itself ; or, as Aristotelian philosophy teaches, the subject can never become its own object. We can, in this connection, refer back to our earlier arguments which led to the statement that self-observation is a late, and observation by others an early, primary disposition. What, then, is susceptible of self-observation ? We understand by this the phenomena of consciousness, the mode and manner in which objects—things in the external world, realities, verities and values—present themselves to us. Comprehension itself—the relation of the ego to its objects—we do not comprehend ; we know perhaps, about it, we live on the road to comprehension, but the moment we reflect on it, it melts away into a new image based on memory and therefore not on vivid perception, an image that has already become indefinite, ghostly and inflexible. If this be true of objectively directed dispositions, of the manifestations of the ego in action, it is even more true of the ego, which is the fountain-head of all actions. The ego—the person itself may transcend that incomprehensible something of which we are aware in all our experience as constituting our ego—can never be its own object. If it contemplates itself, or, rather, imagines that it does so, it sees only a shadowy figure of itself, as in a glass darkly, as it was a moment ago, never as it is at the actual moment ; for the ego is always in the place from which it gazes outwards, and never in the place at which its gaze is directed. We shall see later that this fundamental fact about the experiencing of self renders continuous self-knowledge impossible, and justifies the need of guidance ; yet we are still unwilling to yield to that conclusion. In order fully to meet the objection formulated above, it is important to establish the fact that the ego or the person is quite unable to direct its attention to itself, and therefore the perfecting of the individual person in the commonly understood sense cannot possibly determine the direction of a person's goal, striving or effort. It is clear that if our purpose is to be the modification of something, that something must be supposed to be already in existence ; this does not apply to the person.

Or, to put it differently, it is impossible to make the person and his make-up one's direct target. Those who believe that this is possible in their own case and in that of others are mistaken ; it is one of those mistakes that arise partly out of certain prejudices, from a certain dogmatism in matters of psychology and education, and partly from a preference for a genetic solution of problems with a disregard for their phenomenological aspects. The confusion that prevails on the points in question arises, I believe, because two essentially different modes of thought meet in the realm of educational psychology or characterology, modes of thought that are scarcely compatible, unless some reconciling factor, at present non-existent, is discovered. One of these incompatible avenues of approach is a traditionally conditioned conception of man's nature, deriving in part from the old faculty-psychology ; the other is founded on a biologically coloured conception, which is influenced by the methods of natural science, and according to which a problem is capable of solution only when it is stated in terms of causality, origin and direction. However, what is needed is a simple descriptive method, an observation of what is there to be observed, unhampered by " origins " or already established principles of methodology. It is not convincing to conclude, because the moral perfection of the person is the goal—not indeed the ultimate goal, nevertheless a goal of human conduct, and hence also the goal of education, which serves to mould the conduct—that it necessarily follows that all efforts must be directly concentrated on the person. In fact that by no means follows ; it is indeed impossible, for the reason that the person can never be taken as a premise.

The above dilemma, then, arises from a false hypothesis and a false statement of the problem ; it need not occupy us further. We must, however, turn our attention to a further problem. If one is not entitled to take the person as a premise, then it seems impossible for the person to direct his efforts with the purpose of his (*i.e.*, the person's) perfection ; it also seems impossible for the person to recognize the suitability or unsuitability of his own nature for any given ideal. Does one not really harbour the suspicion that the doctrine of the essential unknowableness of the person, carried to its logical conclusion, excludes all upbringing, or at least all self-upbringing ?

We shall postpone the answer to this question for the time being, because it is necessary, at this stage, to introduce a concept we have not yet touched upon ; this concept, " conscience," is very important for the theory and practice of characterology.

9. CONSCIENCE

We are not called upon here to consider this difficult question in all its aspects ; we can disregard the theological and metaphysical significance of conscience and its purely psychological aspects. Our present concern is restricted exclusively to the characterological side of the problem. In order that the relation between conscience and character may be elucidated, a brief consideration of the facts and phenomena presented by what is comprised within the term " conscience " is unavoidable.

When a man speaks of having a good or a bad conscience, he generally implies that by means of a corresponding experience he is aware that an action contemplated, commenced or completed harmonizes or conflicts with his moral code. This definition, although very vague, is on the whole correct ; but there are certain indications that it does not altogether get to the root of the matter. Thus, it sometimes happens that a man admits that he has done this or that, well knowing that his action was forbidden, or that he was breaking a commandment, and nevertheless that his conscience was quite clear. In stating this, he does not mean that he has only just this moment become aware of the unlawful nature of his action ; he means precisely that he acted with full knowledge that he was transgressing a commandment, but that nevertheless his conscience is untroubled. This seems at first sight to be incomprehensible, and one is inclined to doubt the speaker's honesty, to regard him as unusually flippant, or to suppose that he has not fully appreciated the consequences of his action. These are quite obvious interpretations ; but I think it is unjust to cast doubt on the subjective truth and reliability of all such statements, or to condemn them as frivolous. It seems to me that the above definition of conscience is mistaken in one respect. It is not always a matter harmonizing or conflicting with a known or recognized commandment ; *what seems to underlie the phenomenon of conscience is rather harmony or disharmony between the action and the person's make-up.* If we wish to keep the definition of the relation between action and moral awareness within the conceptual limits of conscience, we must understand precisely that by the term " awareness " we mean that " insight resulting from experience " which we previously contrasted with merely " theoretical " knowledge. It is only when an action conflicts with that kind of awareness that the " voice of conscience " is heard, which, like a sensory perception, penetrates the man through the door of understanding, and which, speaking figuratively, has not remained at a superficial level, but has bored its way through the deepest strata of the person's being. If we may so describe it, the voice of conscience is heard only if there is disagreement between the quality of the action and the quality of the person.

It is noteworthy that the " voice of conscience " always conveys a warning or a reproof; it admonishes us to be good, it addresses our " better self," but only when that better self has not been party to the action. The " good " conscience is determined only by the absence of the " bad." Just as we are unaware of our bodily sensations when our organs function normally, and become conscious of them when function is disturbed, so the absence of conflict does not produce in us any unusual experience, only its presence being noticeable.

Conflict, then, is noticed between what should be and what actually is done, provided that the " should be " harmonizes with the nature of the person. As we have seen, the person is of necessity unknowable to himself. But how, then, can he become at all aware of a " should be " in harmony with his own make-up? A recognition of that make-up seems implicit in such awareness; in other words, if the person is to be able to make a comparison between the " should be " that is in harmony with himself and the actual completed action, he must have some knowledge of his own make-up. Moral judgment of one's own conduct, pronounced by the voice of conscience, is unlikely to contain anything other than a relation between the " should be " corresponding to the person and the fundamental principle of the action or the principle followed in the action ; that is, it is the judgment of a relation. There must, however, be two components to a relation. Consequently, if conscience is to be at all possible, the make-up of the person must be an objectively presented premise, which obviously it is not and cannot be. Indeed, the position is still more complicated : the recognition of a relation formulated by the voice of conscience—even if not directly in the form of a judgment, although that is frequently the form—does in fact make a comparison or at least establish a relation between the " should be " that is in harmony with the person and the principle of the action. The qualifying phrase, " in harmony with the person," assumes a second recognition of a relation, the recognition that a particular " should be " not only exists in the abstract, but has regard to the actual person, is his concern, or however one may put it ; and this recognition of relation seems definitely to demand that the person should be an object to himself.

This difficulty cannot be avoided by maintaining that the person is objective to himself, but only vaguely as a " general impression " or simply as a " feeling." Such vague premises undoubtedly do exist ; we come across them in those not infrequent cases in which we pronounce the judgment that something is not quite right, without being able to formulate clearly what it is that is wrong ; for this also presents a relationship. For the present problem, what matters is, not that the person cannot clearly and distinctly recognize himself, but that he cannot be objective to himself at all.

In order to clear up the whole problem, which, as we have seen, is by no means simple, a somewhat more extensive

examination is necessary ; and we must link it up with
certain facts of experimental psychology. Long experience
has convinced us that there can be comprehension of a
relation, even if one of the components is not presented to us
as a premise. Thus, for example, we can by the comparison
of successive notes of different intensity or tone recognize
the second as being louder or higher, softer or lower, without
having retained the first note in our minds ; we experience
simply what W. Köhler[1] calls " a step upward or down-
ward," even if we are unable to remind ourselves of the
starting-point of that step. This fact, it is true, is on quite
a different level from that of our particular problem ; for in
the case we have just considered we are dealing with a
relation, one of whose components, although not present, can
by its nature be present and objective. In our particular
problem, on the other hand, one of the components of the
relation, namely the person, can by its very nature never be
objective. Yet we perceive a certain analogy. We are led a
step further by an observation that can easily be made, when
we are trying to recall a forgotten name, word, or tune.
Something occurs to us, but we know it to be wrong ;
perhaps it resembles what we are seeking, but it is not the
thing itself. In such a recognition of the unsuitability or
resemblance, a relation is set up between the actual mistaken
recollection and the forgotten word, which is not present ;
but even in this case the difference cited above with reference
to the relation of two tones also applies. These examples are
only intended to show us that the recognition of a relation
is possible even if one only of the two components is actually
present ; but in these cases it was present at one time. We
are now faced with a still more remarkable situation. It is
possible to comprehend a relation between something that
actually exists and a second something that has never

[1] *Zur Theorie des sukzessiven Vergleiches*, in *Psychol. Forschung*, vol. IV. (1923).

existed. This occurs in what we may call, with N. Hartmann[1], the " problem-consciousness " ; the nature of this quite astonishing phenomenon is as follows : We stand before a fact or a principle and know that there is something beyond it ; or we " see " in a problem that we are not near solving that its solution will lead immediately to further problems, that it will not be a complete solution, even though at the moment we do not know in the least the direction in which its completion is to be sought. In this way, we come only to the point where beyond the known we catch a glimpse of the still unknown ; and if we could not do this, then our knowledge could never progress or widen. If our gaze never reached into the realms of the unknown without our being able to recognize it (otherwise it would cease to be the unknown), we should of necessity remain content with the most elementary and primitive knowledge, or rather there would be no knowledge at all. Carrying this further, we arrive at the certainly surprising but none the less clear and certain conviction that we are in a position, not to know in the strict sense of the term, but yet to comprehend, not only that which is still unknown although fundamentally knowable, but even to some extent that which is essentially unknowable. The emergence of the question of the " limits of knowledge " in the history of the human intellect was, mysteriously enough, only rendered possible because the unknowable, which prescribes the limits of knowledge, is to some extent comprehensible, and that we can approach it and grasp it without being able to understand it.

It must also be borne in mind that the judgment of " intensity of feelings " is based, no less than the judgment of values, on a non-premised maximum, at times even on a maximum that can never be experienced. We cannot discuss this matter further; but it is easy to see that

[1] *Metaphysic der Erkenntnis* (Leipzig, 1925).

here also the main principles of the situation repeat themselves.

From this it appears that such facts as the ability to appreciate the existence of the person without its having objectivity for us are not isolated rarities, but recur constantly in the realm of knowledge, whenever we touch its " boundaries." What further bearing this has on the grasping of the unknowable, both in general and in respect of the comprehension of the person, is not a question which we can investigate here. Moreover this problem, like so many others that we encounter, belongs more to anthropology and metaphysics than to strict characterology.

The fact of problem-consciousness provides, however paradoxical this may sound at first, an analogy to conscience ; it represents in the intellectual sphere a position of affairs similar to that underlying conscience in the moral sphere. Thus, every actually premised intellectual situation in which we become aware, in the problem-consciousness, of a problem extending beyond the given problem determines the quite definite lines for the problem to follow. Since they are relations between the known and the unknown—and the same also applies to the unknowable—these lines are naturally determined by the two component parts of the relation. Thus, in problem-consciousness, there is experienced the fittingness of the problem with regard to the unknown. By this time I believe that the analogy has been made quite plain.

For our purposes, it has been established that the essential unknowableness of the person is no obstacle to the knowableness of the fittingness or unfittingness of a known " should be."

10. REFUTATION OF THE OBJECTION

In what way, then, have we been helped in the task of character-training by the knowledge we have just obtained by these important by-paths? It will be recalled that the occasion for the whole digression was the apparent contradiction between the necessity for " building up " the person, which in its capacity as agent determines conduct in accordance with its dispositions, and the statement that it is a mistake to concentrate on the person as the centre of the picture. However, in order that our discussion may not give the impression of being unduly abstract and speculative, we will recall a saying that exactly describes the idea of the person that we have in mind : " Only he who loses his soul shall save it." This thought contains the most profound truth that philosophy has ever been able to offer us. As we might expect, this saying, which refers to the supernatural life, is analogically transferable to the natural sphere.

The solution of the dilemma can now be formulated in the light of the above quotation from Holy Scripture, as follows : there exists a certain method of approach towards the person, the essential feature of which is that it is not directed towards the person. We have previously remarked that many goals— including the ideal of perfection—are unattainable if directly striven for. Rather does perfection come to him who does not seek it (and is thus not self-seeking) but seeks that which is perfect. " He that keeps My commandments, he it is that loves Me." We can only vaguely indicate the matters concerned with these considerations, and then not with the definition proper to scientific knowledge ; for we are here approaching a mystery, and move as it were in its shadow.

In the first section we demonstrated that man exists and has his place in various levels of existence whose laws permeate him and determine and mould his being. (This is an example of the importance of such theoretical expositions even for questions arising directly from purely practical considerations.) In our analysis of action we pointed out that one of its aspects can be described as the representation, or the affirmative, active incorporation, of man in the collectivities of being that condition him. We have been faced with the paradoxical, but none the less certain, fact that man can of his own volition choose whether he will or will not take an active part in that concatenation of realms which is his birthright ; he can affirm it or deny it. Herein we find the solution of the dilemma that has occupied our attention for so long.

If man goes against the laws of being to which he is by his very nature subject, then at the same time he does violence to his own being, which is determined for him by the principle of cohesion governing the four realms of being. (We need not inquire if this cohesion is by itself an exhaustive determinant of man ; probably it is not, because we are here dealing not with a simple mixture of isolated elements, but with their blending to form a new unity.) If man acquiesces in the laws of being, then he is in harmony with his own being. It should be quite evident that he is unable to realize his own latent potentialities if he takes up an antagonistic position to these laws. Thus, man promotes the development of his own person, and helps the value-potentialities inherent in himself to emerge, only if he actively accepts the laws of being, and of his own volition satisfies the demands that are made on him by those worlds of which he is and must be a member. The more he turns from the ego to the non-ego— of course, in proportion to the higher values he encounters there—and the more he is disposed to serve and freely to surrender himself, the sooner will " that sinister tyrant, the ego," beat a retreat, and he will " save his soul " because he " loses it." The apparent paradox of the approach to the person that leads away from it shows itself, then, to be not a contradiction, but the expression of the antitheses peculiar to human life at all its levels.

One further remark, before reverting to the subject of character-ideals, which we have, perhaps, already left too long. Having regard to the views that have been touched upon—their development would require a whole book to itself—we may ask how it is possible for a man to revolt against the laws of being, which inform him and determine his nature. Our arguments can regress indefinitely, if we say that the antagonism to those laws of being arises out of the person's most individual nature, i.e., is self-generated, since its foundations are those selfsame laws. Here we are inevitably confronted with the immensity of the freedom that, by God's grace, allows us voluntarily to accept or reject salvation, and is itself a mystery.

11. THE CHARACTER-IDEAL

We will now come back once more to the problem of character-ideals. We have seen that the adoption by an individual of an ideal that is overstressed or unduly emphasized is by no means devoid of risk ; consequently, we must utter a warning against implanting such ideals in children too forcibly. At bottom, there is only one ideal—" doing one's job in life "—involving self-surrender and service ; in the same way there is really only one virtue—humble, volitional conformity to the will of God—and only one sin—defiance of God's will. " *Il principio del cader fu il maladetto superbio.*" Pride assumes a multitude of forms, and lurks behind innumerable masks. As Satan appears at times as an angel of light, so pride may often don the garb of humility. It is not by direct manifestation that it can be most readily recognized ; only by its effects, in an inner attitude often deeply hidden from the man himself, is it revealed to us. The nature of pride is the setting up of one's own person as supreme and the rejection of all ties : further, self-isolation, or at least turning one's back on reality, whether represented by common humanity, work or love, or by relation to the divine.

In education, we are faced with the difficult task of steering a middle course between all those measures which tend to weaken the experience of incorporating a personal value (legitimate self-esteem), and those which are calculated to lead to an " absolutizing " of the self. The middle course is hard to find and keep, because it is not a matter of effecting a compromise between two dangerous extremes, but of making a real synthesis of them. Figuratively speaking, the mean that is sought lies not only between, but at the same time above, the two poles. It is not like the mean point between the two extremes of a swinging pendulum, but rather like the mean represented by a resolution of tension. Man should win to the constant awareness of his own inalienable, individual value and the absolute oneness of his person, combined with the knowledge that he has that value only if he knows and feels himself to be a member of totalities greater than himself.

This paradox and antithesis, which is, however, scarcely greater than other antinomous influences in human life, is expressed or exemplified by the fact that Christ continues to live in the Church, regarded as the Community of Saints, but can also live within the individual human breast : " Not I live, but Christ liveth in me."

Thus, the character-ideal that can alone fully satisfy the conditions of man's being must—however much it may vary from case to case in accordance with individual, cultural, national, and situational exigencies—reconcile and synthetize the conflicting claims of the individual and the community, of the value of the individual and the value-giving totality, of the finiteness of the creature and the call to participation in the divine life. As the καθολική not only extends over all peoples, civilizations and eras, but embraces all the qualitative diversities of human individuality, so Catholic life, based on Catholic principles, can reconcile the antitheses of our being and bring about a resolution of tension. To live καθ' ὅλον, according to the whole, should be a possibility, not only for the Church, which does so live, but for each of her members. To describe the living figure of the " Catholic man," and thereby provide a sketch of the positive character-ideal, is a task suited to more skilful pens than mine ; moreover, this ideal figure has many times been depicted in scarcely surpassable ways. We must turn our attention to lesser questions, which are yet of great practical importance.

CHAPTER V

THE CHARACTEROLOGY OF THE SEXES

I. METHOD

In accordance with the intentions expressed in Chapter III, we shall follow up our line of thought by considering next the characterological problems associated with adolescence and puberty, problems which are markedly different for the two sexes. We must first therefore try to obtain a clear conception of such differences as they exist between fully developed individuals ; for all characterological investigation depends on the experience obtained from the study of adults. It is in general a mistake to claim pre-eminence of method for the " genetic " approach ; for the solutions of the problems we approach by such a method, involving reference to earlier stages of development, are for the most part based on an analysis of fully developed stages, an analysis which is undoubtedly often inadequate and unscientific. This applies equally to characterology and to evolutionary and comparative psychology and history ; here there is the danger of projecting, on the evolutionary forms of the past, features they did not possess, but that can, we imagine, be recognized in fully developed form in the evolutionary stage of the present. We must bear this danger fully in mind in the discussions upon which we are about to embark. In particular we must not lose sight of the principle of method which we have so often stressed—a primary search for the possibly reactive origin of this or that peculiarity. If we lose sight of this, we can easily regard certain characteristics, which perhaps distinguish the mature individual of either sex, as primal, essential qualities ; and misled by this view, we may imagine that we have perceived hints of these qualities in earlier years or in some prior evolutionary stage of development.

A great deal has been written on the differences between man and woman. It would be just as well to regard these descriptions and analyses somewhat sceptically. For the most part they are only too obviously one-sided, in the sense either of an exaltation of the male sex, or of a reaction against it. Historically speaking, man was the earlier subject for psychological and characterological investigation. It appears to us almost naive, and yet it is at the same time very indicative, when we read that a woman is " subnormal " in the differential recognition of tactile stimuli, merely because the author found on an average a lower set of values for female than for male experimental subjects ! Obviously, such a prejudiced formulation could have arisen only when these values happened to be lower in the case of women than in men. But " subnormal " ? What is the basis of this conviction that man must be taken as the norm, and that variations from this male " norm " must be ranked as " subnormal " or " supranormal " ? It can only rest on a prejudiced view of the values represented by the two sexes, a form of judgment which should find no place in purely descriptive sciences, such as psychology and characterology ought to be. Even admitting that one has the right to take the man as the norm in many matters, it does not in the least follow that these specifically male qualities ought to be designated as normal in all circumstances and applied in every field.

I have insisted on this matter at some length because the transparency of the method illustrates the way in which the psychology of the sexes is frequently treated. If we desire a theoretical principle on which we can depend for the solution of practical problems, we must do our utmost to keep free of such prejudices. Therefore, we cannot immediately adopt any of the current opinions or any of the ostensibly "certain" tenets as to the psychical differences between the sexes, or any of the deductions arising out of apparently firmly entrenched assumptions. Rather must we endeavour by simple description to collect a mass of facts from which we can develop a more or less reliable point of view.

It necessarily happens, in making a distinction, that one of the two parties of this kind of relation is made the starting-point. The moment one ceases to remain content with a mere description of the respective modes of behaviour of each group in turn, and starts to compare the two, one group must become the basis or starting-point and the other the final point of the comparison ; then it easily comes about that the starting-point, which is possibly chosen merely accidentally, is taken as the standard.

In the present case—the comparison of the two sexes— this temptation is especially great. This is due partly to historical and cultural factors, and partly to the natural inclination of people to adopt their own standpoint as the standard. It is well known that hitherto science has been predominantly the concern of men ; it is men who have, so to speak, developed the scientific method of approach, and women that have occupied themselves with similar problems have worked along the same lines, considering them to be the only existing ones. This involves no danger so long as membership of one or the other sex is not associated with any essential difference in point of view. In mathematics, physics, botany, pathology and many other branches of theoretical and applied science, the sex of the investigator is a matter of indifference. However, in art criticism, and still more in historical research, in biographical writing, in sociological investigation, and also in characterology, the male or female bias of the worker is an important factor to be reckoned with, as it affects the method of treatment. Everyone at one time or another takes the side of his sex ; and we shall see that the factor of " prestige " plays a great part in this, the greater because people are for the most part unaware of it. It is indeed doubtful whether a perfectly objective judgment in the differential psychology or characterology of the sexes is possible at all, for no one can get away from the standpoint of the sex of which he or she is a member.

It might be thought that we could escape from this difficulty by strict adherence to the principles of method that we have always followed—concentrating in the first instance not on experiences but on events, and inquiring not about a person's views on life, its problems and his own attitude to it, but how he reacts on his environment. We should regard that man as normal who is able to fill his place in the world in which he lives with the minimum of internal and external conflicts ; but this assumes that the man's environment is of such a nature that he can take his place in it with relatively little conflict. We all know the fable used by Goethe, of the fox and the stork, who each invited the other to dinner. The fox placed the food before the stork on a shallow dish from which the bird with his long sharp beak could abstract nothing, whereas the stork served the fox in long narrow-necked bottles into which the animal could not put his muzzle. Stork and fox can indeed take their place and live without conflict each in his own world, but neither can do so in the world of the other.

Applied to our problem, this means that if it should prove, for instance, that women more or less consistently fall short of men in some respect or other, it does not directly follow that they are lacking in a particular quality, or are undamentally inferior ; for it may well be that the world in which they are compelled to live is unsuited to their nature. Moreover, it must be borne in mind that disharmony between a person and his environment can depend on his incomplete preparation for the specific demands and conditions of life in the world in which he must live.

Failure or inefficiency in life may thus have three causes : natural insufficiency of the person or, in this case, of the group to which he or she belongs ; unsuitable nature of the environment ; inadequate preparation. In accordance with the procedure that we have hitherto always adopted, regarding it as the only permissible one, we must first of all see whether we cannot refer any shortcomings of the woman as compared with the man to the last two factors ; for we are in a position to discover such connections and intelligently to trace out their effects, whereas a congenital factor can be established only by a process of elimination.

After these preliminary considerations, which have shown us some of the difficulties inherent in our problem and the many different ways in which we may be misled, we can proceed with our attempt to sketch the main outlines of a differential characterology of the sexes. In selecting our material we should do well to restrict ourselves to the purely descriptive, that is, to the material that is as free as possible from the subjective judgments of its compiler. Fortunately we possess such material in the comprehensive studies of his own day made by Heymans.[1] There is no need for us to enter into details, since our present survey can only be quite general.

However, it would seem to me to be more effective if, instead of summing up Heymans's results, we were to adopt another course. If by means of an analysis of the conditions

---

[1] *Die Psychologie der Frau* (Heidelberg, 1914). There is a comprehensive collection of material in O. Lippmann's *Psychische Geschlechtsunterschiede* (Leipzig, 1925). W. Liepman's *Psychologie der Frau* (Berlin-Wien, 1920) is quite incomplete. I have made a partly critical examination of the prevailing opinion in my *Medizinische Charakterologie*.

in which the modern girl grows up and the woman of to-day lives, we were able to establish definite factors to which a precise influence in character-formation could be ascribed with reasonable probability, and if it were further shown that character-traits corresponding to such alleged effects are actually to be encountered in the average woman, then the thesis which we here wish to support will prove to be decidedly more weighty. Our thesis is that a very great number of the traits that are alleged to form part of the nature of woman have risen reactively in response to environment, upbringing and woman's special social status. In that case we should have to distinguish in woman two groups of characterological peculiarities : those which are inseparable from her nature as woman, and those which are adventitiously generated by external circumstances. The same considerations, of course, apply equally to man. In his case also, essentially male characteristics must be distinguished from those resulting from the influence of man's existing cultural and social status. According to this principle, the more or less typical traits met with in the man and woman of today could be of different origin. First, there would be those proper to one sex or another as direct or indirect sexual characteristics ; secondly, there would be modifications of traits not of themselves sexually differentiated, but derived in one direction or another from a neutral common form of human behaviour under the influence of cultural and social conditions. The latter present a not uninteresting analogy to certain biological theories advanced in respect of the so-called secondary sexual characteristics, according to which sexually undifferentiated characteristics develop in a male or female direction under the influence of the ductless glands. If these theories were correct, it would follow that there is a relatively high number of purely human traits belonging in equal measure to the

male and female sex, and undergoing only secondary
modifications, each sex possessing, over and beyond these,
characteristics specifically peculiar to itself.

The opinion just set out above could be directly confirmed
if the conclusions arrived at theoretically could be shown to
agree with actually observed facts. If certain characteristics
in man and woman which we today regard as characteristic
of his or her sex arose reactively, then a cultural system that
provided an essentially different kind of environment should
produce fundamentally different sexual character-traits. If
we could point to a civilization in which the rôles of the
two sexes were almost completely inverted as compared with
our own—a complete reversal is, of course, biologically
impossible—we should expect to find the woman showing
" natural " traits that we are accustomed to see in man,
and *vice versa*. It is important to note that Vaerting,[1] basing
his ideas on ethnological and historical material, supports
the thesis that early civilizations existed in which women
played very much the same part which in most races now
for some thousands of years has devolved on men. Amongst
the more or less matriarchally organized peoples, the women
carried on hunting and fishing, and the men tended the
cattle and occupied the weaver's bench ; consequently, in
those societies the man exhibited " female " traits and the
woman " male " characteristics. I am not in a position to
test the historical and ethnographical validity of these data,
and therefore content myself with merely recording them.
In any event, Vaerting's demands as to method are entirely
sound ; if it is desired to investigate psychical and characterological differences arising out of the sex factor, it is a
mistake to compare the women in a predominantly male
civilization with the men who enjoy hegemony in it ; the

---

[1] *Die psychologische Artung der Frau in Männerstaate und des Mannes in Frauen-
staate* (Karlsruhe, 1921).

parallel must be drawn between ruling men and ruling women, or between the sexes in an appropriately organized system.

In the absence of relevant material on which to work, we cannot follow this course. Even if the statements of Vaerting proved to be entirely sound, perhaps even such collected material would still be insufficient. Nevertheless, it seems possible to proceed towards a solution of the problem, even if we have to confine ourselves to the purely characterological method.

The determination of the extent of the characterological fields common to both sexes and of those peculiar to each is of great importance for the solution of two problems. First, it is probable that the two sexes can understand one another directly only so far as their forms of conduct represent reactively conditioned variations of a common human possession. Secondly, it would help to clear up the controversial point of " equal rights " on a basis of an alleged equality of kind, or of the necessary difference of sociological status and occupation arising out of an alleged qualitative inequality.

2. WOMAN'S ENVIRONMENT

We must start from the undeniable fact that the social status of woman in our present civilization is at any rate different from that of man. There is no need to point out that until recently it was completely different ; we have only to call to mind the conquests of the feminist movement in recent decades. However, I should like to say that, in my opinion, one is liable to make a great mistake in the consideration of these matters. It is assumed that from time immemorial, or in any case since the classical period, woman has been " oppressed," and that it is only in quite recent times that she has begun to " emancipate " herself. It is true that this " emancipation " is very modern ; but why ?

The answer that women lacked education, were entirely restricted to domesticity, and so on, misses the real point ; for the fact that, for instance, women lacked education is not so much the cause as the result of the absence of any effort towards emancipation. I believe that the emancipation movement started so recently because it was only of late that women found themselves in a markedly unfavourable position, a position that did not exist before, but arose out of the industrialization and " technicalizing " of life. So long as the woman was the economic centre of the family, so long as its physical well-being depended on her activities, there was no call for emancipation, because the woman had a position that was different indeed from that of the man, but not less important. One has only to read through any of the household manuals published even as recently as the beginning of the nineteenth century as guides to the housewife and mother in all her activities and duties ; what a wealth of articles were made by the woman at home : cloth, candles, soap, etc., etc. ! And the more the task of satisfying the material requirements of life fell to the housewife, the more important was the part she played. We must not, of course, forget that the process of industrialization, by which the work of the woman in this respect was gradually reduced, had been progressing for a long time ; just as machinery did not emerge suddenly but gradually. But when the nineteenth century witnessed a violent burst of mechanization, it witnessed coincidently a rapid decline in the activities and hence in the importance of women. The absence of a " women's question " in previous centuries was not because women were too stupid, too timid, too uneducated, or even because—according to a rationalism that has degenerated into simple-mindedness—they were forcibly kept in subjection by men, but because their position was not in any way open to question. It only

became so when it was fundamentally altered by the
economic and social factors already mentioned. It seems
that the women of today are incapable of thinking themselves back into the part played by their sex only a few
generations ago ; could they do so, they would be bound to
crave for their lot in bygone centuries, although, of course,
those conditions could not be realized again. There was no
women's question then, because the sexes did not compete
with one another on the same plane ; their lives fulfilled
themselves in different spheres, in which the individuality
of the man and woman could find full expression. From the
fact that women are today dissatisfied with their position, it
does not at all follow that they have always been so, and
have, as it were, only lacked the self-confidence to fight
for improved conditions, or that in dull submission they
surrendered themselves to a lot that could have been
reformed, but was treated by them as inevitable. Those who
hold that belief have fallen victim to the error of which we
have already spoken—that of projecting the conditions of
the present without change into the past.

There are people who loudly and angrily complain of the
deterioration of woman's nature, the depravity of women,
and so on. This attitude is equally false, and derives from
the same intellectual error. Women have not deteriorated ;
only conditions have undergone a sweeping change. We
should therefore not strive to make women go back to a
form of life proper to conditions as they were two or three
centuries ago, which is absurd, but we should seek to create
a form of living in harmony both with woman's essential
nature and with modern conditions. If these conditions
preclude this, we must try to refashion society in order to
make it possible. By merely lamenting the degradation of
woman's nature, and by reproaching women with having
forgotten their true nature, we accomplish nothing.

If we desire—and it is absolutely necessary—to arrest the break-up of the family, which is unquestionably taking place, with all its consequences, and build up the family anew, we must not remain content with warnings and lamentations about the immorality of the times. The *laudator temporis acti* has never been a reformer ; he who looks backward can never go forward. What is primarily required is an intelligent investigation of all the causal factors responsible for the whole fabric of our present existence, our social and economic life, the life of the body and of the spirit. Secondly, we must make a definite avowal of our will to improve it, together with the recognition of the fact that a new age has dawned, which demands new forms. Through all time and change endures the timeless truth, the eternal good, not a tittle of which we can think of surrendering. In this connection we must repeat what we previously said in relation to upbringing. Without detriment to the ideals themselves, which remain eternally the same, the forms in which they are realized or embodied change in the world of finite life. Thus the solution of the " women's question " is not to be sought in the re-establishment of outworn forms, but in the creation of a new form. One does not put new wine into old wine-skins—but it would be more accurate to reverse the comparison : one must put the old wine into new wine-skins if those which have hitherto contained it have perished. Not by keeping woman as she was some centuries ago do we gain anything, but only by showing her what she should and can do in these present times. At another turning-point in history, a great saint and accomplished preacher did not hesitate to say things about marriage and the family that must have appeared very foreign to the customs of the age that had only just drawn to a close. What St. Bernardino of Siena said to his fellow-citizens about the year 1420, towards the end of the Middle Ages, or taught from the cathedral pulpits of Florence, Padua and Bologna, and throughout Northern Italy, sounded new and unheard-of to the ears of the unprogressive ; but that saint was not only a humble son of the Church, and a true disciple of St. Francis, but also a man whose eyes were not blind to the nature of the new age, and whose soul was ready to meet its demands.[1]

Practice always follows on knowledge. That must always be so, for it is understanding that gives action its direction. But if the span between understanding and action be too great, and the latter remain too far behind the former, then disturbances arise in the lives both of individuals and of groups. Today that is often the case in education, especially that of girls and in the general attitude towards women. Most distressing of all, women themselves, who should show more understanding in these matters which concern themselves, are often compelled, under the influence of the views that coloured the education to which they themselves were subjected, to direct their lives not in the light of that understanding which harmonizes with their deepest nature, but in accordance with the principles acquired through the concrete experience undergone in the course of their development. This slashes the soul of woman, and through the gash there may enter in immorality, family estrangement, revolt against motherhood, and much else.

If we look at the status of the young girl in the family circle, we cannot fail to notice that, compared with that of the boy, it is extremely often an inferior one. We have all heard remarks like the following. We meet a young man whose wife has recently had a baby, and on asking him its sex, we receive the answer : " It's only a girl." Why " only " ? There are naturally a number of reasons of historical and social origin— old customs and obsolete laws of inheritance, the idea of the " name " to be continued, that there should be a son to

[1] Cf. Maria Sticco, *Il pensiero di S. Bernardino di Siena* (Milan, 1928).

carry on his father's profession, that it is easier for a man to earn a livelihood and obtain a social position, the strangely incorrect view that boys do not require to be " looked after " so much as girls, and much else of the same kind—but in his heart of hearts everyone knows that this " only " is quite unjustified. Yet the prejudice still exists, with the result that the birth of a girl is a less welcome event than that of a boy, and that the unfortunate " only " clings to her throughout her girlhood and even during adult life. She cannot rid herself of it ; it pursues her to the end.

Thus, from the outset, the girl grows up in an atmosphere of depreciation. This experience is in most cases added to by the girl's quickly discovering that the depreciation is not only a personal affair but is extended to her sex in general. This discovery is made by inference from the position occupied by the mother in the home. If the depreciation applied only to her personally, and favourable circumstances helped to maintain her self-respect, the girl-child could win through to the conviction that the opinions of those around her were mistaken, and would succeed in proving the contrary by achieving something, " making good," and winning a place in life. But, if the depreciation applies to the female sex as such, including even the mother, who is in many respects superior and inaccessible to herself, then there is no escape or hope of rescue. There arises, therefore, without any deliberate intention, a consciousness of inferiority (an "inferiority complex," to use the English term) which is bound up not with her own person, but with her sex, and is therefore the more deeply rooted. The forces which contribute to the development of this sex-inferiority complex are very various. To set them out in full detail would lead us too far afield ; but the importance of the matter and its consequences justifies a further examination.

We have already mentioned the lesser value which is

generally assigned to the girl ; this is particularly striking when the family consists either of a boy and a number of girls or of a girl and a number of boys. This kind of exclusive position is always rather dangerous either for the boy or for the girl. If several girls must rank after a brother, the community-situation provides a counterpoise, which does not suffice to prevent the development of this specifically feminine sense of inferiority, but is sufficient to prevent its having unduly bad consequences. In such circumstances, the boy is rather the person to run the greater risks, for, without any efforts of his own, by the mere fact of his existence, he enjoys a privileged position of a kind already described. On the other hand, the position of a girl sandwiched in between boys is such as to induce a lively sense of inferiority ; if the girl is the eldest of the family, the resultant precedence, and if she is the youngest, the resultant favouritism, sometimes offsets this.

To begin with, many small girls strike out on rather a masculine line of development, even if they receive no stimulus from the side of their brothers. Such girls will not play girls' games, but behave like boys, sometimes very roughly, and often try to surpass their male playfellows, frequently with success, in boldness, endurance and so on. Girls of this kind are frequently blamed and reprimanded for their unmaidenly conduct ; they often hear the phrase, spoken with no element of blame attached : " She ought to have been a boy." Such remarks are often very effectual in strengthening in the girl the resolve to revolt against the feminine rôle unfairly imposed upon her. This is even more marked if the parents, in their disappointment at the gift of " only " a girl instead of the hoped-for male heir, christen the girl with a boy's name and bring her up more or less like a boy, letting her clearly infer that she is only, as it were, a deputy for the son who failed to materialize. Such wrongheaded behaviour on the part of the parents may lead to evil results of a kind that we shall discuss later.

The idea of the inferiority of women, which is early awakened in the girl-child by the treatment meted out to her, is deepened and strengthened by the observation that actually women everywhere play only a secondary part in life. The child can observe this in the first place if, as already pointed out, the mother's position in the family is unfavourable, if the father maltreats the mother, if he belittles her in front of the children, accompanying such remarks with a generally adverse criticism of women as a whole. Secondly, she can observe it, if the mother should happen to complain of her rôle as wife and mother, and warns the girl—as often happens at a very early age—against marriage and the children she may be expected to bear, describing such a lot as pitiable, and advising her to choose a single state. If later the specific sexual functions of women are described to the grown-up daughters as a degradation of their person, as something that at best they can consider as a bargain or endure as a sacrifice, but can never regard in any sense as a fulfilment, and if the tasks of bearing and rearing children are represented as a burden, and never as a source of joy and exaltation—often such things are said at a time when the daughter hardly understands them, even though she absorbs them—it is not surprising if women develop an attitude of open or unconscious (in this case, the attitude is still more strongly determined) revolt against their lot.

It must be admitted that in the minds of many women there is ample justification for the kind of attitude towards women indicated above. One can rightly speak of a predominance of the husband, a predominance that is not based on that natural and supernatural order of which St. Paul speaks in a much-quoted passage in the *Epistle to the Ephesians*, but has become perverted and rendered unjust, with the perversion and exaggeration associated, as we have seen, with authority in general, because it is not exercised as a delegated dignity, bound up with moral obligations, but is simply claimed for the person of the husband. It is as if those who appeal to the words of St. Paul had read only a few lines and had never noticed what came before or after them. Admittedly he says [1] that wives should be subject to their husbands, and that the husband is the head, as Christ is the head of the Church ; but he also says, two verses later, that husbands should love their wives as our Lord loved the Church and sacrificed Himself for it ; and, two verses before, that the members of the Church should be subject to one another and the fear of the Lord. There is no justification either in these words or in any others of Holy Scripture for the offensive arrogance of husbands, their unbridled claims, and their ridiculous conceit at being men and not women. There is no warrant either in the teachings either of Christ, the Apostles or the Fathers of the Church for conduct which so often makes life with such men a burden to their wives, turns the sacrament of marriage into a disreputable farce, and their homes into places of trouble and sorrow, so that their wives and children breathe freely when they leave the home, and dread their return. Is there really anything so magnificent about the husband ? And are not the economic efforts on which he prides himself so much very often inferior to those of the housewife ?

In view of the attitude that men permit themselves towards their wives, it is not surprising that wives no longer correspond to the ideal of the married woman. If, in truth, the husband has to be " the head of the wife," then he must behave appropriately, as the head to the limbs. Just as a man's body fails to function satisfactorily, and a human being is no longer in a position to perfect himself, if he is

[1] *Eph.* v. 23.

" not right in the head," so it is with the family. It is very easy to lay the breaking-up of the family as we see it today at the door of the woman, to decry her depravity and fume about her fashions ; but let the man first put his own house in order. Our Lord's words about the beam and the mote have hardly ever been so grotesquely realized as in man's criticism of woman.

On the whole, I have the impression that there are far more good wives—difficult as things are made for them— than really good husbands, and that the love of the wife comes much nearer to that ideal of love which the Apostle Paul has put before us than that of the husband.

If we investigate the consequences of the experiences, just indicated, which enabled the girl to form an estimate of her own position in the family and the position of woman in general, we must not leave out of account a further series of factors calculated to deepen the impression of woman's subordination, so that this false opinion is never corrected. For example, much more care is bestowed on the future of the sons than of that of the daughters ; more attention is being paid to the son's wishes in the matter of a career than the daughter's ; further, for equal work, a woman receives a smaller wage than a man, and so on. Another series of factors, such as political inequality, unequal treatment under the laws of inheritance and in the facilities for entering a profession, no longer exist in many countries. We shall not inquire whether the removal of such disabilities is of itself, *i.e.*, in all circumstances, a good thing ; but it is self-evident that such sex-distinctions can no longer be maintained under modern social and economic conditions.

Thus we see that there are sufficient grounds for the woman to be conscious—without any very clear ideas about it—that her position is altogether unsatisfactory and second-rate. Almost of necessity her feeling about life is strongly coloured by the thought that success, importance, greatness and power fall to the man alone, that only he is in any full sense a human being, and that the place of the woman is in the background. That peculiar sense of justice which causes mankind to assume that external status must correspond to inner value—an idea which is often misleading in fact, but would be justified in an ideal world-system—leads even women to believe that their worse position and their lesser prospects must correspond to a lesser value, bound up with their nature. As they are bound to recognize early that this worse position is not merely personal, they come to associate their inferiority not with themselves as individuals but with their existence as women. Therefore, all further conse- quences of the sense of inferiority arising in part directly, and in part by way of compensation and over-compensation, are bound up with this factor of " being woman." Individual- psychologists have coined a not very happy term to express the effects of this deep-rooted sense of inferiority in women ; they call it " the masculine protest." This term is intended to indicate that the woman revolts against her position or rather against her nature as a woman, rejects it, protests against it, and therefore craves for the antithesis of that nature—the nature of the man. I feel that this formula is a terminological monstrosity, and we will not make use of it ; but we must never forget that the individual-psychologists were the first to bring these matters clearly to our notice.

It will also become apparent that this unwarranted exaggeration of the importance of the man's rôle within the social system is not without serious consequences even for him. But first we must consider whether we are able to trace any of the character-traits commonly observed in women to the sort of experiences we have described, the sense of inferiority derived from them, and its immediate and remote results.

3. WOMAN'S DISPOSITION

We have already demonstrated several times that the sense of inferiority diminishes the knowledge of one's own value and lessens one's self-confidence. The man who sets a small value on himself at the same time reproaches himself with weakness, since the will to power is a primitive human tendency. Now women, as is well known, are called " the weaker sex." We must therefore first examine this view of women as inferior to, weaker than and subordinate to men, and see how far it is based on objective facts. At first glance it seems plausible, for it is difficult for people to bring themselves to believe that an opinion that is so universal, so traditional and so " obvious " could be founded on error. And there is some support for the argument, although the fact that an opinion has been extensively and continuously held is not necessarily any evidence of its correctness. We shall soon see that this idea contains a very peculiar admixture of the true and the false, and that the true elements are either ignored or regarded as unimportant, whereas the false are accorded the chief significance.

The reasons usually adduced to justify the description of women as the weaker sex are so well known that it is not worth while enumerating them. We will content ourselves with bringing forward a series of facts that are so directly contrary to that description as to throw considerable doubt on its correctness.

When exposed to similar conditions of infection, the frequency of illness with women is in general smaller than with men. The death-rate among women is lower than with men, in spite of the risks attendant on childbirth ; and the average expectation of life is higher among women. That these facts are not to be attributed to external conditions is shown by the circumstance that the infant death-rate is higher for boys than for girls ; more boys are born than girls, but by the end of the first year of life the number of girls surviving exceeds that of boys. The original surplus of boys and its conversion into a surplus of girls is even higher if the number of premature and still births is taken into account.[1] It is indisputable that the female sex is possessed of the greater vitality ; and we can say that in respect of their powers of resistance to noxious influences, women deserve to be called the stronger rather than the weaker sex.

Women's capacity for enduring severe suffering is undoubtedly greater than that of men. It is not only in pregnancy and childbirth that they endure as a matter of course pain and suffering to an extent rarely demanded of men, but they " stick out " other illnesses more patiently than men. The fact that women are biologically selected to bear children does not detract from their ability to meet pain and suffering. Women certainly possess a greater power of resistance to pain, and whether this is biologically or morally determined is of no immediate importance ; enough that it is the fact.

It is in the endurance not only of unavoidable suffering, such as that caused by illness, but also of voluntarily accepted troubles, that women on an average surpass men. Although some men are capable of the greatest self-sacrifice, especially for an ideal, yet in general, woman's capacity in the same respect may be still greater. We have only to consider what they are capable of in the nursing not only of their own children but of the sick generally.

It is customary to refer to the physical weakness of women ; certainly their physical constitution is seldom such as to permit of their employment as dock labourers or blacksmiths ; but quite remarkably robust women do exist,

[1] C. Buccura, *Die Geschlechtsunterschiede* (Leipzig, 1913).

especially amongst the agricultural population and amongst the more primitive races. It must also be borne in mind that many kinds of physical work, such as continuous nursing, which are often performed by women without great difficulty, are by no means light, and only differ in the kind of activity required, and not in the quantity of energy-output, from much of the "heavy" work of a man. Above all we must ask ourselves whether the relative physical weakness which is always present is part and parcel of woman's original make-up, or is a product of upbringing and her general social status. It is already noticeable that with the increasing spread of sport in women's circles, their physical capacities seem to be decidedly on the increase ; for instance, women are able to make the most difficult mountain ascents. Let us recall, further, that in earlier times—as we read, for example, in the historical and mythical accounts of ancient Greece—there were women who were not infrequently victorious over men in contests ; and it is related of the women of Germany that they vied with men in battle—an illustration of this is preserved for us in the figures of the Valkyries and their like. If we add to these facts the data contained in the book of Vaerting already cited (assuming them to be reliable), according to which the women in more or less matriarchially organized societies are men's physical superiors, surpassing them, for instance, in average stature, the idea that the physical weakness of woman is not inseparable from her make-up, but is largely reactively determined, gains greatly in probability. Another circumstance worthy of notice is that where the activity of women is still more hampered than was recently the case with us—in the East, for example—their capacity is apparently even smaller.

A further argument often levelled against women is their small intellectual ability. Even this point is by no means so clear as one might think. Nevertheless, it seems to me to be mistaken for feminists to account for the differences that actually do exist in the matter of the contributions to science made by men and women by the exclusion of women from higher education for centuries, assuming that thereby their scientific abilities have been stunted, just as certain characteristics of wild life in animals disappear after domestication over a long period ; for we know that domestic animals—at any rate many of them—quickly revert to the forms of life of the undomesticated stock. On the other hand three further factors can be adduced. In the first place, the number of women engaged in serious work is still so small, as compared with the number of men, that the probability of striking achievements—which is, as a matter of fact, not too common even with men—is very remote. Anyone who will take the trouble to make a statistical survey, from this point of view, of the works published in the course of a year in any branch of science, can readily convince himself of the justice of this assertion. In the second place, scientific achievement is not only the result of intellectual ability and industry, which are generally not lacking in women, but presupposes a high order of self-confidence and also the confidence of those forming the environment ; but women lack this confidence in their own intellectual ability because they have always been compelled to hear remarks depreciating it. Now, if anyone starts on a piece of work with the secret conviction that he will not be equal to it, it is very likely that this distrust of self will prove to be justified ; and if teachers of science are imbued with the same distrust of the abilities of their female pupils, although they may never openly express their forebodings, this attitude will find reflexion in the minds of women engaged in intellectual work. It deserves to be noticed that recent years, which have witnessed a decline in the general acceptance of the doctrine of women's mental inferiority, have produced a series of first-class, wholly abstract, intellectual and philosophical works by women authors. In this connection, attention may be directed to a very valuable investigation of the top forms of schools in a large city. A comparison of the intelligence and scholarship of the male and female examinees gave on the whole first place to the former, but there were some female candidates of quite exceptionally high intellectual attainments. A survey showed that these girls came without exception from families in which the wife was on an equality with the husband, for example as a partner or co-director of a business. The girls had not been accustomed to observe the subordinate position of the wife, had not learnt that woman was condemned from the start to play a secondary part, had not therefore lost confidence in their ability to fill a rôle in spheres apparently reserved for men, had retained their courage, and had worked on the tasks assigned to them in full assurance of their ability. Thirdly, it may be remarked that we can never know how many great, even world-shaking, ideas originated in the mind of a woman. I know from varied experience how great can be the influence of a woman—wife, sister or friend—even on the intellectual side of a man's life. It is not unknown that many great men have discussed their ideas and schemes with their wives ; but, owing to the vanity of the husbands, the wives' criticism has generally been kept a secret.

The factor of discouragement and lack of self-confidence, the importance of which it is impossible to overstress, may well account for the fact that women have achieved little even in the fields open to them. It has been said in proof of the lesser ability or, as it is commonly expressed, the inferior mental equipment of woman, that she has done nothing outstanding in spheres that were always legitimate for her ; thus in music and the arts she has been only a dilettante.

If discouragement is really so determining a factor, as we are convinced it is, then this need not surprise us ; moreover, in modern times many important contributions to the arts have been made by women. One fact remains and deserves serious investigation, namely woman's apparent lack of ability in musical composition ; but the whole question of the nature of artistic creation, and of musical composition in particular, is still too obscure for any conclusion to be drawn from this fact. Along with the factor of discouragement, there is another which needs careful consideration : one may often observe that women are " not interested " in things that intellectually they could quite well understand and master. Heymans thinks that the reason for this lack of interest lies not in any intellectual inferiority, but in the fact that " cold-blooded, abstract thought is antipathetic to women because it fails to satisfy the emotional needs of their nature." This is one of the many representations of the idea that a special emotionalism, a greater and deeper sensitivity to feeling, is peculiar to women and distinguishes their nature from that of men—an opinion shared by Heymans. We shall see that there is some truth in this, but that the doctrine cannot be wholly accepted. One phenomenon in particular raises some doubt about the validity of that opinion.

There are men of whom it is said in a derogatory way that they are " effeminate." These men by no means always deviate physically from the normal male type ; even those of virile appearance can behave effeminately. It is not our intention to describe this behaviour in detail, but rather to see how it can be explained. We must inquire how far such behaviour can be derived in an intelligible manner from other traits, and especially from the early history, experiences and impressions. Apart from all sorts of merely external traits, such men for the most part more or less avowedly dislike definitely " masculine " activities. They are also usually very much concerned with their health, often to a point almost amounting to hypochondria. Many of them reject some sphere of activity completely : often it is their profession in which they " do not come up to scratch," often it is the erotic life that they reject, often merely that of ordinary friendship, for many such men seek and find friends and acquaintances outside those circles and social strata to which they belong by birth, education, and profession. They either attach themselves to pronouncedly masculine types as a sort of disciple—sometimes with a more or less clearly marked homosexuality, but also frequently without it—or frequent almost exclusively female society, where they often play a strange hybrid rôle and are not taken seriously as real men ; or they belong to an exclusive, would-be æsthetic coterie of people like themselves ; or they associate entirely with their social inferiors. In forming a judgment of the kind of nature we are discussing, these features are far more important than the effeminacy, which is at first more striking. It would be more appropriate, instead of calling these men " effeminate " or womanish, to describe them as unmanly. The essential feature about them is their negative attitude towards the rôle proper to their sex. Analogous to them are those women who quarrel with the obligations and status devolving upon them as women, and consequently with their very membership of the sex. Naturally they cannot rid themselves of their feminine nature ; they can only act as if they had got rid of it ; and the man can only act as if he had renounced his manhood. Both the woman who behaves like a man and the womanish man are persons who for some reason or other seek to escape their peculiar obligations, or at least would like to do so. What is of interest to us in all this is the fact that these womanish men display a tendency to a stronger emotionalism, in the same way that those women who seek to play a masculine rôle, of which there are many varieties, are marked by a relative display of indifference.

It could be argued that the degree of emotionalism depends on the rôles played by people in life, therefore that the state of affairs described above is no evidence against the assertion that a more lively emotional life characterizes woman's nature. However, on this point it must be said that whereas it is just conceivable that one could adopt a greater emotionalism at will, or follow a line of conduct giving that appearance, it is quite unthinkable that a human being whose innermost nature was imbued with a lively emotional receptivity, as is asserted to be the case with women, could exhibit emotional poverty. Such behaviour presumes a degree of self-control and self-mastery with which the champions of this view of women would never be disposed to credit them. Thus, we conclude that the opinion that the emotionalism of woman, which on the average is unquestionably greater, is at least in part reactively determined, enjoys a certain degree of probability.

4. WOMAN'S LACK OF COURAGE AND ITS EFFECTS

Amongst those emotional forms of conduct which are generally considered to be more marked in women than in men, mention must be made of that group which has timidity for its central point : addiction to fear, cowardice and the like. Heymans mentions lack of courage as a characteristic feature of woman, and considers that it is a consequence of that emotionalism which he regards as a primary quality. However, it is legitimate to inquire whether the relation may not be directly reversed, so that the greater emotionalism is regarded as a consequence of a deep-seated lack of courage ; in which case the lack of courage would not be of quite the same order as that which Heymans has in mind. We are already sufficiently aware of the fact that lack of courage is a correlate of an insufficient sense of one's own value, and, further, that man is and always must be strenuously exerting himself to prevent this apprehension of worthlessness from crossing the threshold of consciousness. Consequently there arises, secondarily, from the original sense of inferiority, a cowardice as it were of the second order, as a defence-mechanism, which serves the purpose of shielding the person from all situations that put his courage to the test and so contain the danger of revealing his utter worthlessness. Now, we are not dealing here with the primary and original lack of courage, arising directly out of the sense of inferiority, and which we should more accurately describe as discouragement, for we do not believe that it is here a question of an inborn trait necessarily inseparable from woman's nature ; it seems to us to be rather a modification of an originally entirely fearless disposition, resulting from experience. It is instructive to observe how in the case of a large number of women this lack of courage has arisen in the course of life, mostly in the later years of childhood ; though puberty and the awaking of specifically feminine qualities in fact play only a subordinate and subsidiary part, for this type of discouragement usually sets in long before puberty, somewhere about the sixth to the eighth year. We are thus dealing not with an original absence of courage but with a secondary loss occurring later. Now, the question arises as to whether it is possible to discover a nexus between a sense of inferiority and emotionalism. If this nexus can be shown to exist, and if it can be further shown that all those effeminate men who are characterized by a high degree of emotionalism also suffer from a sense of inferiority, which is responsible for their hypersensitiveness, then the contention that emotionalism is a fundamental feature of woman's nature can no longer be said to hold good, or at any rate, not to the usual extent.

Now, it is obvious, as we have frequently shown, that the desire to " explain " a human being or a human type in terms of a single principle is mistaken and fruitless. However, if at a given time any single factor in a person is functionally predominant, it will probably express itself in some way in all his behaviour. The desire to sum up the woman's subjective and objective life solely in terms of the inferiority-feeling must no more be ascribed to us than the wish to conceive of all specifically female traits as determined by discouragement and the primary realization of inferiority. Our point of view is rather that all doctrines involving a kind of " spiritual alchemy," by which spiritual events of one kind are transformed into those of another kind, start from entirely false theoretical principles. We wish to dissociate ourselves entirely from such ingenuous reasoning. What we assert is simply this : that according to our fundamental rule of method, it is not possible to postulate primary female qualities without first of all investigating the possibility of their having been reactively determined ; and that the emotionalism of woman is to a large extent bound up with the factor of discouragement.

It is obvious that timidity and discouragement are connected, the former being the consequence of the latter ; for apprehension, looked at purely biologically, is a protective mechanism of the weak ; the feeling acts as a warning to an individual in threatening situations to which he does not feel himself to be equal. We have already dealt sufficiently with this point. Thus the susceptibility to fear is clearly associated with lack of courage ; but discouragement and the timidity generated by it have still further effects. Just as we tend to depreciate things beyond our grasp, as is exemplified in the fable of the fox and the grapes, so do we tend to depreciate those things which we do not allow ourselves to covet. The man who is afraid of mountains can either run away from them and settle in the plains, or explain that mountains are hateful and mountaineering foolish, or he can simply state that mountains have no interest for him.

How would it be if it turned out that women's lack of interest in abstract matters and much else, as catalogued by Heymans, were derived from her lack of confidence to tackle such matters? It is somewhat remarkable that Heymans, no doubt rightly, attributes to women the intellectual ability to occupy themselves with such matters, but explains the smallness of their achievement by their lack of interest. The opinion advanced here—that women have, indeed, sufficient intelligence, but are lacking in confidence—seems to me to be the more plausible. We will not follow up the matter in detail, but simply indicate the final result ; for we are less concerned with a descriptive and derivative characterology than with the need to establish practical principles as a guide for upbringing. We hold, then, that woman's alleged emotionalism can be regarded largely as the consequence or expression of a general discouragement. This applies especially, and possibly exclusively, to all those emotionally determined reactions to which a negative value is customarily assigned. Without attempting an exhaustive enumeration, we may mention inconsistency, irritability, "touchiness," pettiness, "not playing the game," all of which can be shown in a variety of ways. Many of these qualities, however, can be exhibited in a positive form, although admittedly they are then somewhat different. Everyone will readily recognize the difference between saying "Women disregard facts," and saying "Women pay more attention to persons than to facts." Let us consider the attitude towards a crime : The man will be pre-eminently the representative of the abstract idea of law, whereas the woman will have in mind not so much the violation of an article of the law as the fate of the individual concerned. The phrase, *summum jus, summa injuria*, might have been coined by a woman. Münsterberg once maintained that women are little suited to judicial office or to serve on a jury because they allow themselves to be too much influenced by their first impressions, and too little by the weight of the evidence ; and there is some truth in this, though whether the first impression must necessarily be misleading is another matter. It may well be that this kind of feminine attitude arises out of the woman's concern for the individual case at the cost of the general principle involved.

We think, then, that the feminine qualities that we have just mentioned are closely connected with discouragement so far as they are thought of expressly in terms of negative value. A man who doubts the success of constant effort is himself inconstant ; even children often show lack of perseverance because success comes too slowly, or because they become aware of the limitations of their powers. Irritability, impatience and the like are, on the one hand, tools used by the will to power of the weak, and, on the other, a form of conduct that provides a means of escape or flight from some situation or other, by the introduction of factors foreign to the situation. He who cannot hope for success in great things will jealously guard his rights in small, and will strain after small victories.

As we have said, we do not propose to enter into further details. It seems more important to realize that in indicating the nexus between a high degree of emotionalism and the sense of inferiority, we have not said all that there is to be said on the subject. We might with good reason adopt the standpoint that in intellectual equipment there is no essential difference—not even necessarily one of degree—between man and woman, for what has been said in this connection about the size of the female brain has long been recognized as irrelevant. And we might justly maintain that many apparently specifically feminine peculiarities are secondary characteristics, arising out of an avoidable sense of inferiority. Yet we must steer clear of that false extreme which seeks entirely to abolish all the differences between the male and female natures, deriving them entirely from environmental differences. The conception of psycho-physical unity which we developed earlier (although for a real elucidation of these difficult matters a very much more elaborate discussion would be required), greatly limits the causal significance of bodily make-up as a determining factor in a person's nature. This concept, however, makes it necessary to regard existent biological differences, not indeed as causes, but as indices of deep-seated personal differences. Now, we have defined character as the principle governing a man's actions, and his action as a relation between the person and the universe. Therefore it is clear that corresponding with the essential differences in the nature of man and woman, as expressed by biological differentiation—that is, corresponding to the differences distinguishing each single member of the relation —there must be differences within the relation, and hence also in the formal factor common to a person's every action, that is, his or her character.

Little as we may be inclined to postulate an ultimate equality of the inmost personal make-up—for, however enthusiastically it may be asserted, it is after all only a postulate—we must, on the other hand, be equally wary in proceeding to practical deductions. For in dealing with the nature of man and woman, which we have already described and will subsequently define more precisely, we cannot arbitrarily exclude the possibility that certain forms of life and activity are closed to women from the start, or that their intrusion there must prove unsatisfactory. Even persons of the same sex differ vastly among themselves in the matter of character, and very diverse characters are found among men who have made equally valuable contributions in the same sphere of activity. Although, as we previously pointed out, there is such a thing as an " occupational type "—determined partly by the fact that men of a particular type gravitate towards a particular occupation, and partly by the influence of environment and special qualifications on character-formation—yet it is indisputable that amongst those engaged in the same occupation a great diversity of character is encountered. Consequently, nothing is gained by maintaining, for instance, that because woman is essentially different from man, and because an occupation has hitherto been exclusively reserved for men, she is therefore unsuited for that occupation. Judged from the standpoint of practical, communal interests and the attainment of individual goals, it is naturally quite a different question whether it is *desirable* for a woman to take up such an occupation. When one looks at things as a comprehensive whole, *suitability does not yet provide sufficient grounds for actual employment*. A person may have a perfect aptitude for thieving, and yet it would not occur to anyone to train the person along such lines.

It is not possible here to deal fully with the specific nature of the two sexes ; such an analysis would require too much space and demand a too extensive preliminary investigation involving a peculiarly critical method of selection. We must content ourselves with presenting a few of what seem to us to be the more important facts, more or less aphoristically and dogmatically.

5. MOTHERHOOD

The relationship between mother and child is possibly the most intimate of all the forms of association between two persons, its closeness not being equalled even by the greatest love between man and woman. It is expressed on the biological plane by the common life led by the two in the period of pregnancy. The intimate association is deepened and brought home to the mother in the clearest possible way by the experience of birth ; she recognizes the child immediately as in a certain sense *her* creation, so that in her mouth the term " my child " has a different sound and meaning from the same words as pronounced by the father. The unique nature of the mother:child relationship finds reflection in the fact that, as Scheler has rightly observed, the term " mother-love " is current in speech, whereas the term " father-love " is unusual and sounds strangely. With the fact of the allocation to woman of the function of motherhood—and in this respect it is irrelevant whether this potentiality is realized or not—there is connected, I believe, the circumstance already mentioned, that women pay attention more to persons than to things, more to individual concrete facts than to general abstract relations. If woman's nature has sometimes been described as materialistic, obtuse, less spiritual, intimately bound up with the " chthonic powers," and so forth, this description, which is usually regarded as somewhat dogmatic, is not so far wrong ; but, in my judgment, it does not imply a lowering of woman's value, but only indicates a difference, and one that should raise the value of woman's nature rather than the reverse. For the relation between mother and child is the most primitive and at the same time the most complete expression of the human relationship.

Of the two Commandments dealing with the love of God and the love of one's neighbour, " the second is like unto the first," and thus both are binding without distinction of sex on all mankind. However, it is tempting to adopt the notion of the division of the Commandments between the two sexes, not in the sense of obedience, but, if the expression is admissible, in the sense of their " incorporation " ; for the man's calling to the priestly office makes him competent in a specific manner for the "service of God," and the calling of woman to the function of motherhood makes her the exemplar of the love of one's neighbour. Inasmuch as all women are called to motherhood, but only a few men are chosen for the priesthood, it might well be thought that, generally speaking, the woman fills her place in the plan of creation and the scheme of salvation better than the man.

It is now time for us to turn our attention to the practical conclusions to be drawn from this exposition for character-training in boys and girls. We have enumerated a series of educational errors which may have serious consequences for the development of girls ; there is one further remark to be made on this point. The existence of an absolute difference between the natures of man and woman in no way justifies the evil circumstances we have mentioned ; and so long as this difference is brought home to woman's consciousness as inferiority only harm can result. If society cannot attain to a full and ceaseless recognition of the value of woman in her own sphere, then there is no prospect of success for the efforts to win her back for the service of the home, the family and the children. The fact that for a long time past the struggle has been not for the freedom, the rights and the recognition of women as women, but for placing them on the same footing as men and in the position of men, shows that the feminist movement is born of resentment ; consequently, many feminists employ undesirable methods, and some of their efforts either overshoot the mark or are directed towards objects that cannot be approved. It should also not be forgotten that the prevailing social and economic system makes it necessary for a large number of women to adopt " masculine " occupations ; it is all very well to say that women should restrict themselves to feminine occupations when there are insufficient openings for all those seeking employment. Doubtless district-visiting and nursing are professions to which women are particularly well suited ; but how many women can obtain posts of this kind ? In this, as in everything else, efforts at reform can be made only in relation to the whole situation, and cannot start with women, who are largely the victims of conditions for which they are the least to blame.

6. THE BRINGING-UP OF BOYS AND GIRLS

Consequently, character-training is harder in the case of girls than with boys, although the contrary belief is generally held ; for, as things are today, the girl must be prepared for two eventualities—for motherhood, with all that it involves, and for the life of an independent wage-earner. This alone is a good reason against the parallel education of boys and girls ; and the careful investigations of K. Bühler show that the time-factor in the development of the two sexes is so different that co-education is impracticable except in the period before school and the early school years. Even if considerations of possible moral risk be ignored, the idea of complete co-education throughout the whole period of youth is shown to be completely mistaken ; but this by no means justifies the segregation of the sexes. A part of the preparation for the realities of life is social intercourse and collaboration between the two sexes. People who to a large extent grow up isolated from persons of the opposite sex often learn only with difficulty to enter into relations with them when the occasion demands it. Many marital and even occupational difficulties are attributable to this. Finally, many professions require an understanding of both sexes ; teachers, doctors and ministers of religion, for example, serve and must understand both sexes, and their understanding should not be derived from books, but from that direct and vital insight which demands reality for its acquisition.

In the matter of the character-training of the sexes and of the assistance that education ought to provide for the bringing out of specific potentialities, it is, broadly speaking, easier to give negative than positive advice. Possibly, human nature would take the right path unassisted, if no obstacles were opposed to it, if it had the support of its most important and natural ally, the will to community, and if parents and teachers were to avoid misdirecting it into unnatural channels by unintelligent methods and behaviour. If the girl is to become a woman, and the boy a man, it is surely necessary that in addition to the realization of themselves as members of the community, they should feel themselves to be sexual beings without this feeling's being in any way accompanied by a sense of degradation or disharmony with the high values they incorporate, and that they should acquire confidence in their ability to discharge the obligations devolving on them in consequence of their physical nature. In this respect also, the maintenance of courage or the avoidance of discouragement is a *sine qua non*.

Nobody would be prepared to dispute the fact that present social conditions are very far from satisfactory ; nobody can be blind to the fact that the position of women is, generally speaking, not a good one, although happily there are a large number of women whose lot is pleasant, and whose attitude towards life is right. Although the number of male neurotics is by no means small, women still form the main body of those who suffer in this way, which shows that, on the whole, women are in a worse state of conflict than men—not that it proves anything about a special constitutional predisposition in the case of women. It is a matter of urgent necessity for the maintenance of individual and communal normality and a desirable level of morals and religion that a serious start should be made to analyse the problems at which we have only just hinted here. At this point we immediately find ourselves faced with insuperable obstacles, as in the case of the education of children and adults. If our efforts fail, it is only in the smallest degree due to the operation of natural limitations ; nor is it due to the fact that we are brought up against people who are stubborn and whose disposition, constitution—call it what you will—renders a change of mind impossible. Such a failure *is* due to the obstacles imposed by existing social, economic and world-wide political conditions, and ultimately to the fact that the minds of the great mass of mankind are so lacking in a true communal consciousness that the real sense of humanity has to a large extent been lost. It is unnecessary to refer to the way in which man may lose the feeling for human things to the same degree as he has alienated himself from things divine. The Austrian Chancellor, Monsignor Seipel, once coined the term " hygiene of souls " ; it has passed out of use, but it would be wise to reflect on its deep meaning, and the demands it imposes, more seriously than hitherto. The problems—nowadays acute—of women's education, women's occupation, the position of the woman in the family and communal life, and, bound up with these, the future of the children, the race, and the Church, can only be solved by intensive and all-embracing reforms. Neither by a trivial attempt to creep back to past conditions—always illusory— nor by grumbling and effecting improvements first in one direction and then in another, but only by a genuine and deep change of heart (*metanoia*) affecting our whole civiliza- tion can there be any improvement. Where is he who shall summon us to prepare the way of the Lord ? We hear many who cry out in the wilderness ; but there is no voice possessed of the power and urgency of John the Baptist. It is high time for someone to seek to awaken and stir up mankind. Μετανοείτε· change your hearts !

CHAPTER VI

THE LATER YEARS OF CHILDHOOD, SCHOOL, ADOLESCENCE AND THE PROBLEM OF SEX

1. YOUTH AND THE SOCIAL ENVIRONMENT

IT was not without intention that our remarks in the last few pages were pitched in such a key ; for much as the matters we shall now discuss may warrant optimism—so long as we confine our attention to the character-formation of the child within the family circle, and the exclusion of essentially avoidable mistakes in upbringing—a review of actual social conditions gives little ground for it. In spite of all these obstacles, fine characters do develop ; there are people who grow up able to accept all their personal shortcomings and the imperfections of life because such things do not mean for them the true and the essential. However, as regards the mass of people, exceptional and heroic efforts would be required for them to live tranquil and upright lives ; to go through life *integer vitae scelerisque purus* is made difficult enough for the present generation, and the *scelera* are to a large extent not the outcome of personal guilt.

It is not hard to prepare a child for the trials and obligations of life, and to teach him that success is not everything and greatness of no account. It *is* hard to prepare him to live with those who crave only for success, who regard their fellow-men merely as means to their selfish ends, whose ways are dark and devious, who have no understanding of frankness and kindness, but believe everyone's conduct to be dissimulation, who regard the people in their environment as enemies instead of as fellow-workers, who are unable to conceive of any values that are absolute and not relative, because they are the centre of their own cosmos, who therefore know of nothing more worth striving for than self-exaltation and exhausting the transitory possibilities of pleasure. Despite all counter-efforts, this type is enormously on the increase ; we shall come to know it more fully, when we shall see that the above description is by no means exaggerated.

It is the type of man without backbone or stability. This is not the place for us to inquire why so large a number of people today have lost their balance, and wander in a state of complete bewilderment ; what primarily concerns us is the fact that this type corresponds to a transitional phase of human development ; for the period of adolescence exhibits a similar attitude and line of conduct. (It could be said with some reason that our epoch suffers from a kind of " fixation at the juvenile level " ; it shows a shortage of people who are fully adult. Such an assertion will undoubtedly be contested ; but that it can be justified will be shown in the chapter dealing with neurosis.)

Over the period of adolescence [1] there already lies that shadow which, owing to the undesirable social conditions of the present day, darkens the lives of adults. Adolescence is the period of transition from the life of the child to that of the adult. One can sympathize with those who consciously or unconsciously dread the transition to adult life, with its obligations of manhood or womanhood, and try to put off the evil day. One cannot maintain that their attitude is mistaken so long as one bears in mind only the realities of the moment ; their mistake becomes apparent only in relation to the essential laws, the final cause and goal of life.

---

[1] An elaboration of these observations is to be found in my book, *Psychologie des Geschlechtslebens* (Munich, 1922), and in *Medizinische Characterologie*.

2. PUBERTY AND ADOLESCENCE

In most of the studies of the period of adolescence and puberty, and the psychical and characterological changes associated therewith, the sexual factor is usually put in the foreground. For the young people themselves, the physical experience of sex, and for the observers, the physical manifestations noticeable at this time, which are evidently connected with the genital organs, are certainly very striking ; but this is only one side of the whole process of adolescence, and it is perhaps open to question whether it should be regarded as the primary factor or whether it plays the leading part in the changes associated with puberty. In support of the opinion that accords the sexual factor the chief importance, which we take leave to doubt here, there is the fact that, in the absence of somatic puberty, the secondary manifestations of sex, both physical and psychical, fail to appear.

This observation is admittedly relevant ; it has been too often confirmed to allow of any doubt ; but it can be questioned whether the conclusions drawn from it can be immediately accepted. If one believes that the person is an indissoluble psycho-physical unity, and that changes of any kind must affect the whole, it can be seen that the problem can be viewed from a different aspect. Certainly, the removal of the genital glands—castration—renders certain processes of development impossible, but it does not check development entirely. The adult eunuch is still an adult, although of a different kind from the individual whose development has been undisturbed. It is as though, with the removal of the ductless glands, there had been withdrawn from development a region which would have developed as normally as other parts of the organism ; but the processes of development as such cannot be regarded as fully excluded, because, although they are determined in their effects, they are not causally or derivatively determined by the existence and functional activities of certain other organs. In the first and the last instance, the reason for the appearance of developmental processes is to be found in the psycho-physical organic unit in whose depths they have been latent. Normal adolescence is distinguished as a rule by a special rapidity of development. I know of no data to indicate whether after the loss of the genital glands—of course before the age of sexual maturity—such a quickening-up of development is absent, or whether it is still traceable, a possibility which cannot be excluded.

Thus we see in the sexual development of adolescence only one side of a process of change coincidently affecting the whole person. This point of view is confirmed by pathology, for remarkable cases are known in which, in consequence of pathological changes brought about by disease in very early childhood, the physical symptoms of puberty, together with a marked increase of growth, occur in childhood with no sort of corresponding psychical development. This shows that the part played by the physical side of sexual maturity is commonly overestimated. The sexual manifestations are the most striking, but not for that reason the most important in the whole process ; in the same way, in epilepsy, the convulsive attacks occupied the sole attention of investigators until it was realized that the fits, although the most dramatic symptom, form only part of a far more comprehensive syndrome.

The nature of the changes occurring in adolescence escapes us if the sex-development factors and the consciousness and expression of erotic emotion are placed in the foreground. Apart from the fact that, especially in the case of girls, the psychical and characterological phenomena distinguishing this period of life can occur in the absence of any conscious experience of sex, and that the difficulties experienced by adolescents are not always and exclusively bound up with the " question of sex," a more thorough analysis reveals other and obviously far more deep-seated factors. To these we will now direct our attention ; the part played by the sexual factor will be discussed later.

There can be no doubt that childhood does not present a steady development whose peaceful progress is suddenly shattered by the " storm and stress " of youth. Even in the years of childhood there are periods of accelerated or retarded change. Just as the increase in weight and height is both absolutely and relatively greater in infancy than subsequently, so naturally the first phase of psychical development is one of particularly rapid progress. If a comparison is made between the sum of what an infant learns in his earliest years—walking, talking, the use of things and so on—and all the knowledge acquired later, the latter appears very small in comparison to the former. But knowledge and faculties are already present in ample measure, before there is any marked crystallization of idiosyncrasies or of character. Particular traits appear very early, and it is often possible to prophesy in the years of infancy what the child of six or seven will be like ; but such expectations may end in bitter disillusion. Often undesirable new qualities appear, and others, which seem to be strongly marked, disappear, the whole conduct undergoing a change of tone which to the observer seems at first sight to be quite causeless.

It is only about the sixth or seventh year—sometimes rather earlier, sometimes rather later—that the child gives the impression of being a finished product, a complete child. The years immediately following do not produce any immediate changes ; definitely infantile traits that have more or less persisted become continuously less marked, but there is hardly any change of a far-reaching kind, or the addition of really new elements. It is only at puberty or in the year or two preceding it that something new begins to emerge. The stability mentioned as being reached at about the beginning of the school age is evidently closely related to the fact that by that time the child has a fairly coherent picture of the world. If he is intelligent and alert—which means, generally, if the free development of his faculties has not been checked by timidity and discouragement and the eternal " you can't understand "—he is by this time more or less clear about the main laws governing the world. Of course he has not acquired this knowledge by systematic reasoning (although by means of processes approximating to it), and there is much that he does not know, but he is also aware of this ignorance, and is therefore perpetually asking innumerable questions about details. These details, however, are of an eminently practical nature, and have to be fitted in, often not without violence, into a previously constructed framework. Many children at this time build up world-systems that are often very complicated and comprehensive. Now since, as we know, character, as a principle attaching to the relation of the ego to the non-ego, is dependent on the non-ego—that is, the world or the world-picture that the subject has constructed, which in these years has become relatively concrete—the stability which we have already mentioned appears in the child's nature and conduct.

This world-picture and the attitude the child takes up towards it form in all circumstances the material on which the further transforming forces take hold and in which the processes of change occur. Since the psycho-characterological faculties of man have a special " time of manifestation," as is clearly shown at the period of physical puberty, it may be that something hitherto completely unnoticed appears as something quasi-new ; but this novelty can influence only something that is already present.

These considerations help to establish the truth of the decisive importance attaching to the earliest years of life ; and consequently, after all that we have said of the environmental influences to which at that time the person is exposed, for the whole later development of character, the experiences of the first six years, the period before school, are all-important. Therefore those people to whom the small child is entrusted bear the very greatest responsibility for his later characterological disposition.

3. SCHOOL INFLUENCES

It is, of course, indisputable that the subsequent years also exert a constructive and, reconstructive influence ; this applies particularly to the school influence. The school can do an immense amount of harm ; the question whether it can, apart from certain exceptional cases, help to correct long-standing anomalies may remain in abeyance. If a desirable change occurs in the school years, this is as a rule to be attributed not to the school, but either to the abolition of the sense of isolation, brought about by the social life of the classroom, or to the human contact with one or other of the teachers. It must always be strongly emphasized that all subsequent improvements, whether brought about by conscious efforts or by fortunate circumstance, operate in, and are co-determined by, a medium that is already to hand. Therefore the upbringing that takes place in the parental home, which begins with the very first days of life, and in a certain sense even earlier, is by far the most important for character-formation.

This is the proper place in which to say a word on upbringing in boarding-schools. This usually takes place in the school years, but the distressing social conditions of our times compel many parents to entrust their infant children to a crèche or day-nursery, at any rate during the course of the day. As we have already said, certain circumstances justify this procedure ; for example, it may be expedient to educate an only child away from home in order to avoid for him all the possible undesirable consequences of his position of isolation. Apart from economic pressure, that kind of consideration is the only one that justifies the removal of the child from the family circle. (We are here, of course, considering only " normal " families and " normal " children ; the problem of difficult, criminal or otherwise abnormal children will be dealt with later.) Apart from the fact that boarding-school education can never replace the individual care, the sympathy and the close personal relations that ought to exist between parents and children, there are three serious disadvantages inseparable from it. First, the child at a boarding-school lives in an artificial community, which is in no sense a copy of reality—that is, of the community in which as an adult he will have to live and move and have his being ; consequently the boarding-school, generally speaking, is an inadequate preparation for the realities of life. The artificiality of the community is caused by the fact of living with persons of only one sex and in the main of the same age ; further, the fact that the adults in this community only play the parts of teachers, prefects and the like, exaggerates the distance, because the factor of natural personal affection, which helps to abolish or diminish distance, is lacking. Secondly, life in a boarding-school is very strictly regulated according to a time-table ; teaching, preparation, leisure, games and so on are all prescribed by rule. Thus, the child does not learn how to divide up his time on his own, to estimate the time necessary for the completion of a piece of work, and to regulate his work and recreation on his own initiative—all things that he will have to learn in later life, even at the university. Thirdly, the aims set before children in boarding-schools are for the most part not those of real life. As an Old Etonian once remarked to the translator of this book, "Membership of 'Pop' and distinction at games are not the real objects of life." That comment was possibly rather too cutting, if meant to cover all the aims put before children at boarding-schools, but it does go to the root of the matter. We do not wish to ignore the fact that boarding-school education is sometimes unavoidable, because, for many parents, it is the only possible way of imparting the desired kind of culture to their children, and also because, leaving the case of orphans on one side, there are a number of cases in which for several reasons—without the parents being necessarily to blame—life in a boarding-school is to be preferred to that in the home. Our protest is levelled only against unconditional preference for institutional as opposed to family upbringing, and against those parents—whose name is unfortunately legion—who send their children away from home solely for reasons of convenience, whether their decision is animated by their own happy experiences in such institutions, by family tradition, or by a feeling of their own incompetence to shoulder their educational responsibilities.

Before reverting to the subject of puberty, we should like to make some further remark on the school and its influence on character-formation. We have stated that the school can do much harm ; the amount is naturally proportionate to the counter-influence exerted by the parents. There is only one corrective—parental influence—for the undesirable results of school life, whether these arise from association with contemporaries or from any other cause. In order that this influence may be felt in the later years of childhood, various conditions are necessary, amongst which the most important is the continuance of mutual confidence.

The unamiable influences that may be operative in the school environment are very various ; some are avoidable ; others are possibly inherent in the school system. It is evident that with large school classes individual attention is impracticable ; for instance, a teacher cannot be expected in every case of misbehaviour to take the child's individual make-up into consideration. It is therefore the more important that the teacher should be fully acquainted with the general principles of child psychology and character-formation. He cannot know all the factors that determine the behaviour of this or that child, for some of these are conditioned purely domestically and others depend on the child's relations with his school-fellows ; but he should realize that misconduct is by no means always a manifestation of naughtiness, stupidity, depravity and so on. If a child is exceptionally naughty, the teacher should take the trouble to investigate the causes, before immediately condemning him.

For school-children, the teacher is the representative of authority ; even with the greatest latitude in the class-room, a modicum of discipline and of authority to uphold his position is indispensable. Even in those " self-governing schools " [1] where a more or less extensive " autonomy " is cultivated, authority exists, even though it is exercised by an elected committee ; thus, the constitution of such communities of young people and children shows that the members themselves are convinced that without some form of authority they cannot succeed.

The scope of the teacher's authority is bound up with two sets of conditions : the first comprises everything that may be called the preparation of the child for school life ; the second depends on the personal make-up and conduct of the teacher himself.

[1] See Ferrière, *L'Autonomie Scolaire* (Geneva, 1922).

The child may be conceived of as having received a proper preparation for school life if his will to community has been adequately fostered and his will to power directed into the right channels. Secondly, the idea of authority should not have become hateful to a child, nor submission to it be regarded as a belittlement of himself; he should have learnt to conceive of subordination as a necessary part of discipline. He fully understands the nature of social relationships, especially his personal relation to adults, including, of course, the teaching staff. This understanding is effected by means of a scheme that he has worked out on the basis of his own experience, or, if one is disposed to give less credit to the constructive thought of children, has been impressed or forced upon him. The psychoanalysts of the Freudian school [1] interpret this in terms of the " father-imago." Although I am not in agreement with their views, this conception is one which admirably describes the position ; actually the child sees in all persons in authority who happen to come his way an " imago " or copy of the father or parents, and behaves towards them in accordance with the experience associated with his own parents.

Although it cannot be doubted that many mistakes are made by the school authorities, nevertheless, in numberless cases, the parents who complain of the bad relations existing between the pupils and teachers, almost always putting the teachers in the wrong, have themselves laid the foundations of the trouble in question by their own mistakes in upbringing. The same applies in the case of those parents who lay all the blame at the door of the child, unreservedly taking sides with the teacher ; their attitude only intensifies the

[1] The translator is aware that the phrase " psychoanalysts of the Freudian school " is tautological ; he has used it intentionally, as many of his readers may not be aware that the Freudians designate themselves as psychoanalysts, denying the title to adherents of other analytical schools ; Jung and his disciples call themselves " analytical psychologists," and the Adlerians, " individual-psychologists."—TRANS.

disagreeable situation. All parents should bear in mind that these alternatives—blame the teacher or blame the child—by no means exhaust the situation ; there is a third factor, which is much more likely to prove to be the responsible one, namely their own mistakes.

With regard to the teaching-staff, school masters and mistresses are liable to make the same kind of blunders, with the same undesirable results, which we have already investigated, when dealing with the child:parent relationship. We need not consider these in detail ; we will permit ourselves to make only a few general observations.

If we examine the situation closely, we shall see that the position of the teacher is not without danger for the formation of his own character. Anyone who spends most of his time with people to whom he feels himself superior, both in the sense of an adult in the presence of children and as a learned person dealing with the ignorant, can easily come to exaggerate his own importance and fall a victim to a sort of subjective infallibility. It is notorious how readily teachers are inclined to extend towards adults the attitude they adopt to children ; they show themselves dogmatic and pedantic in their own family circle ; they are always better informed than everyone else, intolerant of contradiction, and so on. Such characterological distortions are related only secondarily to the teacher's profession, and have their roots in a form of character antecedent to and partly determining their choice of career—a matter which we shall discuss in the chapter on abnormal and neurotic characters. For those children who for some reason or other are insufficiently prepared for school life this kind of attitude on the part of the teacher causes serious difficulties ; their introduction to school life and its discipline is not only not facilitated but often rendered impossible. There are a number of people who acquire from it a lasting and lively hatred of school and all its associations ; they have been compelled to adopt a permanent attitude of revolt, which not only prevented them as children from acquiring the communal standpoint, but bars their entry, as adults, into the life of the community, which is associated in their minds with the idea of coercion.

On the other hand, in many cases, the school can correct a variety of mistakes made by the parents. First and foremost, the school-fellows act as valuable educational auxiliaries. For this influence to be effectual, the child must already be more or less a sociable being. Unusually timid children, the victims of an exaggerated sense of inferiority and its attendant anxiety, are unable to establish the requisite contact ; they are immune from the influences of the school community, which are naturally exercised not consciously but artlessly. Therefore, after a few vain attempts on the part of their school-fellows, they are promptly pushed aside, left in the cold, and despised as being either proud, stupid or tiresome. The isolation of certain children brought about in this way should not escape the careful observation of the teacher ; he enjoys many opportunities for helpful intervention, not necessarily in school hours— although even then his encouragement may be very welcome —but on school walks, excursions, in the playground, and so on. I have repeatedly noticed the beneficial results of such sympathetic behaviour. The teacher should bear in mind that the verbal form in which he attempts to offer encouragement is not without importance. I know of an unsatisfactory pupil, who, on the rare occasions when he showed up good work, was greeted, with the best intentions, with the following remark : "Now, then, you have done well this time; don't let's have such a falling-off again." This formulation, in which the teacher's anticipation of a relapse was implicit, had very undesirable results. On his reformulating his remarks in a more positive form, which implied his cheerful confidence in the pupil's future efforts, the results were very gratifying. It must be borne in mind that a goal that objectively is not a lofty one seems very high to one who has to scramble up to it from a great depth ; I am in the habit of expressing this idea as follows. If the mercury rises from 0° to 16° C. the rise is higher than if it rose from 12° to 16°, but, despite the greater " achievement," the temperature is no warmer.[1] Regarded from the standpoint of characterology, the case we have just mentioned may not seem to be very important, because it appeared to relate to intelligence more than to character ; but similar cases could be quoted in which only questions of character were involved.

It should be noted that the relation of poor scholarship to abnormal character—the nexus has frequently been observed—is by no means always that which is commonly assumed ; this point will be made clearer in the discussion on abnormal character. According to the current view, a child learns badly because he has a bad character, is idle, careless, mischievous or lacking in self-respect. But in many instances the situation is reversed ; the child is inattentive, insubordinate, a nuisance, etc., because he learns badly, and this may in turn be due to the fact that he has lost his confidence in his capacity for learning. This attitude is usually strengthened—in a series of easily understandable progressions—by the reaction of the teaching staff. We have learnt from observation that auxiliary tuition, enabling the child to show his ability, can frequently straighten out the warped character, even in those cases in which the child has been diagnosed as " degenerate," " evilly disposed," or " congenitally afflicted." Before undertaking to pronounce such a sentence of moral death, one must know infinitely more about children and the human soul than most of the persons

---

[1] Cf. the work cited in the footnote on p. 156 ; also Allers, *Scheinbar unbegabte Kinder*, vol. I, 1925.

who pass such verdicts, and, above all, one must understand the individual case far better than most of those who sit in judgment.

We will not dwell further on the subject of school influences, however interesting it might prove to study the subject in detail, and however necessary a psychological investigation of the school system may seem to us. What has been said may suffice to demonstrate that the experiences of school life contribute their share to the characterological development of children, preparing them for puberty—in a favourable as well as in an unfavourable sense.

4. THE CHANGE OF OBJECTIVE OUTLOOK OCCURRING AT ADOLESCENCE

We will now resume our interrupted discussion on adolescence and the changes accompanying puberty. We have seen that these changes are more than an epiphenomenon of physical puberty and the conscious experiences directly related to it—that is, experiences that are more or less definitely sexual. It has already been indicated that adolescence must be regarded above all as a period of transformation. It must not be imagined that sexual factors are added as novel elements of experience to an existing body of experiences and its appropriate reaction-patterns, and that these factors added in this way modify the entire pre-existent situation and conduct. Puberty, in the specific sense of the term, is rather a partial phenomenon running parallel to others, a fact which is by no means unknown. With reference to this, it is instructive to recall the by no means uncommon cases that show a normal and orderly progress of physical puberty without a corresponding appearance of the other changes associated with adolescence, there being a discrepancy between the physical and psychical maturing processes. We previously had occasion to consider the " Peter Pan " situation, in which the person clings to the child attitude ; we left it open to doubt whether one is always entitled in these cases to speak of a genuine "clinging," implying behaviour, or whether external obstacles to development are involved ; in any case, we cannot get away from the fact of such discrepancies with a subsequent retrieval in the psychical and characterological spheres, which would normally take place more or less coincidently with the physical ones. This shows that an explanation of the phenomena of adolescence solely in terms of reaction to physical processes and conscious sexual experience is insufficient.

The essential feature of the changes accompanying puberty and adolescence appear to us to be a breaking away from the old and, as we saw, relatively stable outlook on the world, and the adoption of a revised attitude to the universe.

Before proceeding further, this conception of outlook on the world—" world-philosophy," individual cosmogony, call it what you will—demands a more detailed explanation. In the adult it involves a picture not of the " universe contrasted with myself," but of the " universe which includes me as a part of it." It does not express the relation of two members, " I and the universe," which are ontological equals, mutually independent and brought into relation one with another more or less accidentally, but it describes the relation expressed in the formula, " I-in-the-universe and the universe." This formulation involves the objectivization, to a certain degree, of one's own ego ; but we have already asserted that the subject can never be objective to itself. As a general proposition, this assertion is perfectly obvious, but we made it apply to a person at the very moment of completing an action ; nevertheless, he possesses at that moment an image of himself, above all as a member of all the relations in which he is involved. The person is not comprehensible to himself at the moment of deliberate action, in the same way as the action itself is not comprehensible ; but he is capable of apprehending the action, and himself also in a certain sense. Schilder, in a lecture hitherto unpublished as far as we know, made use of the following very helpful analogy to illustrate this situation. When we gaze at the dead body of someone we loved in life, we cannot altogether regard it as a mere lifeless corpse, but invest it with a faint gleam of the vitality that has left it ; in the same way, there is a kind of breath of life in a recollected action, although as a completed event it has ceased to exist.

It is not our intention to proceed further with the phenomenological and ontological aspects of this very difficult problem. We only wish to point out that there is no inconsistency between the two assertions that the subject cannot be its own object, and that a certain kind of objectivization does exist.

The cosmogony of the adult, then, " contains " the ego, as we indicated in the above formula. The cosmogony of the child also includes the ego ; but this " inclusion " is of a different kind. For to the small child the universe, its components and laws, are a mystery, but his own ego is not so. It is true that tendencies to make a problem of himself are detectable even in the small child, the ever-present question of " Whence came I ? " being inseparable from such all-embracing problems ; but, as a rule, it is not more than a matter of tendencies, which in subsequent years become scarcely noticeable. " I," as a problem, is, so to speak, first discovered at the period of puberty ; we must not, of course, set any strict or definite temporal limits to this period, for the problem can take shape in the mind before the actual years of adolescence in specially disposed individuals or under the influence of particular environmental circumstances.

In that period, then, there occurs what may be described as " self-discovery." From what we have previously said, it should be clear that thereby we do not mean the first emergence of the ego, which would be absurd, but a special attitude adopted by the ego towards itself. Before this attitude is fixed, and while—to keep to the analogy—the ego is being sought for or is searching for itself, as yet unsuccessfully, the situational totality must of necessity be extremely problematical. Further, the element of uncertainty is unavoidable, for once again, as in the years of childhood, the person is faced with the necessity of gaining a position that is as yet not clearly defined, all the approaches to which are insecure, dangerous and adventurous.

The physical accompaniments of puberty contribute in no small measure to the feeling of insecurity in adolescence. Here, again, we are not primarily considering purely sexual development. It is well known that young people, especially in the first phase of pubescence, are noticeably clumsy ; the natural psychomotor gracefulness of childhood has departed, adult psychomotility has not been established, because the rapid growth of the body does not permit of a fixed rhythm. Even in the matter of physique, or, to express it better, of the consciousness of himself as a physical being, the youth does not know overnight, so to speak, what he will be like when he wakes up in the morning. As is well known, these physical changes not only involve the growth and movement of the various parts of the body, but also affect other, possibly all the other, organs, even though these changes may not always be apparent. We need only recall the change of voice, which is more marked in the case of boys but is not absent in girls. Thus there is brought about a change, which is often far-reaching, in the vital consciousness and which, as always, leads to an increase of the sense of insecurity.

As in many similar situations, there is a vicious circle here. The uncertainty and insecurity born of changes in the vital consciousness increase the youthful maladjustment, clumsiness and sulkiness, which in their turn still further increase the sense of insecurity. We can already see how many character-traits of these years can be intelligibly regarded as corollaries of the totality of circumstances in which young people find themselves, and that we are not bound to content ourselves with the mere affirmation of a dependence upon natural processes. As in our treatment of the part played by constitutional factors in character-formation, we must again be on the look-out for " occasions," rather than lose ourselves in a welter of " causes," which may, on investigation, turn out not to be strictly speaking " causal."

5. THE DIFFICULTIES EXPERIENCED IN ADOLESCENCE

As a result of the insecurity and uncertainty characterizing the critical years of puberty, there is at that time a repetition of all the difficulties and problems of early childhood which we have already discussed. Naturally, it is not a photographic kind of repetition, because the human being who finds himself once more a victim to a sense of insecurity has become a different being, and his environment has also changed. In the intervening years he has assimilated a number of experiences, and a variety of constructive influences have played upon him ; consequently, he is not nearly as plastic as he was in his childhood. This provides a certain safeguard, for there seems to be less risk of undesirable circumstances leaving their traces behind them. On the other hand, the danger is greater ; to remove a scratch on a waxed surface it is sufficient merely to smooth it over lightly, but to remove scratches and stains from a polished metal surface one must refurbish it. Further, positively acting forces make less impression than formerly, not because the character is now more closely bound up with the organism, but because all behaviour is at this stage on a more conscious level. The now self-conscious ego is prepared, and the resistances that every human being offers to all external influences are strengthened by the co-operative assistance of rationalization and knowledge. *Therefore, for the upbringing during these years, far more love, tact and selflessness are required than ever before.* The word " selflessness " must here be understood in its literal sense ; in seeking to influence young people, the upbringer must more than ever surrender himself.

Sometimes people have the impression that puberty destroys all their educational efforts, or at least all the visible results, and that the whole ground must be re-traversed. In a certain sense this impression is justified ; of course, in reality, none of the influences of childhood are lost, but much is for the time being forced into the background. It must be borne in mind that this process of self-discovery involves not only occasion for feelings of insecurity and the complexity of things, but also a factor that can greatly strengthen his positive self-feeling ; if the youth has experience of " himself "—using the word in its literal sense—for the first time he will in many cases, disregarding those occasions of extensive discouragement, become aware of himself as an independent value. This increased sense of self, which impels him to test everything which he has hitherto simply accepted, to take nothing for granted, to make his own affirmation the sole criterion of truth, has yet another source, namely, the sense of insecurity that colours—though often faintly—the whole mood during these years. We are already sufficiently familiar with the mechanisms of compensation and over-compensation, which again become operative, for us to be able to dispense with any further explanation.

It is quite understandable, bearing in mind the train of events we have just sketched, that the idea of authority is the first thing about which youth begins to experience doubts. It must again be emphasized that enforced authority will lead to no good, certainly to no lasting result, and that there is need of special love, patience and devotion if the required attitude towards authority is to be re-established. This applies equally to the attitude towards the community. As is well known, young people tend to isolate themselves, go their own way and so on, and so far as they cultivate society at all, they prefer that of their own kind, and ignore any other. This attitude evidently derives from the new consciousness of their own value, which itself primarily as well as secondarily is brought about by the operation of compensation. The man has now actually made the discovery of his own ego, and he discovers it as an incorporation of possible values—it could not be otherwise. Consequently, we are given the possibility of helping people who are deficient in this respect to acquire a sense of positive self-feeling ; at the same time we are always in danger of depriving people of such an experience for years and possibly for the whole of their lives.

Although in our opinion the process and the problem of " self-discovery " is the central factor in pubescence, it must not be thought that it sums up everything that matters in the lives of young people. It is true that the ego as such becomes a problem—one might almost say a theorem—but first and foremost in its relation to those great realms of being to which man belongs and the fields of activity open to him. Therefore the problem of their common humanity, their membership of the community, their share in the burden of toil which falls to the lot of all men—that is, their choice of occupation—and finally all those questions which have sexual love as their focus, become deeply-moving experiences for young people. Above these, there rises the religious problem, which according to recent investigation seems never to be absent from the experiences of these years.

Youth is disposed to theorize ; world-systems are built up and cast down with equal rapidity, problems are enunciated, debated and just as quickly discarded. A certain instability has always been regarded as characteristic of the years of development. This instability and the theorizing attitude, together with the tendency to preoccupation with highly abstract problems, are closely connected with a sense of insecurity. Grappling at the purely theoretical level with a problem that at bottom involves very personal issues, may be a defence-mechanism and an evasion serving to blunt the acuteness of the personal situation. Seizing upon problems and letting them drop, accepting solutions and as soon rejecting them, indicate an attitude that is due to the same cause, so far as one is inclined to avoid ultimate obligations and to escape binding consequences.

For with the complete discovery and crystallization of the ego, man awakens to the consciousness of his unavoidable, ultimate loneliness, his final dependence upon himself, and therewith of his absolute responsibility towards himself. The " shelter " of childhood is gone for ever ; the youth feels this, without so far having attained that measure of equanimity and assurance which will enable him to stand really alone. The loneliness of which we have just spoken must not be regarded as antithetical to membership of the community or to the will to community, which, as we are never tired of emphasizing, are essential for man. This loneliness lies, as it were, much deeper ; it is more cryptic than that aloneness usually complained of. It is the necessary corollary of the absolute " once-and-for-all-ness " of the human person, which is bound up with his metaphysical existence, and can be only partly abolished, the degree depending on the extent to which he enjoys the supernatural life.

We have already said that in the period of adolescence upbringing is peculiarly difficult, and calls for an even greater measure of understanding, tact and devotion than in childhood. Now, upbringing is a relation between one who is engaged in the task of upbringing, and one who is brought up, and as in the case with all relations, is dependent on its two members. In this case we must not forget the second member ; to expect him to behave in such a way as to render his upbringing an easy task is an impossible require-ment, for the production of receptivity to positive influences is the chief educational function. What *can* be done is to *prepare* the youth, to guide him from the outset, so that in spite of all the difficulties inseparable from pubescence, he does not isolate himself from the positive educational forces.

If this is to be successful, the youth must have retained his confidence in those concerned with his upbringing ; this is natural to the child. We have frequently emphasized the importance of that factor, and it is now seen that its significance extends beyond the period of childhood. Many educational difficulties met with in the years of adolescence could be avoided if those responsible had access to the more intimate experiences of youth. If there existed a real bond of confidence between parent and child, if the latter were sure that in all circumstances his advances would not be rejected nor his conduct condemned, if he were accustomed from the beginning to share his inward struggles with his parents, it would not be so difficult to keep this relation alive beyond the years of childhood and through those of pubescence right up to maturity. Then there would not occur that estrangement between parents and children which is so frequently a source of sorrow to both.

6. THE FORCES THAT SHAPE CHARACTER

In considering the kinds of alteration undergone by the character during the years of pubescence, and the forces assisting in the transformation, it must not be forgotten that the latter work on a medium that has already taken form, contributing materially to the character that develops at puberty and shows persistence. An adolescent who has met with discouragement will certainly not gain in courage by experiencing insecurity in later years ; his receptivity to external influences, however sympathetic and tactful, will always remain at a low level.

The forces that shape character are of three kinds, not only in the period now under discussion, but generally speaking. The reason for our postponement of this matter is that one of these groups of forces does not seem to be of importance in the years preceding adolescence. The three groups are as follows : (i) The directly discerned motives of action ; (ii) the demands coming from the outside world, which are felt to be more or less binding, though the reason for them is not always entirely discerned ; (iii) the undiscerned, unreflective motives, which are largely bound up with vital values, and on this account are frequently regarded as " impulsive," although this is incorrect if the usual connotation of " impulse " be retained in this connection.

It is the second group that, in our opinion, has small significance before adolescence. This assertion may be considered surprising ; it will be alleged that it is the small child who obviously acts without clearly discerning his motives, for example on receipt of an order, that is, in response to imperfectly understood demands. In this connection it is necessary to draw two distinctions. A discerned motive is one to which the person gives his substantial assent—we are using the term in the sense of Newman's "real assent." Discernment in this case means that "experienced understanding" which, we maintained in an earlier chapter of this book, should be distinguished from the merely "theoretical" or rational understanding. It is not a matter of insight in the sense of possible logical reference of the occasional requirement or intended action to some fundamental principle already accepted. The possibility of such a "discerning," but by no means unconditionally "understanding," attitude is irrefutably demonstrated by the sort of behaviour that is described as being "in conformity with the will of God," in connection with which it would be absurd to speak of rational understanding proceeding by way of logical deduction. Underlying the attitude we have in mind, at the very kernel of the person's being, there is an affirmation of something that one not only does not understand, but does not seek to understand. It is natural for the normal child unthinkingly to accept demands arising out of his parental and communal relationships, without seeking—apart from a few questions, which are usually satisfied with casual and inconclusive answers—for rational justification.

The conscious analysis of the demands coming from the world of the non-ego begins only with pubescence ; these exogenous demands are clearly experienced as demands, and meet with a kind of instinctive resistance. Therefore the years of adolescence are characterized, on the one hand, by doubt magnified to the point of extreme scepticism, and on the other by a marked need for support, by a lively desire for clearness, and by a struggle to get a hold of reality, which is felt to be unavoidable and at the same time incomprehensible.

7. SEXUALITY

There is no need to discuss in greater detail the matters dealt with in the previous chapter ; possibly we have said enough to indicate the educational implications. It is our present intention to consider the third group of motives that influence character-formation, and at the same time to discuss the problem of sexuality ; by way of introduction, some brief general remarks on the position held by sex in the total make-up of the person may not seem to be superfluous.

In most of the treatises on sexual psychology, sexual psychopathology and the educational aspects of these branches of study, the subject in my opinion is not seen in quite true perspective, because sexuality is seen " in bits " instead of as a whole—a methodological error. There is a prevalent tendency to regard the sexual element as a relatively independent " part " of man, almost as if the content of sexual experience were not amalgamated with the rest of the person into a whole unity. One has the impression that the sexual factor has established itself as a kind of independent force, foreign to the person, which indeed in a sense dwells within the person, but yet does not wholly belong to him. It is impossible here to investigate the origins of this conception, the factors giving it plausibility or the causes of its wide dissemination. I must content myself by opposing to it a second contention ; here I have had to rely on somewhat dogmatic assertions instead of on con- clusive arguments. I have, however, been able to deal with the matter in greater detail in another place.

My contention is as follows. Despite all the uniqueness of the sexual experience and its inclusion in the organic sphere, the same principles that apply to human conduct in general, and that we have come to recognize as being fundamental, still hold good. For what is of importance in the matter of upbringing is not the facts of sexual experience, but sexual acts and conduct, even though the latter are conditioned by the former. We shall soon see, however, that the converse is equally true ; the experience is largely conditioned, one might sometimes say even evoked, by the action—in the sense, that is, of the latter's purposive direction.

Let us be true to our methodological principles and recall that an action or a behaviour-pattern can be understood only in the light of the actual consequences, and that the mere consideration of a subjective experience is insufficient to provide us with a clear indication of the position of a particular act in the totality of a person's life. Doubtless, when regarded only as a subjective experience, sex appears to be specifically directed to the gratification of the pleasure-principle ; but sexual acts regarded in a more comprehensive connection are seen to contain various other factors. Once we can rid ourselves of that false conception, already considered, which accords sexuality a kind of external autonomy, and come to regard sexual conduct in the same way as conduct in general, from the five aspects discussed in the first chapter of this book—and in so doing focus our attention on the expressional functions of all behaviour— it at once becomes clear that even *sexual behaviour must take its stamp not only from the " sex-impulse," but also and essentially from the person as a whole.* A man's sexuality is, no less than his conduct at any other level, the expression of his person and his character.

This perhaps calls for further explanation. It is evident that sexuality in its individual manifestations, both as a function and as an experience, is partly conditioned by a person's physical nature. This is proved by those cases in which disease or anomalies of development weaken or abolish sexuality ; the cases of increased sexuality following on disease are, however, less convincing. The first-mentioned disturbances are due to a weakening or a destruction of the organs concerned with the phenomena of the sexual life ; it can easily be imagined that hypoplasia of the organs should result in a weakening of the sexual processes. But the converse of the proposition—that such a weakening indicates a functional weakness of the organs concerned—does not follow. Such a possibility must, of course, always be taken into account, but not immediately taken for granted, because other factors may well be responsible. The incursion of these other factors is more easily understood if we conceive of all the organic functions as forming part of a kind of hierarchical scale, so arranged that the most peripheral functions form the foundations of the functional totality, even enjoying a measure of independence, but normally under more central control. The interruption, removal or abolition of this central control by a predominant impulse can give rise to the same set of phenomena as would be caused by a deficiency of the more peripheral function. For the un-deniable fact of the control exerted by " higher " levels demands the transmission of both excitatory and inhibitory impulses to the peripheral or " lower " levels, and therefore that the removal of control should give rise to an increase of function, through the discontinuance of inhibitory impulses. It is true that an increase of function can originate entirely peripherally, depending on local changes ; thus hypertrophic changes in the thyroid gland and the conse-quent absorption into the blood-stream of an excessive or a perverted secretion give rise to the syndrome known as Graves' disease ; this is only one of a large number of similar conditions. An analogous disturbance localized in the genital glands cannot be assumed with any certainty ; there is no proof of a condition of " hypersexualization." Even in the case of those persons who regard themselves as especially highly sexed, or, whose conduct seems to warrant this assumption, we hardly ever find local changes in the sexual organs indicating functional excess ; in the same way, as we have already remarked, those whose sexual impulse is abnormally orientated do not always show physical signs indicating a constitutional or organic basis for their abnormality. It is more expedient to seek for the causes of increased or " perverted " sexuality, not in the actual organs of sex, nor in the rest of the physical organism, but in the man's total disposition. Adler has coined the happy term *Organdialekt*, " organ-language," in describing how abnormal phenomena manifest in the field of, but not generated by, a particular organ, and deriving from more centrally situated and in the last instance more psychical impulses, can naturally be manifest only in the sphere of the organ concerned. To express it more colloquially : it is possible to have palpitation of the heart only in the heart, and stomach-ache only in the stomach ; if for reasons that do not concern us here there are gastric disturbances that are due not to local, but, let us say, to psychical causes, the symptoms are nevertheless located in the stomach. If an abnormal attitude expresses itself in the sexual life, sexual symptoms such as hypersexuality, impotence or perversion will result. The hierarchical arrangement of every function, including the sexual function, in the psycho-physical personal unit, results in the fact that all organic phenomena are the expression of the person's entire make-up. The degree of adaptation to it is various for the different functions ; the more they form part of the content of conscious experience, the more suitably do they express psychical dispositions. Thus the activity of the liver is not subjectively experienced ; that of the heart or the stomach is more so ; and that of the sexual organs is still more so. Other factors rendering functions more suitably expressive of psychical dispositions are their capacity for

being modified by experience, and their normal association
with affective responses—for example, palpitation of the
heart from excitement, vomiting from disgust, and so on.

All these three factors apply to the sexual organs. Changes
occurring in them can be experienced ; they can be
influenced by way of the imagination ; and these changes
not only accompany the affect proper to sexual love, but
can evoke it.

The assertion that a man's sexual behaviour and his
sexual experience, right down to the (apparently organically
conditioned) so-called " strength of impulse," are largely
dependent on his general disposition, is also biologically—
or, if the term is preferred, anthropologically—supported.
If we think of a person's whole disposition and the fundamental principles that direct his life as analogous to a
consciously constructed plan—an over-simplified and somewhat narrow point of view—it can then be said that every
human being possesses a sexuality appropriate to his schema.
This implies that *a person's sexual behaviour is by no means fixed
and unchangeable*, but can be transformed *pari passu* with the
changes in his general disposition ; nor is the " strength of
impulse " an unchanging factor ; it varies according to the
attitude and requirements of the moment. Although this
opinion may seem somewhat unusual, it can bring forward
a large body of practical evidence in its support. If anyone
desires to confirm this, he should not go to work in the
ordinary way, but should carefully, laboriously and patiently
explore a man's whole attitude and dispositions to their very
depths ; and if he has succeeded in revealing and influencing
these, he will at the same time have been able to discover
the transmutability of sexual life and emotion.

It will be seen that we find ourselves in direct opposition
to those authors who regard the constitution of the sexual
impulse as unchangeable, and man's sexual behaviour as an

index of an original predisposition or something of that order. Therefore we are equally opposed to the psycho-analytical school, and to the view that represents sexual conflicts—that is, conflicts between sexuality and morality—as unavoidable trials and sufferings, which have to be endured with resignation. In my own opinion, in educating the child and later the adult, it is possible to keep sexuality itself and both its normal and perverted manifestations within tolerable limits. That result, however, will seldom be attained by simply waging a war against sexual experience ; it is necessary to investigate a person's fundamental dispositions, which express or mirror themselves in his sexual experience, and bring about a modification in them.

The conception of the problem of sexuality formulated above, and its position within the totality of the person, assists us to elucidate the educational side of the sexual question. In so doing, it will be advisable to start with negative and avoidable factors, before proceeding to consider the more positive aspects. Such a method should not be regarded as inadmissible ; although disease by itself does not enable us to understand health, it provides us with problems that suggest methods of approach to health, and the knowledge we have gained from the study of disease in relation to health can be confirmed or corrected. This is very frequently the method of approach in medical research, but in relation to morals the situation is even simpler ; for there is a certain minimum of moral health, which every human being can and must attain. Beyond this minimum point there are many, possibly innumerable, roads—varying according to individual needs—leading in the direction of perfection ; but the minimum is the same for all mankind. In the Catholic system it is called the state of grace, the state of being a child of God, for the maintenance of which there are merely negative requirements, namely the avoidance of mortal sin.

Consequently, in the sphere of morality it follows that by indicating how errors may be avoided, that is, by means of a negative condition, a corresponding positive demand is involved. Thus, for character-training, which is very much the same thing as moral training, the approach by way of the abnormal is less likely to lead us into error than might otherwise be the case. In this context, the word " abnormal " should not be considered as equivalent to " diseased " in the medical sense ; its justification is that so many moral defects have so frequently been described as " diseases," and the person who tries to remedy them as a " physician of the soul."

There is no need here to concern ourselves with the psychology of the sexual life in general or with all the aspects of sexual education. We shall confine our attention to these questions only so far as they affect character-formation ; we must therefore investigate *the phenomena of the sexual life*, on the one hand, in their aspects as *character-forming factors*, and, on the other hand, as *indices of a person's total disposition*.

We will first consider the second point, paying particular attention to the sort of conduct that is experienced as an insoluble problem and an insuperable difficulty both by its perpetrators, whether they be adolescent or adult, and by those concerned with their moral education. It is an un-doubted fact that a man repeatedly commits sexual acts of which he completely disapproves and which awaken remorse and pangs of conscience. Here, if nowhere else, the passage from the *Confessions* of St. Augustine previously quoted is singularly apposite : " Whence and wherefore this inexplicable fact ? " And we are also reminded of the saying of St. Paul : " The good which I will, I do not ; but the evil which I will not, that I do." [1]

We are here clearly dealing only with a special instance of a form of conduct that is repeated in very various forms in

[1] *Rom.* vii. 19.

every conceivable condition of life ; it is a special instance of the " *doing of the forbidden thing,*" for which St. Augustine supplied us with a meaning. In itself it presents no problem ; but a problem does arise because, with certain individuals, acts of this kind provide the only instances of the commission of forbidden acts, and it is somewhat surprising that this so widely spread disloyalty to principle should be met with in this one particular connection.

Before investigating this matter more closely, there is one further observation to be made. Here, as elsewhere, the principle that prevention is better than cure holds good ; but, in this connection, preventative measures can only be of a general kind. It is not expedient to direct expressly to sexual dangers the attention of a young man who is as yet unacquainted with conflicts of this kind, because knowledge without actual experience is calculated to excite curiosity, and lead to the very thing it is desired to avoid. Preventative measures can only consist in preparing the young man for conflicts and difficulties in general, enabling him to overcome them and imbuing him with a proper attitude towards real values and commandments. In this way, much can in fact be prevented, though undesirable events will occur often enough. However, the first outcropping of such occurrences should not be taken too tragically, not because they are unimportant—this we are far from asserting—but because it is highly probable that to begin with they take place with incomplete realization of their import. If, at that time, there is still a persistent confidence between parents and child, then these conflicts will not remain too long repressed, and their resolution should not prove to be an insuperable task. If, however, such conduct persists into adulthood, the chief problem is not how it originally came about, but why it is maintained in the face of condemnation.

We must not be misunderstood in the sense of being

thought to advocate the total exclusion of so-called *sexual enlightenment*; quite the contrary. We hold strongly that a knowledge of the facts of sex is essential, and that this knowledge must be imparted to the child before he acquires it unsuitably from unqualified sources. *This enlightenment is the duty of the parents and not that of the school authorities;* of course, if the parents are incapable of this, or if they do not possess the child's confidence, it devolves upon others. But it must *always be given by way of individual explanation,* never in the form of class-room teaching; the latter can, at most, only prepare the ground by careful instruction in biology. Sexual instruction can and should only take place by stages, the moment for its necessity being shown by relevant questions on the part of the child, always assuming that the requisite confidence is not lacking. Questions of this kind, like all children's questions, must be answered; the remark, "You can't understand that," is more out of place here than anywhere. It would lead us too far astray were we to deal with this matter in detail, but we believe that we have hinted at the main points.

Let us now return to the question why men allow themselves to commit sexual errors in spite of the fact that in other matters they are eager, and endeavour successfully, to do right. If we remember that every error and every sin contains the element of revolt and of making oneself superior to the Lawgiver, the question takes the following form : Why is this overweening pride, which we have seen to be the direct outcome of the corruption of human nature by original sin, manifested particularly in the sphere of sex, and most especially in sins against the sixth [1] Commandment?

If solitary sexual offences are regarded from the standpoint of rebellion against a commandment, it will be found that, apart from the sixth, there is no single commandment

---

[1] According to the Catholic enumeration.

so easy for man to revolt against, for it is almost the only one whose transgression does not necessarily involve external consequences. The sixth Commandment is, as it were, the Tom Tiddler's ground in which the coward can revolt. In addition to this, there is the fact that it is unnecessary in such acts to emerge from the sphere of one's own person ; there is no need to take a single step into the world of the non-ego—an action that fills a person with a sense of discouragement and a secret dread, since every such step involves a certain " conquest " of the world. Now the contention that such sexual offences are, when deeply examined, expressions of revolt or rebellion, and that sex is, so to speak, only an accidental medium in which this attitude manifests itself, is, as I am well aware, somewhat startling. However, this is confirmed by psychotherapeutic experience, in which much light is thrown on the bizarre fantasies accompanying actions of this kind, fantasies in which the self-assertive tendencies are paramount, and in which the will to power and rebellion are often blatantly displayed or easily recognized in symbolic guise.

With the secret and deep-seated disinclination to cross the boundaries of self into the world of realities there is connected a second motive behind the behaviour under consideration, which can be formulated somewhat as follows. Even when nature and impulse seem to direct me expressly beyond myself and towards the rest of mankind, I disregard the summons, and, master of myself, curled up in my own shell, I am self-sufficient. This is the most extreme denial of community, although in a sphere in which communal obligations in the form of actions are not unconditional, and in many cases not yet imposed. If a man cannot bring himself to deny his communal obligations in social and professional life, he is still able to express his negative attitude in his erotic life. It has constantly been observed that persons who are addicted to such sexual offences show defects of conduct in other respects. This frequently applies, but by no means always. The imputation of unsociability, reserve, pessimism, reduced efficiency and the like to sexual mal-practices, together with various and special kinds of injury to health and morals, *is unquestionably mistaken.* The above-mentioned consequences are in no way attributable to sexual malpractice, as such. They are either the result of the conflict in which the addict involves himself, with its coin-cident self-reproach and self-condemnation, or more fre-quently they are not, strictly speaking, consequences, but incidental indices of a special fundamental disposition of the person as a whole. Because the person's disposition is of such-and-such a kind—this means, of a kind that we shall later learn to recognize as " neurotic "—he develops anomalies which find expression in the sphere of social life just as much as in that of sexuality.

It therefore follows almost invariably that *an isolated campaign against sexual offences is both inexpedient and unsuccessful.* To lead a man to fight against something he feels to be too strong for him is to expose him to certain defeat and dis-courage him still further ; he comes to imagine that he is permanently addicted to his practices, and that his addiction results from lack of will power, degeneracy, temperamental predisposition, congenital taint and so on. As elsewhere, education and re-education should not be peripherally but centrally directed ; the object must be to bring about an internal change of attitude and above all to bring about a new self-confidence and a quickened sense of personal value.

Anyone who has investigated youthful or adult addicts to such practices is aware that they are not depressed and discouraged on account of their sexual habits, but that they are enslaved by these habits on account of their discourage-ment. There is here yet another example of the vicious circle—from discouragement to defeat and from defeat to discouragement.

Consequently, all attempts to meet the situation by the use of threats and prophecies of disaster are wholly undesirable ; they can only do harm and sometimes inflict injury of the most serious kind. To assure a man that any particular sexual habit will ruin his health only serves to add yet another conflict to the moral conflicts which are already proving too much for him ; his discouragement is increased, and new fuel is added to the secret fires which consume him and which he imagines he is fighting. Apart from this, it has long been known that the assertion that health suffers from such practices *is quite false.* It is a survival from an antiquated period of medical knowledge and arose from inadequate or insufficiently understood observations and various prejudices which cannot stand examination. *The time has come to remove such false teaching from educational literature, and to stamp out the various " popular " writings on this subject.* Such threats are occasionally justified on the grounds of their alleged " deterrent effect " ; this is not only psychologically unsound, but morally objectionable, because the use of falsehood as a means to an end is inadmissible, and can never be of real use in the long run. Here also the principle holds good that it is more important and more effective to stress the positive than throw emphasis on the negative.

Actions of which the perpetrator disapproves and which he nevertheless constantly repeats have a third kind of importance, if they are considered not in themselves, but in their relation to the person's life as a whole, with special reference to future conduct. In considering undesirable actions of every kind, one should always ask oneself what the situation would be upon their cessation. In numerous instances it will be noticed that such actions represent a peculiar kind of defence-mechanism for the person concerned.

This does not apply only to sexual offences ; theft can, for example, play the same part. The situation can be formulated as follows. " So long as I remain constantly addicted to such practices, I cannot expect myself, and it cannot be expected of me, to make moral progress in any direction." It is evident that in this way the offences can exercise a protective function, if the person disbelieves in his ability to make any moral progress whatever, or if, obsessed by a somewhat exaggerated ambition in regard to the extent and rapidity of such progress, he does not believe that he can make sufficient progress to bolster up his self-esteem. Many people say straight out : " I must break myself of these habits, and then I shall be able to work for my complete moral development, think about becoming worthy of my fellow-men, making good at my job and so on." Metaphorically speaking, *sotto voce*, he will add : " But I cannot break myself, and so I need not bother about all the rest ; if I were only free, you would soon see how nearly perfect I should become." But there is no guarantee for anyone to attain to perfection.

In conversing with a girl of about eighteen, who had sought advice on account of recurrent sexual offences, I chanced to mention St. Theresa. The girl admitted that one could be saintly even in these days, but, for her, being saintly meant being a great saint. To my question, " And if you could break yourself of your sexual habits, would you be a great saint to-morrow ? " she blushingly answered " Yes."

In this connection, it should be pointed out that actions of a sexual kind—and of other kinds—of which the person who commits them disapproves, constantly remind him of his " weakness of will." Thereby the man convinces himself and sometimes others—possibly his confessor—that he is quite incapable of " getting the upper hand over his passions."

This is especially impressive when the person agrees that the temptation in itself is not remarkably strong ; for it is plausible to argue that, whereas a considerable effort of will is required to resist really great temptation, violent excitement and so on, the capitulation to small temptations must surely indicate " weakness of the will," moral degeneracy and the like. In innumerable cases, to talk about a permanent weakness of the will is only to use a phrase covering the following meaning : " I should be capable of all things if I only had the will ; how can anyone expect me to get the better of the difficulties of life, when I am always defeated in my own private struggle." In such behaviour, however, neither the " strength " of the impulse nor the " weakness " of the will are truly primary ; the primary factor is the apprehension of testing oneself in the sphere of reality, and the deficient sense of one's own value generating this apprehension.

In addition, let it be remembered that despair, remorse, and the everlasting struggle against temptation of every kind waste a vast amount of time, thought and attention, which could be more profitably spent in tackling other problems ; further, under the cloak of a moral conflict and a struggle against sin, such a man may be exclusively concerned with himself.

It frequently happens in the case of adults, but less frequently with children and adolescents, that they indulge themselves sexually from a subjective motive ; they imagine that life does not offer them any pleasure, and that sexual gratification is indispensable to them as a compensation for everything else. It is very interesting to note that for a large number of such people the gratification is experienced as slight. On closer investigation, we frequently discover that the chief thing is not the sexual pleasure as such, not even the relief of sexual tension, but the content of the fantasies accompanying or even generating the sexual act. These fantasies are, of course, mostly, although not invariably, of a sexual nature, but they are the expression " in the language of sex " of the man's inmost motives, of the goals for which he strives and which seem to him to be unattainable.

The psychoanalysts regard the non-sexual fantasies accompanying sexual acts as symbols covering sexual dispositions. I myself am much more inclined to regard such fantasies primarily as symbols of other tendencies ; and it has often been my experience that on the interpretation of these symbols and on the reorientation of the tendencies they represented, the apparently insuperable sexual conflicts can be resolved.

I am therefore not of the opinion that some sort of a " sexual constitution," however one may picture it, is an essential determining feature of character. What matters is not the nature of a man's sexuality as such, but how he experiences it, his attitude towards it and the position he is prepared to accord it in his general system of life and in relation to ultimate values. *Therefore, the problem of sexual education is summed up in an inculcation of a proper appreciation of values.* A moral sexual life is possible only for the man who has succeeded in attaining the right attitude to commandments in general and to super-individual and communal obligations. For this a man must be free from any over-valuation of his own person, so far as the weaknesses of human nature permit. If one regards auto-erotic actions as the expression of a sort of being-in-love-with-oneself, one is certainly right ; one is wrong if one imagines this " love " to be primarily erotic. It is first and foremost *an expression of the supremacy of one's own person*, an attitude that is forced to adopt every kind of disguise on account of its inherent impossibility. We mentioned above that people who are constantly preoccupied with this kind of conflict and problem

THE PSYCHOLOGY OF CHARACTER

almost exclusively focus all their thought and attention on themselves. This side of their fundamental disposition also expresses itself in their sexual conduct. When analysed psychologically, it comes almost to the same thing whether a man makes himself the sole content of his experience because he admires himself or because he hates himself, or because he hypochondriacally fusses and worries about himself incessantly. In discussing certain phenomena, such as scrupulosity, we shall later have occasion to return to this point.

Amongst the young people whose sexual behaviour is a cause of great anxiety to themselves or to those responsible for their upbringing, I have learnt to distinguish two main groups, those who have been too strictly brought up, the joyless, and those who have been spoilt, the inordinately exigent. Both are at bottom thoroughly discouraged ; both can be helped by encouragement.

Encouragement can, however, exist only in an atmosphere in which man's isolation is abolished, *i.e.*, the community. The discouraged are, as we have perhaps too persistently repeated, incapable of community. The parent, teacher, physician or priest must first break through this circle. This can only be done through confidence and by a loving desire to sympathize and understand. Such difficulties cannot be resolved by restricting one's efforts to fighting them, suppressing them, or even discussing them. We are never dealing with an isolated phenomenon, however much appearances may suggest it ; it is always a matter of disturbances, disharmonies and false dispositions affecting the whole *psyche*. Very illuminating in this connection are the numerous cases, in my own experience, in which sexual anomalies, with or without corresponding actions, have disappeared in the course of therapeutic conversations, although they were hardly mentioned, if mentioned at all. They were only one form of expression of false dispositions affecting the whole person.

I shall have occasion in the next chapter to make some additions to what I have said here. I wish to point out that it was impossible for me to present a comprehensive psychology of adolescence and all the problems connected with it ; that would have demanded a whole monograph. I merely desired to indicate some of the factors that seem to me to be essential, together with their practical application in education.

CHAPTER VII

ABNORMAL AND NEUROTIC CHARACTERS

I. THE COMMON BASIS

IN the previous chapters we have frequently made reference to unusual characterological dispositions which demanded our attention either because they resulted from errors in upbringing, or because they threw light on certain normal characteristics, of which they were caricatures or distortions. These considerations and their practical significance for education warrant an exposition of the developmental processes encountered in the backward, the "nervous," the perverted, the anti-social, the criminal and so on. At first sight it may seem strange that behaviour-patterns so diverse as those indicated by the above list should be grouped together under one heading, and still more strange that we should be able to assert that they possess more in common than the factor of undesirability, so much so, that they in fact form an essentially coherent group. In support of this simplification we may first of all adduce the fact that not only may these various forms of abnormality be encountered together in many diverse kinds of combination, but different abnormal states may manifest themselves in one and the same individual during the course of his life. A thorough investigation of a person's disposition reveals more frequently than one imagines a change or succession of behaviour-patterns, which at first sight show abnormalities of vastly different kinds. In such cases, one can generally convince oneself that the transition from one form of behaviour to another was determined by the situation of the moment, and was an intelligible reaction to temporary conditions, obligations, or experiences.

In our first chapter we expressly opposed the conception of an " inborn character," in the sense that a man is as it were inevitably compelled by fate to take a certain course from the outset, even though it may lead him astray. All our previous remarks demonstrate clearly that reactive factors play too important a part in character-formation to allow of a characterological theory entirely dependent on the conception of congenital diathesis. We prefer to regard congenital differences of make-up in terms of greater or smaller resistance to certain influences, which implies that in every man there are the possibilities of abnormal development and behaviour. It clearly depends largely on the intensity of the strain to which the individual is exposed, especially in those critical periods of life in which conduct is still relatively fluid. We started by supporting the thesis that character is essentially changeable. When we apply this principle to the problems of characterological abnormality, it is clear that apparent " normality " cannot exclude the possible appearance of abnormal phenomena, and that abnormalities of the moment do not preclude later development in a normal direction. Many great men who stand out on account of their intellectual or artistic achievements or holiness of life have exhibited phases of more or less gross abnormality. Above all, in the lives of many saints we find such phases, the significance of which we shall come to understand more clearly.

Nervous symptoms and neurotic episodes imply nothing against the " normality " of the person concerned, since it is possible for anyone to react neurotically to circumstances, and in any event an isolated symptom proves nothing. Clinical psychiatry has taught emphatically for a long time that life has psychological significance only when regarded as a connected and synthetic whole. It cannot be too strongly stressed that terms like " neurotic," " nervous " and " hysterical " are not judgments of value. The person may conceal higher value-potentialities—which are by no means affected by the neurosis of the moment—than the ignoramus who misjudges him can possibly imagine. Attempts to interpret artistic or spiritual distinction in terms of " neurosis " are therefore futile and ridiculous. One point, however, I do concede ; namely, that neurosis and true saintliness are incompatible. I shall have more to say on this later.

A study of educational characterology cannot afford to neglect the question of abnormalities, since these respond very successfully to educational or re-educational methods.

A careful investigation of the past history of a man exhibiting abnormal conduct (except those cases whose abnormalities are definitely organically determined), shows that his condition originated in childhood, and usually in very early childhood. It is a mistake to conclude from this that such disturbances are congenitally determined ; as we have repeatedly demonstrated, such an assumption would be permissible only after excluding the likelihood or the possibility of their being reactively generated. Those who deduce the existence of a " morbid diathesis " from the abnormalities of childhood have not usually taken the trouble to search for possible reactive factors, because they are fascinated or obsessed by the dogma of the constitutional (physical) determination of character and the omnipotence of heredity. It is one of the greatest services rendered by the Freudian school of psychoanalysis that it established the importance of the experiences of childhood for the later development of character. For this achievement no one, not even the opponents of psychoanalysis, can withhold credit from Freud's researches, although there can be many different theoretical interpretations of the observed nexus. It is true that the psychoanalysts were not the first to detect the connection between character and destiny, but they were the first to establish it on a basis of comprehensive individual investigation, and to record their observations in a way which will always redound to their glory. It must be admitted that the influence exerted by character on a person's fate remains extremely obscure, if an explanation of the problem is attempted in accordance with psycho-analytical theories. Even individual-psychology, which has a somewhat wider outlook on this matter, cannot draw any wholly satisfactory conclusions. A naturalistic, or even a simply non-metaphysical, conception of the problem can only lead to the most elementary and superficial conclusions ; for only a metaphysic of the person can prepare the ground for a solution of this difficult problem, and help us to consider it in its final implications. Psychoanalysis taught us that the foundations of normal and abnormal character are laid in the years of childhood, and we have learnt from individual-psychology that there is no essential difference between the abnormal behaviour-patterns of the adult and those of the child, whether these abnormalities are termed "neurosis," " perversion," " criminality " or anything else, and that the larval forms of such characters are already met with in those children who, for reasons of convenience, are grouped together as " difficult to bring up." Of course, apart from characterological abnormalities, organic illness can also be responsible for difficulties in upbringing. We have already pointed out that purely physical factors can lead to *secondary* characterological anomalies, as is best exemplified in endocrine disturbances, which may lead to various forms of mental deficiency and stunting. Psychotherapy in cases of this kind is out of the question ; any sort of treatment undertaken must be physical. Mental defectives whose lack of development is due to pathological cerebral changes do not respond to ordinary educational methods, but require a special kind of pedagogic technique which cannot be dealt with here. Since, however, as we have said, secondary characterological anomalies can arise from organic causes, it is essential that *every child and young person who is " difficult to bring up " should be examined by a competent physician*. This applies to all cases, for even when cerebral or glandular disturbances and mental defect are not in question, some possibly unexpected organic factor can be responsible for the characterological symptoms, by generally lowering the vitality, decreasing the sense of " vital " security, and leading to discouragement. Thus, defective vision, adenoids, slight vertigo secondary to middle-ear trouble, and many conditions of this kind, which can exercise the most unfavourable influence on the psyche of the developing child, may pass unnoticed by even the most intelligent lay observers. The education of so-called " psychopathic " children should therefore never be undertaken without the close co-operation of an expert physician. It is a grave mistake to consult unqualified " experts," however well-intentioned and well-read in psychology such people may be, in the case of backward and difficult children ; the results may be as dangerous as those associated with the most unscrupulous forms of quackery.[1]

2. " DIFFICULT " CHILDREN

We are here applying the word " difficult " only to those children or young people who show undesirable characterological anomalies of a kind that renders them unresponsive to ordinary educational methods, and for which no organic

[1] Obviously a great deal more could be said against " lay analysis " or " lay psychotherapy," advocated by many members of both the psycho-analytical and individual-psychology schools.

basis can be detected. This definition involves and depends
on a judgment of value, which cannot be uncritically
accepted ; for unamiable characteristics or difficulties in
upbringing are not objectively measurable phenomena, but
are asserted as a judgment of value by the upbringer, the
nature of whose demands colours the whole situation. There
are parents who describe a child as difficult if he only shows
a little liveliness, quite within normal limits, and some whose
sergeant-major-like ideas on discipline require a kind of
obedience and regulated behaviour of which only an
essentially timid child is capable, and a healthy child never.
One is accustomed to discount as obvious exaggerations the
eulogistic descriptions of their children given by doting
parents ; but it is even more important to accept the
opposite kind of account with considerable reserve. Frequently children are represented to us by parents as being
" totally ungifted," whereas anyone with only a modicum
of experience could have " spotted " the child's intelligence
and receptivity ; and we have often been asked, without
the slightest grounds for the assumption, whether a child
were not weak-minded or insane. Moreover, remarks of this
kind are generally made in the presence of the children
themselves ! " Difficulty " can be established only if the
demands of the upbringer are within reasonable limits ;
but it is impossible to lay down these limits precisely.
Consequently, one is thrown back on a merely approximate
judgment, an estimate of the existing difficulties and the
educational situation in each individual case, without being
able to formulate general rules. Obviously, there is a
sufficiency of cases in which the behaviour immediately
warrants the description, being so unsocial that there can
be no doubt of their deviation from the norm, even though
it is never possible to define the norm precisely.

In attempting to describe the factors common to all cases

showing difficulty in upbringing, we must refer to an observation we have previously had occasion to make, namely, that *fear, visible or concealed, is present in all such children.* Even in those cases in which the description given by the parents or teachers does not at first sight suggest the element of timidity, the child's conduct being characterized rather by recklessness, foolhardiness, rudeness, defiance or dull indifference, it is not difficult to unearth the factor of fear, if one goes beyond the range of parental observation and description and inquires into certain idiosyncrasies of conduct. For example, a small boy may be mischievous, addicted to silly pranks, a daring pilferer, able to balance on the window-ledge of the top storey, to run across the road in front of fast motor-cars, to stay away from home for hours at a time, and to roam the streets—and this enterprising boy, admired by his playfellows as a hero, is perhaps afraid of the dark or of certain animals, or shows himself strangely backward in learning to swim. The last-mentioned disability often reveals the inner uncertainty of the child ; in this case, where it is a matter of an entirely new and unfamiliar situation, the child is frequently unable to call up the energy deriving from compensation, which in more familiar situations helps to conceal from himself and others his deficient sense of security behind an exaggerated display of courage.

We have already seen that fear and the will to power, self-assertiveness, overweening ambition, or whatever else one may call the hypertrophy of this tendency, are closely related. Only the man who feels it absolutely necessary to conquer, and at the same time sees the probability of defeat, will experience fear ; renunciation of victory or exclusion of the possibility of defeat are both incompatible with fear. And, *vice versa*, in the presence of fear a man shows the disposition to fight against life or reality, and to assert himself as an individual. Anxiety about one's own " standing " and value cannot be experienced as such, for such a stark experience would involve the admission of a doubt of one's own value, and therewith its denial ; the anxiety is therefore disguised or is transferred to other matters whose rôles as substitutes are more or less determined by individual experiences and diverse influences. Thus if, for instance, we come across a " difficult " child who has a terrible dread of dogs because he was once chased by a big butcher's dog, or of fire because he once saw a house on fire, or of burglars since he heard about a burglary next door, and so on, it is to be assumed that these experiences are only the occasion for displays of anxiety which have their sources in the person at a far deeper level. It is therefore foolish as a rule to try to " harden " the child against the cause of his fear, for that does not remove its actual roots, quite apart from the fact that it hardly ever succeeds unless it is associated with some other kind of encouragement. In the event of success, it is likely that some other circumstance has led to an increase of the child's courage, self-esteem and self-confidence, so that fear, which to a certain extent was merely a habit, has lost its significance and function in his scheme of life, and can readily be abandoned.

This ambivalent situation, self-assertion on the one hand, and the desire for security and protection on the other, throws much light on much of the behaviour associated with difficulty in upbringing. The close connection between this difficulty and an exaggerated sense of insecurity in the child is supported by the fact that many and possibly all anomalies of behaviour exhibited by difficult children reveal themselves as exaggerations of traits encountered in " normal " children who present no difficulties in up-bringing.

We are not called upon here to give, as it were, a clinical

description and symptomatology of " difficult " childhood. Only by reference to certain typical forms is it possible to indicate the general nature of this defective development, and to hint at the general lines that should be followed in bringing up such children.

The most frequent complaints made by teachers and parents against difficult children—lying, disobedience, laziness, defiance, sulkiness, vulgar talk and behaviour, an inclination for madly reckless pranks, and pilfering—all these are typical of the definitely unmoral and antisocial behaviour encountered in these cases. Typical " nervous " symptoms are absentmindedness, inattention, lack of concentration, lack of natural talents, apprehension, shyness, unsociability, unadaptability, night-terrors, bed-wetting, fearfulness, touchiness, gloominess, secretiveness. Close observation reveals the fact that anti-social traits are always combined with some of the nervous symptoms mentioned above. Sometimes apparently incompatible traits are associated in one and the same child, in which case it is necessary to search for a formula common to both factors. This will always be successful if one does not view the various forms of conduct as isolated, disconnected phenomena, but attempts to interpret their possible functions in the child's total scheme of life ; it is therefore necessary to determine the kind of situation in which the one trait predominates, and the kind that is governed by the other.

I was once called in consultation in the case of a boy five years old. This boy had a younger brother of two and a half who was developing great independence, and had already begun to dress himself alone. The elder one showed himself remarkably clumsy ; he was unable, as a rule, to put on his clothes or shoes properly, although sometimes, quite unexpectedly, he performed these tasks quite well. He had to be washed and dressed by his mother, he was defiant, aggressive to smaller children, disobedient, timid, and hopelessly afraid of the dark. In striking contrast to his timidity and dependence, he had once or twice run away from home and wandered about alone for hours at a stretch, and he had been turned out of a kindergarten because it was alleged that he had led the other children into mischief ; also in certain matters he showed unusual sharpness, enterprise and courage. What he most craved was to obtain as much sugar and milk as possible, though the latter was specially reserved for the younger child. The family—the father was a metal-turner—occupied a small, primitive house, which contained no larder, so the mother used to place the milk on the top of a high cupboard to protect it from the greedy elder boy ; but the boy piled stools upon the table and mounted this tottering structure to obtain the milk. This feat certainly called for more courage than was attributed to him in view of his fearfulness in other circumstances. At first he had shown himself to be a very cheerful child, easy to deal with ; and it was only towards the end of his third year that he began to be difficult. This time witnessed far-reaching changes in his life, associated with the birth of his little brother and a change of house. The parents had moved from a large suburban house belonging to the grandmother, where they had lived together with her and her unmarried daughter. In contrast with their present small house, there had been evidently all sorts of things to see and do ; and the grandmother had taken the first-born straight to her heart, as is the way with grandmothers, and even the little brother had not been able to supplant him in his privileged place. It must have appeared to the scarcely three-year-old boy that the advent of his small rival had made him take a secondary place in his mother's eyes, since he was bound to notice how the maternal care was diverted to the baby, the more so because in the first months the latter was very delicate. Then came the removal, away from the grandmother and the aunt, away from the big house where he was already known and liked, into a loneliness where he had no longer a retreat provided by the love of the two women, all alone except for his little brother, who had usurped his mother's favour and care. His conduct was now governed by ideas connected with the punishment of his rival ; he was determined to make him feel that he, the elder, was still there and had his rights, to compel the attention of his mother—scenes when dressing !—to claim for himself anything especially reserved for the little one, even when this involved some risk and danger. Further, he attempted to play the rôle of leader in all those situations in which the small brother was not by the mother's favour already paramount ; and occasionally he sought to impress her with his own importance and make himself conspicuous by running away and causing her trouble and anxiety, and by being generally naughty to attract her attention even at the cost of punishment. Is not this from the point of view of the " dethroned " elder child a quite intelligible and logical line of conduct, which in design and execution closely resembles an intelligently conceived plan, carefully adapted to the purpose in hand ? This was so evident that there was no need for further investigation, especially as the mother, as soon as she guessed the trend of our inquiries, voluntarily supplied a mass of relevant additional details.

What was to be done ? Obviously it was impossible to recreate for the child the desired position of favour ; but one could try to help him to understand that this position was neither the most desirable nor the only one capable of satisfying his natural need of appreciation and recognition. At the same time, one could try to find some way of gratifying not only the child's subjective, but also his objective demands by procuring him satisfaction through achievement. I advised the mother first of all not to hold up the younger child as an example, as she had frequently done in the past—" See what baby can do already, and you, the elder, are so clumsy ! "—and secondly, to develop the child's self-esteem by giving him tasks to carry out, and praising him for them. Thus instead of putting the milk up on the cupboard out of his reach, she was to make him the guardian of the milk so that the dog should not get it. This advice and more tending in the same direction—the strengthening of the child's positive self-feeling by achievement and its recognition—was so successful that, according to the mother when she came back some weeks later to make a report, he had become " quite a different boy." It is true that I was dealing with an exceptionally intelligent woman who was inclined from the first to listen to what I had to say, and was animated by a true and quite unselfish love of her child.

That case is very simple and very clear ; but perhaps it will be admitted that not everyone who might have had to deal with it would have diagnosed and treated it in the same way. This new method of approach, which we owe largely to individual-psychology, has taught us to view things differently, to pay attention to details that would previously have been regarded as unworthy of notice, and to draw from them conclusions whose importance is demonstrated by the test of practical success. This method of approach and procedure explains many somewhat obscure and prognostically gloomy cases surprisingly quickly ; but often, admittedly, only a laborious change of educational method can divert the child's development into normal channels, after the ground has been prepared for the development of an anti-social disposition. For a case to be successful it is essential for the upbringer and the consultant to be in complete agreement ; for in the face of the former's opposition, it is impossible for the latter to achieve anything. It is sometimes possible for older children to fight their own way through to a relative independence, but younger children apparently find this impossible. However, such a result, achieved apart from the co-operation of the parents, is not entirely satisfactory ; it is scarcely possible to guard such a young person from misanthropy and neurosis without coincidently " turning him against " his parents, even though the external forms of cordiality may be retained. If parents and teachers obstinately maintain their own standpoint and close their minds to that of the child, we maintain that ignorance, even when innocent, must be made to pay the penalty of its mistakes. It is more important to make a young person immune against possibly lifelong trouble, permanent inadequacy and the incapacity to hold a living, personal, religious faith—the last-mentioned is often an associated disability—than to be squeamish in the matter of offending the susceptibilities of the adults.

Our large experience in cases of children guilty of repeated pilfering throws light on the causes, not only of juvenile cleptomania, but on those of other childish aberrations. For pilfering in children we have been able to determine the following motives.

One is the need to " play a part," combined with the deep-rooted disbelief in the possibility of being able to do this by means of positive achievement. The desire is satisfied sometimes by " heroism "—theft, for instance, in the presence of playfellows, or theft of which he can afterwards boast, so as to arouse their admiration. Sometimes the theft is committed not for the sake of the stolen article itself, but in order to obtain money or other articles to give away and thus purchase a band of supporters. If, for instance, a boy cannot establish his position by excelling in work or games, or as a natural leader in enterprises requiring cunning, he will, assuming he is greatly discouraged, light upon the idea of purchasing his position. If he can do this lawfully, by giving away his own property—his lunch, postage-stamps, and so on—he will do so ; otherwise—if, for example, he is poor or under strict parental control—he will take to evil ways.

A second motive, which is rather more out of the ordinary, is pleasure in one's own wickedness. We have already encountered this trait in our discussion of sexual offences, and shall come across it again when we come to consider neurotic characters. This motive presents itself in various forms. Firstly, the child who is repeatedly pilfering convinces himself and others that he is incapable of moral progress and that there is nothing to be done for him—a remark which is often repeated in his hearing. In such cases the disposition often approximates to that met with in compulsion-neurosis ; for the child often experiences a more or less irresistible impulse to acquire articles or money, even when he has no immediate use for them. Secondly, the theft or the possession of the stolen article serves to provide a momentary gratification when the child despairs of sharing in other pleasures ; and he wishes to assure himself of at least a transient pleasure, even if he expects to be found out and punished. This is a frequent occurrence when the child has been brought up excessively strictly, and trivial faults and acts of disobedience have met with severe punishment ; in such circumstances it is a matter of indifference to the child whether he commits a small or large offence, seeing that in any case he will incur severe punishment. Further, the last two motives mentioned may be combined so that the conduct is calculated to demonstrate the " greatness " of one's own wickedness. Thus a girl once told me that she intended " either to be an angel or a devil," meaning that if she could not possibly obtain a leading place by being good, she would do so by being as bad as she could. Clearly, lack of recognition and praise, as well as favouritism shown to brothers and sisters, can occasion this sort of conduct.

A third group of motives may be closely associated with the group we have just considered ; this group covers what may be called " acts of revenge." The following story may serve as an example. A boy was playing with bare hands in a heap of snow. A horrified passer-by said, " Your hands will be frozen " ; to which the boy replied, " It will serve my father right if my hands are frozen. Why doesn't he buy me some warm gloves ? " This is a splendid illustration of the motives behind the conduct of many children, and even adults. Many a child who steals believes that by his action he will be revenged on his parents ; for not infrequently theft is the offence that is most abhorrent to the parent, the thing that touches his most sensitive spot. The child seems to know that his actions will bring disgrace upon his parents and upon the whole family. Occasionally the motive of revenge immediately reveals itself, as for instance, when a child removes things from the house that he cannot possibly want, and hides them somewhere, simply because he knows that they are treasured by his parents. Theft, then, can simply be a means of causing distress to the parents, as well as the expression of an unconscious attitude of revolt ; this applies, of course, like all the foregoing, to other sorts of misdeeds. In these cases, the differential diagnosis from compulsion-neurosis is often a difficult matter.

We have already drawn attention to the association between theft and sexual aberrations, an association that has long been known. Either the two abnormal forms of conduct exist in one and the same person, or sexual excitement acts as a stimulus to theft or *vice versa*, or an act of theft is followed by sexual relief. It is therefore often asserted that compulsive theft (cleptomania) represents a disturbance of the sexual impulse, and is in itself at bottom a specifically " sexual " equivalent. This opinion is maintained in particular by the psychoanalytical school. Although the facts themselves are not in dispute, being fully borne out by my own experience, I am not myself convinced of the inevitability of the above conclusion. The far-reaching analogy between theft and sexual acts and between the motives actuating both gives plausibility to the assumption that both forms of conduct, separately or in combination, may be the expression of the same basic disposition of the person concerned. However, even the observation that in many cases masturbation may be substituted for theft, if measures have been undertaken to overcome the latter habit, does not necessarily, in my opinion, support the sexual theory of theft. The associated forms of conduct resemble in every respect a type of behaviour not uncommonly encountered in neurosis, namely, the abandonment of one symptom which threatens to involve the patient in undue difficulties, and its replacement by another. I cannot interpret this, as do the psychoanalysts, as the " conversion " of one occurrence into another, or as the transference of a special kind of " impulse-energy," the *libido*, from one aim to another ; I regard it only as a change of method or means, the same end being retained.

The motive of revenge also plays a great part in the *suicide of children and young people*. Such tragic occurrences naturally attract much public attention, for they cause everyone to ask himself what circumstances could possibly have driven a young person to take his life. Usually, a superficial survey of the facts does not make it possible to determine the precise motives of the act. In some cases, the whole setting of the scene lets us see that the intention was to frighten and impress the school-teachers ; indeed, sometimes the latter receive a direct warning. The teacher or parent

who, from the point of view of the young person, is over-strict
or unjust, is to have the terrible results of his conduct
brought home to him. The same motive lies behind a large
number of cases of suicide or attempted suicide in adults.
Many such attempts are consciously actuated by the desire
for revenge, in which case the act is intended merely as a
highly impressive piece of play-acting without a tragic
culmination ; in other cases, the motive is entirely unconscious, and the " demonstration " is more likely to end in
disaster. It perhaps sounds frivolous to apply the anecdote
of the boy and the warm gloves to such tragic events, but it
does go to the root of the matter. If one has won the
confidence of any depressive children who are lacking in the
normal childish zest for life, one is sometimes treated to the
most amazing fantasies and day-dreams. Such a child often
pictures to himself how the parents will stand in tears at his
coffin, what an impression the funeral procession will make,
how the teacher who threatened him with a bad report will
despair and reproach himself (" It would serve him right if
I were dead," as an eleven-year-old boy once said to me
about his form-master), how the whole world will lament
him, as sacrificed by his fellow-men, and will condemn their
conduct. Obviously, on the one side we have the idea of
taking the centre of the stage, if only in death, and on the
other the avowed need for revenge.

Thus, up to a point, it is right to lay the blame for such
occurrences at the door of the adults in charge of the
children ; however, it must be added that this blame often
does not carry any responsibility with it, for the adult in
question may have had no conception of the child's difficulties, or understanding of the way in which the child
looked at the world in general. Many of these tragedies
could certainly be avoided if someone were there able to
understand the child and his inmost feelings, and to put

him on the right path ; we are assuming, of course, that it is possible to convince adults, who in the child's cosmogony play the greatest and the most decisive parts, of the necessity of reforming their own attitude.

Let us picture to ourselves for one moment the terrible inward journey a child must have travelled to have been led so far away from the natural, simple joy of life appropriate to his years, and his natural courage and life-hopes, to a condition in which he counts his life as nothing, and casts it away. It can only be the brief years of experience that have warped his attitude ; and his experiences have been largely determined by the adults in his environment. Truly every child suicide or attempted suicide is a terrible indictment of those who should protect the child, guide and direct him, and provide him with a true world-picture.

It would occupy too much space to treat of these matters more fully. We have perhaps indicated clearly enough the main outlines of the problem of " difficulty " in upbringing, and some prophylactic measures. There will be a few additions on this matter in the following section, which deals with the problem of neurosis.

3. NEUROSIS

It is, of course, impossible to give here an elaborate clinical description of the various forms of neurosis, or to deal with the theoretical side of the problem comprehensively. Neither does it come within the scope of this book to give a detailed description of the abnormal phenomena met with in human character. Our principal object is the exposition of a few important fundamental principles for the upbringing of the normal man ; abnormal behaviour should serve to illustrate only the undesirable results of a wrong procedure. Consequently, our remarks on neurotic characterology can only be of a general character, and relate to fundamental principles.

As we do not intend to start a theoretical discussion on the nature and origin of the neuroses, we may also omit a critical exposition of current doctrines. We would only remark briefly that together with the vast majority of modern investigators in this field, we reject any theory that attributes the neuroses to organic changes in the human body. The idea of a " weak nervous system " as the primary cause of neurotic symptoms is entirely fallacious, and arose out of an essentially materialistic conception, which could and would not recognize any disturbances in man's being and conduct other than those conditioned by physical changes. Nowadays this view is held only by those writers who cannot break away from that antiquated method of approach, or have made no attempt to obtain any clear conceptions of causes and origins in this field of psychopathology. Such writers have naturally grossly misunderstood the doctrine of the individual-psychologists in the matter of organ-inferiority in neurosis-formation. Secondly, we are unable to associate ourselves with the psychoanalytical conception, against which we have a series of what seem to us to be weighty objections to raise. With the fullest recognition of the number of valuable discoveries in the realm of fact which we owe to psychoanalytical research—and especially, indeed almost exclusively, to that of Freud, the founder of the school—we are bound to assert that the theory is very defectively constructed ; its faulty logic is such that it cannot stand up to criticism even within its own premises. We must remember that the fundamental hypotheses that form the starting-point of psychoanalysis are unacceptable when regarded from the standpoint of a positive metaphysic and from a Catholic conception of the universe. It seems to me out of the question to seek to reconcile Catholic philosophy, and the fundamental truths it incorporates, with psychoanalytical theories. Anyone who attempts this synthesis must have lost sight either of the axioms upon which the whole psycho-analytical theory is based or of the ultimate meaning of Catholic philosophy. Thirdly, we must point out that, from the standpoint of both theoretical and practical psychology, certain tenets forming integral parts of the psychoanalytical system are open to serious criticism. As I have said, it is not my intention to include here a critical review of psycho-analysis, and I may therefore refer to pronouncements I have made elsewhere.[1] It will suffice, in the following brief statement which emphasizes our own views, to adduce some reasons for our rejection of psychoanalytical theories.

On the other hand, we are equally indisposed to give an uncritical assent to the theories of individual-psychology as set forth today by most of the adherents of this school, although we are of the opinion that it enables us to approach the truth more nearly than psychoanalysis.[2] It must not be

[1] See the article mentioned in note 1 on p. 49. Further : *Über Psychoanalyse* (Berlin, 1920) ; *Psychologie des Geschlechtslebens* (Munich, 1922) ; *Glück und Ende der Psychoanalyse* in the *Schweizer Rundschau*, 1928, Nos. 1 and 2. As the essential hypotheses of psychoanalysis are entirely naturalistic, and their rejection would lead to the collapse of the whole system, any attempt at a compromise between the psychoanalytical approach and Catholic philosophy is mistaken from the outset. The pronounced anti-religious tendencies of most psychoanalysts, not excluding Freud himself, Reik and others, follows logically from its theoretical foundations. This cannot be " got over " by the efforts of Pfister, a Protestant theologian and psychoanalyst (*Hysterie und Religiosität ; Psychoanalyse und Weltanschauung*, both Vienna, 1928). A spiritualistic or even merely a non-materialistic conception destroys the whole theoretical system ; for which reason I cannot concur with the voluminous expositions of R. Liertz (*Die Pyschoneurosen*, Munich, 1928). It is, of course, to be willingly admitted that psychoanalysis has taken the right view of many facts ; but its exponents are in the habit, almost without exception, of assuming the whole theory. It is therefore necessary to detach the body of facts from its theoretical framework, in order to get them in proper perspective. In my opinion, there is an unbridgeable gulf dividing the psychoanalytical and the Catholic theories of human nature.

[2] To believe that individual-psychology is only a variant of psychoanalysis, or that it starts from the same premises, is to take account of only one small part of the body of facts with which the former deals. Such a view can be held only by someone who has understood clearly neither the foundations of the one nor the complete thesis and methodology of the other. The approximate identity of the two schools could be maintained only by those psychoanalysts who accept their own doctrines almost as a matter of faith, as being above

forgotten that the facts, as such, are in many cases identical, and that the differences consist in their theoretical inter-pretation and formulation, and often only in the terminology employed. Psychoanalytical expositions are so formulated that the theories completely colour what should be the plain description of a situation, so that what is offered us as fact and proof of a theory actually already assumes and contains the whole theory. The data offered by individual-psychology are, so to speak, more naive, more human and less overloaded with theoretical and metaphysical assumptions. Naturally, all sorts of philosophical doctrines, not necessarily relevant to or consistent with the facts under consideration, intrude into the writings of certain individual-psychologists ; such views are no more acceptable to us, without critical examination and evaluation, than the others. With this proviso—that we do not without reserve adopt and subscribe to every one of the theses of individual-psychology—the following brief sketch of the nature of neurotic disturbances will, in the main, conform with the ideas of that school.

Before seeking to investigate the nature of neurosis, we must first inquire whether it is proper to use the term " neurosis " as though it were a definite psychopathological entity, for the conditions covered by it are so various that the use of a single clinical conception may give rise to objections. As a matter of fact, purely descriptive accounts of the different varieties—hysteria, phobia, compulsion-neurosis, hypochondria, neurasthenia, stammering, gastric and cardiac neuroses, etc.—give the impression that we are dealing in each case with discrete clinical conditions. However, our experience convinces us that in one and the same individual one form of neurosis can be substituted for

criticism, and who are never able to " get away from " their own standpoint, although they imagine themselves to be exercising an objective judgment. This observation is directed as much against Schultz-Henke (at the Third Psychotherapeutic Congress) as against Liertz and Kunz (see note 1, p. 94).

or alternate with another. This argues against a constitutional diathesis for a specific kind of neurosis, and suggests that the variations in the neurotic syndrome are determined by the patient's experiences, in other words, reactively. It is therefore probable that from the outset the form taken by the illness depends upon environmental factors, and that we are entitled to regard neurosis as a single clinical entity with a symptomatology varying in accordance with purely accidental influences. On analysis, we can detect in all the varieties of neurosis certain features common to all of them ; and these features are essentially the same as those encountered in " difficult " children. We maintained that the behaviour met with in such children represented the reaction to particular experiences of a person with a particular disposition ; in the same way, it is probable that the same is true of neurosis.

If, being unable to give a clinical account of neurosis, we content ourselves here with establishing the essential unity of its various forms, this does not mean that we have closed our eyes to the fact that a whole series of problems are still awaiting solution, and in particular that our knowledge of the factors of experience that determine the symptomatological picture in neurosis must be greatly enlarged. However, we believe that we can judge the connections between individual experience and the form of the neurosis sufficiently well for us to apply our opinions to the subject of character-training. Ætiologically considered, *neurosis is due to the exaggeration of the tension between the will to power and the possibility of power ;* in other words, it is the direct outcome of the purely human situation following the Fall. One can even say that it is the form taken by illness and aberration of *the consequence of the revolt of the creature against his natural mortality and impotence.*

All situations involving a feeling of impotence give rise to fear, and fear lurks in the background of all the experiences of childhood. If the development is unfavourable, the factor of fear becomes more and more significant, as we saw in the case of difficult children. *Fear is a fundamental factor in all forms of neurosis ;* it is the corollary of the struggle against superior power. It can arise only when a person puts up some sort of a fight, and when defeat is regarded as probable ; when victory is despaired of, other states of mind take the place of fear. People led out to execution, says St. Thomas Aquinas, have no fear because they have no hope of escape ; and Spinoza remarks that fear can exist only where hope also exists ; if the latter is lost, it is not fear but despair that results. In hopeless situations a man may show despair and also resignation ; if the factor of acquiescence in his fate is added to the situation, his attitude is modified to one of submission.

Experience amply confirms the fact that fear is an essential element in all forms of neurosis ; there follows the deduction that the neurotic person is incapable of submission to the sovereignty of the non-ego over the will to power of the ego. Accordingly, *rebellion* accompanies fear as a second characteristic of neurosis.

Now, this rebellion is directed against the unchangeable facts of existence and of the rule of law in the universe, against man's inevitable limitations as a creature, against the supremacy of nature and of other fellow-men, against existing law and custom and civilization, and finally against the overshadowing greatness of God, of the " *Deus incompre-hensibilis et absconditus.*" As we have repeatedly demonstrated, all these various realms of being and the laws governing them are interwoven and synthetized in man ; in fact, the complex construction of his being constitutes his uniqueness in the scheme of creation. Therefore, man's rebellion against the non-ego is coincidently rebellion against himself, so far as it is directed against something essentially unchangeable, for example, the inevitability of his human limitations.

If this revolt were experienced in consciousness, it would annihilate a man ; the person puts up a defence against it with every possible weapon. The primary effort, as we have seen, is directed towards the preservation of the sense of personal value, real or pretended, and especially at those times when it is most called in doubt.

4. ARTIFICIALITY AS A CHARACTERISTIC OF NEUROSIS

Since neurotic behaviour conflicts with the laws governing a person's being, a third essential factor of neurosis arises, which we call the characteristic of artificiality.

Artificiality has two, or perhaps three, separate connotations which have not hitherto, as far as I am aware, been sufficiently sharply distinguished. In the first place we have an *artificiality of experience*, or of the individual factors of experience, which is discernible to introspection or to the psychologically trained observer. This sort of artificiality arises when a man finds himself drawn at one and the same moment in two or more different and mutually exclusive directions. It is a pose, but it also comprises every state of not-being wholly and entirely in an experience. We genuinely experience a work of art if we surrender ourselves entirely to it and are permeated by it, so that all other experiences of the moment are entirely obliterated. We act genuinely if we concentrate wholly on the purpose in hand without secondary considerations, such as the impression we are making on others. This form of artificiality might be described as " immanent," because in this kind of experience there is a conflict between two experienced tendencies, which need not always be equally clear, but are potentially so. In the second kind of artificiality, the antinomy is between *the person's being* (or his conception of himself) *and his behaviour.* This does not always mean that the individual entertains too good an opinion of himself, is a *poseur*, or gives himself airs ; not infrequently the reverse is the case, and the outside observer receives the impression that the individual is " really," or has the potentiality of being, bigger, richer, more profound, more alert, more resolute and generally better than his actual behaviour would suggest. Just as we have a quite impalpable, almost unaccountable feeling of malaise, disharmony and falseness when we become aware of the artificiality of " immanent " experience, so we cannot catch hold of the indications that enable us to recognize the second form of artificiality, which, when applied to experience, may be termed " transcendental." Nevertheless, both experiences undoubtedly occur.

There is possibly a third form of artificiality, which is, however, much harder to define. The uniqueness of man, as we have already pointed out, is his ability not only to exist, but to take up an attitude towards his existence—to affirm or deny it. It is clear that neither affirmation nor denial can in any way modify the person's real situation and make-up, which are independent of such subjective attitudes ; but human action and behaviour are not determined solely by the person's being, as such, but also by his attitude towards his existence. When the attitude is negative, the denial is not a revolt against, but an abnegation of, existence, seeing that it cannot lead to any change there. If we could apply psychological phraseology to psychical events occurring at the deepest, most secret levels of a person's being, far below the strata of moral consciousness, it might be said that there is never a real denial but only a " doing as if." Perhaps it would be more proper to say that it is a case not so much of denial as of the refusal of affirmation. This situation gives rise to a further variety of artificiality, which derives from a conflict between the being of the person as he actually is and, as one might almost say, that which is demanded of it. In this sense, therefore, the only genuine man is he who ceaselessly, freely, in the very core of his being, and therefore gladly—all these psychological terms being only analogical descriptions deriving from the person's basal attitude towards his life and experience—has definitely affirmed his general human finiteness and in particular his own shortcomings and impotence.

All these three forms of artificiality—if it is permissible to regard the third as a special variety—are to be found in those people whom we call neurotics. I myself am convinced that artificiality, especially in its second and third forms, is the essential and fundamental characteristic of neurosis, all the other characteristics being secondary and more or less directly derived from it.

Regarded more closely, these two kinds of artificiality are not alien to or a perversion of human nature, but are the direct result of human nature consequent and subsequent to the Fall. In neurosis, therefore, we can perceive an exaggeration and distortion of general characteristics, and can apply the knowledge gained from the study of neurosis —of course making due allowance for the distortion—to educational and re-educational problems. We recognize that between the " normal " and the " neurotic " person no line of demarcation based on principle can be drawn, and that *every man is, in a sense, a potential neurotic.* We repeat again emphatically that " weak nerves " and the like are nothing more than a colloquialism, a feeble relic of antiquated scientific systems ; or if these ideas, in some distorted form, can still be regarded as constituting a nuisance in scientific literature, they arise from complete ignorance of the subject, and inability to reason things out to their final conclusions on the part of their exponents.

Certainly there are " *occasions* " *for neurosis ;* there are all those occasions which we have considered under the head of mistakes and difficulties in upbringing, organic defects, inferior social conditions, and so on ; but it is necessary to repeat that no man is condemned by fate to a life of neurosis without hope of rescue. In principle, the development in the direction of neurosis can be checked in every case, and if it is already established, it can be made to regress. Naturally, intervention in some cases is very much more difficult than in others ; those cases are especially resistant in which various contributory circumstances render the process of re-orientation impracticable or almost impossible. We cannot go into this matter, but we considered it wise to make mention of it, to avoid possible misunderstandings.

From the fact that artificiality is an essential component of neurotic behaviour, it follows that *the only person who can be entirely free from neurosis is the man whose life is spent in genuine devotion to the natural and supernatural obligations of life*, and who has steadfastly accepted and affirmed his position as a creature and his place in the order of creation ; in other words, *beyond the neurotic there stands only the saint*. This enables us more easily to understand the frequent occurrence of neurotic episodes, or of phases bearing an extraordinary resemblance to them, in the lives of so many saints. This should not lead us to the foolish and pseudo-scientific conclusion that saintliness is in itself a true or modified neurotic attitude to life. The neurotic phases are always only episodic, as can be proved from the study of such lives ; they represent periods of transition in which the battle against the " dark despotic self " is fought out to a victory, raising the man to a higher plane of life. The repetition of such episodes is thereby rendered more understandable, for they correspond to the various stages in the man's upward progress and lead to a more and more complete absorbtion into the Godhead. On the other hand, it must not be forgotten that in dealing with the spiritual life, psychology can only proceed very cautiously and tentatively in its attempts to explain things, for there factors and forces are involved that are outside the categories of this science, and even the most delicate psychological analysis and description prove inadequate. It seems, for example, to be altogether mistaken to interpret " the night of the soul " and similar phenomena in terms of neurosis or of purely natural categories.

If we maintain that the ultimate conquest of the artificiality which characterizes and is of the essence of neurosis can be achieved only by saintly living, it follows further that *moral health, in the strict sense, can develop only in the soil of a saintly life*, or at least a life that aims at saintliness.

We arrive at the same conclusion by another method of approach—practical observation. I have never yet come across a case of neurosis which did not eventually reveal as the ultimate conflict and problem an unsolved metaphysical problem—so to designate the problem that deals with man's position in general, no matter whether the person concerned is religious or not religious, a Catholic or a non-Catholic. This possibly accounts for the frequently noticed preoccupation with philosophy of so many neurotics. It is mistaken to regard this " metaphysical " problem as a cover for other problems or as the expression of another impulse, as is so often done. It conceals nothing, neither the will to power nor other impulsive tendencies ; it is in truth the ultimate and most important problem which disquietens those people, and which they do not trust themselves to answer or even to formulate properly. Thus we understand how it is that an intelligent, loving, tolerant, patient, purely religious guidance may in many cases lead not only to a correction of the religious attitude, but also simultaneously to a " cure " of a coincident neurosis, for such an influence actually touches the most central problem of all. Not every neurotic, it is true, is immediately able to recognize the " metaphysical " nature of the problem that is troubling him. Such cases demand a protracted " course " of enlightenment and education in order to bring them to the point where they will be competent to deal with the problem ; in other words, they require systematic psychotherapy.

5. THE EGOCENTRICITY OF NEUROSIS

In his anxious—because it is necessarily hopeless—struggle against the non-ego, in his artificial attitude, which prevents his affirmation of man's place in the scheme of the universe, the neurotic is always defending a lost position. His insecurity, which arises from the impossibility of his final attitude, compels him in part to evade the consequences of his disposition, to flee reality and safeguard himself against it, and in part to pursue the appearances of success which gloss over the hopelessness and unreality of his position. Consequently, he is filled with an incessant concern for his own ego, which is in constant peril. Thus we find an obvious, more or less successfully disguised, egocentricity as a further essential component of the neurotic character. The neurotic is like a man gazing into a small hand-mirror which reflects his own features, but excludes the outside world.

The assertion that every neurotic is always concentrating on himself will be readily admitted in the case of certain forms of hysteria, in which auto-eroticism plays the chief rôle, and hypochondria, in which preoccupation with one's own person dominates the picture. This principle is not so easy of acceptance in the case of neurotics whose conduct seems unexceptionable and modest, and who appear rather to conceal their trouble than to make capital out of it. Moreover, it may be thought strange that a man should pursue his ostensibly selfish ends by means that must be clearly incompatible with his most personal interests, and to take upon himself sufferings that are not demanded by the real situation. It may be thought still more surprising if we assert that these neurotics use their symptoms and sufferings to serve definite ends, and at the same time honestly believe that their dearest wish is to be freed from their illness, with which, as they are always asserting, they are powerless to cope.

Let us refer yet again to the passage from the *Confessions* of St. Augustine in which he speaks of the two wills in man. To understand neurosis, we need only assume that the neurotic is unaware of the second will, " which lacketh that which the other possesseth." If we recall how often we all conceal things from ourselves, how we consciously or half-consciously turn away from external and internal difficulties, how often we deny to ourselves things we know to be true, such as our own mistakes, we shall, I think, realize that between this attitude and that of the neurotic proper there is only a series of intermediate stages which merge one into another.

This conception enables us to understand the apparent anomalies just mentioned, which are encountered in the picture of neurosis.

Let us first consider the sufferings of the neurotic person— pains of all kinds, organic symptoms like heart-attacks or indigestion, mental symptoms like obsessions and anxiety, and various others whose exposition belongs rather to clinical psycho-pathology. In many cases this suffering is made use of by the patient as a convincing excuse for evading his obligations, or for increasing his subjective sense of achievement. The neurotic is like a child who is allowed to stay away from school on account of stomach-ache, but is made to pay in some way for this privilege by being deprived of his favourite dishes and placed on an uninteresting diet.

Perhaps the analogy with those guilty of self-mutilation in war-time is even more illuminating. Moreover, we have previously called attention to the fact that small achievements accomplished under difficulties appear subjectively greater than objectively greater achievements which do not demand from the person any conquest of self.

It must never be forgotten that however " unreal " the causes of such sufferings may be, they are in themselves absolutely genuine, and not, as is so often foolishly asserted, " imaginary." The man who has to endure constant suffering and who can only achieve anything, however small, by overcoming it, leads a life of martyrdom. But martyrdom is the heroism of the weak, and, as we have already said, can easily be accepted as a character-ideal— not with full consciousness, on account of inner resistances— by a man who regards heroism as something worth striving for, but which is denied him by fate. On this level there is no true distinction between bodily pain and moral suffering, between the endurance of harassing organic symptoms and the necessity of living in a world which by the neurotic pessimist is regarded as a vale of tears.

6. NEUROTIC AIMS AND NEUROTIC CHARACTER-TRAITS

The tension a man feels between the demands imposed by his ideal and the consciousness of his achievement is all-important. The dominating feeling of insecurity, arising out of his inferiority-experiences, demands a measure of compensation proportionate to the man's feeling of his own unworthiness ; this steady growth of discrepancy between claims and achievement still further increases the feeling of insecurity. If a man could only be satisfied with his inferiority and the corresponding limitations of what he can achieve, if he could, in other words, content himself with his " one talent," he would not require the artifices and self-deception of neurosis ; he would even enjoy the astonishing experience of discovering that even if his possibilities were not as extensive as he would desire, they were very much greater than his fears usually led him to believe. A patient suffering from compulsion-neurosis once said to me, " I used to have a tower, it was unfinished and the rain came in ; now I only possess a pile of bricks. You have pulled down my tower." I told him he ought to start building a modest little house for a family out of his bricks, a piece of advice he apparently followed surprisingly closely by getting married two years later. But there are many people who evidently receive more satisfaction from an incomplete tower than from a little house complete with roof and all.

We will rapidly run through some of the characteristics that are hardly ever absent from a case of neurosis, and which are to a very slight extent also present in people who are free from any neurotic symptoms. These characteristics enable one to suspect an inner disequilibrium tending in the direction of neurosis, and encourage us to trace the connection between such features and the fundamental nature of the neurosis. Neurotics are said to be unusually ambitious, self-assertive, pushful, tyrannical and proud ; and we believe that the fundamental characteristic of neurosis is to be recognized under every such kind of disguise. If we ask such a man whether he is ambitious, the answer will be sometimes "Yes," more often "No," and occasionally a hesitating reply will be received. If he denies that he is in any way ambitious, and is then asked if he is not very sensitive or easily offended, the answer will almost invariably be in the affirmative.

Sensitiveness is, however, undoubtedly one of the disguises of pride ; for the " touchy" man almost incessantly dictates to his fellow-men how they ought to behave towards him. It is as if he were carrying about with him unwritten and unpromulgated rules of court etiquette, whose infringement should be unmercifully punished ; but since he lacks the power to expel from his court anyone who has shown disregard for his rules, he himself withdraws, shows offence, and experiences a sense of injury, becoming unapproachable and repelling every advance. The situation is the converse of the well-known saying : " If the mountain won't come to Mahomet, Mahomet must go to the mountain." Further, if the small everyday annoyances irritate the man so much that the iron—in this case filings—enters into his soul, how he must suffer in really serious troubles ! Sensitiveness is, then, an alarm-signal displayed by the man who doubts his own ability to meet troublesome situations in which he may be called upon to show what he is worth.

Many people, especially neurotics, are constantly experiencing disillusionment. As an example, a much-travelled lady patient of mine once told me : " Whenever I come into a strange town, I am always disappointed ; it never looks like what I imagined it." There is, in fact, in all disappointment a factor of angry surprise, of astonishment that the world and people presume to be different from what the person in question expected. Such a person not only holds the belief that, if things were as they should be, the world would be run in accordance with his ideas, but he is so obsessed by this that he is quite unable to perceive the paradox of such a demand, which in its extreme form is a craving for omnipotence. These people maintain that they have already been so often disappointed that in future they wish to avoid people, to look forward to nothing, to do nothing.

Such an inner attitude is also connected with *superstition*, in one of its aspects, a trait not infrequently encountered among neurotics. Many have a predilection for " magical " practices, which are to avert harm or bring good luck ; or such ideas are manifested in their obsessions.   As an example of this, one of my patients believed that he had the " evil eye," and therefore avoided people out of regard for them ; he was further convinced that he could " exorcize " the evil influence from all conceivable objects if he stared at them long enough. At bottom, all such people attribute to themselves more or less supernatural powers. Closely related to this are the many " presentiments " of which they are capable, and the premonitions that come to them ; this is easily understandable.

The man who is uncertain of success, but believes it to be indispensable for him, will have to set about things more cautiously than the man who just " gets on " with it and is prepared to take a risk. The neurotic is therefore characterized by what individual-psychologists aptly term the " hesitant attitude," which manifests itself in various ways.

Inability to make up one's mind, or at least great difficulty in coming to a decision, is one of its commonest forms. Long wavering, the constant weighing of the pros and cons of an undertaking which is often ridiculously trivial, the justification of such behaviour by rationalizations—such as the desire to do absolutely the right thing—and similar conduct, eventually have two main results. Either the time for action is entirely wasted : the housewife hesitates so long that she fails to get what she wanted at the sales ; when it is too late, she thinks she has certainly had bad luck, but who knows if she would have made a good bargain—better not buy at all than buy badly. Or, if circumstances make it essential for the matter to be attended to, it is put off until the last minute, when the person acts as if he had been rushed into a decision. This manœuvre always enables him to say, if things go wrong : " Yes, but it would have turned out better if I had had more time to think things over." Some people conceal the same mental disposition by acting with undue haste ; they explain it as being due to " tempera-ment."

The habit of constantly seeking *advice* is also an indication of this attitude of mind. If we carefully analyse the reason for anyone's seeking advice from a second party, we shall find that it is very seldom the latter's true opinion that is desired ; more frequently the person merely wishes to have his own previously formed opinion confirmed, and if the other person disagrees, " he knows nothing about it." Usually the seeking of advice is a device for shifting one's own responsibilities to another's shoulders. A " generous " person will not reproach his adviser, if the advice was bad ; but, at the same time, he has evaded the necessity of self-reproach.

We have already remarked that *doubt* about the right course to be taken can postpone an undertaking indefinitely. As in the debate preceding a decision, it is rare for a single new idea to emerge after the first five or ten minutes' dis-cussion, so, in the case of morbid doubt, the final situation remains substantially unaltered.

It must not be supposed that morbid doubt and the obses-sive rumination is always concentrated on the alleged matter in hand. Such meditation often only serves as an excuse for preoccupation with other doubts and reflections at the expense of really important problems, or for idleness com-bined with the appearance of activity. If the problem seems to be of extreme importance—if, for instance, it is a question of the soul's salvation, the validity of confession, or the pro-priety of taking Communion—the person thinks that the necessity for arriving at absolute certainty on such a matter fully entitles him to disregard everything else. One variety of this kind of futile reflection is *preoccupation with the past*. This is sometimes useful when one is concerned, for example, with the reconstruction of facts, seeking an analogy with the existing situation, or endeavouring to correct the mistakes of the past—such as unfavourable opinions on the actions of others—in the light of new experience. On the other hand, there are people whose thoughts revolve incessantly round past experiences, their mistakes, their culpable blunders, their supposed grievances, and so on. The man who stands still and wrings his hands because he has blundered only wastes time ; and at this such persons are experts. Now, such an attitude serves other purposes : in the first place experiences kept alive in this way serve as excuses for many kinds of failure, which they simply cannot accept or for which they refuse to acknowledge responsibility : " If the confounded professor had not failed me in Greek, heaven alone knows where I might not have got to by now ! " Secondly, many such people imagine that their terrible past experience—often the dreadful event is absurdly trivial— makes it impossible for them to go on living—not that they commit suicide ; achievement, energy and endurance can no longer be expected of them, and naturally, for the most part, other people or " fate " are to blame. Thirdly, " there are horrible things, which one has always to bear in mind, but of which one cannot speak to other people." This attitude, in the first place, constantly reminds the person of the absolute uniqueness of his own tragic fate—uniqueness, of course, in a different sense to that in which everyone's life can be said to be unique—and, in the second place, it provides him with an excuse for reticence, isolation and reserve, for it is better to close up altogether like an oyster than to run the risk of betraying such secrets. They cannot be confided even to one's husband or wife, even to one's confessor ; if these secret matters are conceived of as sinful, the problem gains alarmingly in significance—all confession is useless, all Communion unavailing, and so on.

This leads us to a consideration of *scrupulousness*, of which we previously spoke, when dealing with the subject of doubt. This is a true neurosis, and a source of unending trouble to its victim and to his spiritual advisers ; it can show itself in various ways. In the first place, the scruple provides a means of making constant demands upon the person's spiritual adviser, for sometimes other people enjoy his confidence, and, in his eyes, exist simply to listen to him and offer consolation. Secondly, the scrupulous person is always wiser than his spiritual adviser ; however much the latter may assure him that there is no question of sin, and it is only a case of morbid imagination, although the person will perhaps be convinced of this in the confessional and for a few minutes afterwards, he will then relapse into his previous attitude : the spiritual adviser has not understood him— one of my women patients used to confess four times a day in as many churches without ever being understood !—he has expressed himself badly, etc., etc. At bottom it simply means, "The confessor can say what he likes ; I am right." A young girl was obsessed by sexual fantasies ; both her confessor and her doctor assured her it was the result of ill health. She declared it was sin. Why ? The fantasies increased when she was at work, met people, and went out of doors, and could only be kept within tolerable limits if she stayed at home and " fought against the temptation " ; the struggle occupied her wholly, to the exclusion of everything else. It might be supposed that a Catholic would find relief on being assured by a priest and a doctor that her condition was due to illness and curable ; it might be tormenting, but it was certainly not sin. But no—it must be sin, because only then is the " struggle " against it inevitable, making every other kind of activity impossible. Moreover, the scrupulous person is very conscious, even if somewhat vaguely, that his is a most delicately constructed soul, a soul which will be sullied by the slightest straying from the path of rectitude. Gerson calls scruples a mask of pride. There is pride behind the idea of not being understood even by specialists and experts, a pride that inordinately exaggerates the already existing uniqueness of the individual. Last, but not least, the scrupulous person, who is the moral hypochondriac *par excellence*, concentrates continuously and exclusively on his own ego. I have never come across such people who entertain scruples with regard to the Commandment dealing with love for one's neighbour ; sex, the rules of fasting, evil gossip, distraction at Mass, in fact, anything except the love of one's neighbour can form the substance of the scruple. Most of the scrupulous people I have known were at the same time unusually sensitive—another instance of the " delicate organization of their souls " and their obvious egocentricity. A scrupulous person is quite capable of postponing the presentation of a birthday gift, if the birthday should happen to fall on a Sunday, because carrying the parcel would constitute " servile work " ; he can entertain the most ridiculous apprehensions about fasting, and create a terrible scene because a junior colleague— *horribile dictu*—is allotted a better room in the office, say, for reasons of health ; a scrupulous woman can send her old mother out shopping, because otherwise she would be prevented from saying her rosary between ten and twelve—a self-imposed penance. Scrupulousness differs in no essential respect from other varieties of obsessive or compulsion-neurosis ; here, too, the ego is the real and final goal of thought and action, fellow-men just being regarded as instruments for selfish purposes.

Being unable to occupy ourselves with the matter in greater detail, we may remind ourselves, *en passant*, of the similar disposition shown in certain cases of addiction to solitary sexual offences. Such people also care only for themselves, being quite incapable of reaching out beyond their own person, or, if they do so in imagination or reality, the fellow-man is only a means to an end. The end, apparently only the gratification of sexual desire, is in reality the exaltation of self and the debasement of others.

We are not concerned here with the treatment of neurosis or with the correction of characterological abnormalities in adults. The above analyses of character are intended only to illustrate the motives governing many kinds of normal as well as abnormal behaviour.

CHAPTER VIII

SELF-KNOWLEDGE AND SELF-UPBRINGING

I. THE POSSIBILITY OF SELF-KNOWLEDGE

THE subject of this chapter may appear somewhat out of place in an essay on applied characterology ; for we are accustomed to think of upbringing objectively, and as especially applying to children and adolescents. However, the possibilities of self-upbringing and, as a necessary antecedent, self-knowledge, constitute an important problem for many people, who will welcome a few remarks on this subject in this place. As we have just remarked, self-knowledge must precede self-upbringing ; but we already know that it is impossible for the person to be objective to itself. Therefore, self-knowledge can never be a knowledge founded on one's ultimate being, but only a recognition of certain data, providing us with terms of reference to something deeper. Consequently, in seeking self-knowledge we can only employ the same technique, and no other, which we have laid down for acquiring knowledge of other people. The main guide to a knowledge of human action is the principle that such knowledge is primarily to be derived from the results of a man's conduct. Just as in our efforts to understand a fellow-man we must be guided not so much by his assertions on his thoughts, feelings, desires and aims, as by the evaluation of their actual effects, the changes brought about in the sphere of reality by the man and his actions, so in arriving at a judgment of self we must adopt the same criteria.

2. OUR RELATION TO OUR FELLOW-MEN

When we discussed the theory of human conduct and character, we demonstrated the primal importance of that aspect of reality which, in the natural sphere, can first be called specifically human, namely community, the community of one's fellow-men. Now, as man's behaviour in general, and in particular towards the community, is largely determined by the conflict or balance of the two primal tendencies, the will to power and the will to community, we are provided with a reliable criterion for our own fundamental attitude, namely the degree of harmony existing between ourselves and our fellows. Behaviour that tends to destroy that concord will, in general, cause us to doubt the purity and moral level of our motives. The converse is not entirely true ; for it cannot be immediately assumed that behaviour that has no adverse effect on such concord is on that account immune from criticism. There is a wrong kind of concord ; and the difficulty lies in the ambiguity of the term. The kind of concord that is described as " howling with the wolves " should clearly not meet with immediate approval ; for in this case discord may be a higher duty. Even this hardly justifies aggressive behaviour, apart from certain cases in which aggression may happen to be a professional duty. Even " professional " aggression, like that of the clergyman who is bound on occasions to criticize and condemn behaviour that is inconsistent with morality, should never contain the factor of hostility. That form of aggression is dictated by love and should bear its stamp ; it exists for the sake of others, not for its own sake, and still less for the personal advantage of the aggressor. This serves to distinguish it from enmity or other kinds of discord born of the will to power : " Love seeketh not its own." If enmity were to manifest itself, stripped of all disguise, as hatred, desire for revenge, ill-will and so on, the man who was anxious to uproot such a tendency from his own nature would soon become aware of its presence, and even if he could not master his emotions, would deny them all expression. The disguises adopted by the will to power and self-seeking are dangerous. Especially fraught with danger are self-delusion and self-deception.

Clearly, the highest demand made on man as a moral person is not that he should conduct himself as if he were not actuated by hostile sentiments and the urge to self-seeking, but that he should continuously deny their access to his psychic stronghold. This demand makes itself felt outside the abstract realm of pure morality, for its fulfilment reacts visibly in the living world of external reality, showing the intimate connections, both causal and effective, between all human behaviour and morality and religion. A man may make every effort to suppress all outward expression of hostility in all its forms, but so long as his mind is coloured by hostile sentiments, it will somehow come to the notice of his fellow-men and be countered by corresponding reactions. Even the greatest show of friendliness fails to deceive children as to the existence of inner coldness and unapproachableness ; nor does an affectation of coldness prevent them from detecting the true warmth of feeling behind the mask. The complaint of many people, " I take the greatest trouble to be friendly to everybody, yet I cannot get on with them and they hold themselves aloof," is usually wrongly formulated ; one small word must be changed ; such people do not exert themselves to *be* friendly, but only to *act* as though they were. The man may reject the claims of a demand, or only its fulfilment ; this involves a great difference of inner attitude, which the most consummate arts of simulation and self-control eventually fail to conceal. How many people do not give, although they really wish to receive ! How many more give in order that they may receive ! Many people who give do so with a faint display of condescension and patronage. This attitude of superiority often escapes detection even by the most lynx-eyed analysis, but the man " gives himself away " when observed not in the act of giving, but in the act of taking. Whoever gives gladly, readily and generously, but feels it very galling to receive kindness or accept gifts from others, should subject his own ultimate motives and disposition to a careful scrutiny. A wise man once said truly that there is a sordid element in taking as well as in giving. Inability to take springs just as much from a false pride born of a lack of consciousness of one's own value, as avarice is at bottom only the coward's variety of the will to power—the coward who contents himself with the means of power without possessing the courage to make use of it. The man who is seeking self-knowledge should put to himself the following question : " Canst thou request, canst thou accept ? "

The question of the ability to accept is capable of a generalization on the one hand, but demands a restriction on the other. The restriction refers to the fact that there exists a type of man who is quite capable of requesting and even of demanding, with no sense of shame or degradation, regarding it rather as the exercise of a right ; one rightly regards such people as being " shameless." Here, as elsewhere, the carrying of a thing to extremes converts it into its opposite ; a balance must always be maintained. The " shameless " person is usually characterized by the fact that he feels the fulfilment of his request or demand to be a right, and therefore acknowledges its non-fulfilment with a certain resentment. It is easy to see that this attitude is comparable to " sensitiveness," whose mechanisms we have already attempted to explain. The differences are of degree and courage rather than of kind ; for the sensitive person makes demands, but usually only in a disguised form, whereas the shameless man, who is possibly more courageous, puts forward his demands openly.

Usually, the sort of man who is interested in self-knowledge and self-training will not be shameless and exigent in his demands ; but sensitiveness will often enough be a part of his nature, and consequently the relevant parts of this book will cause him anxiety.

The general formulation of the question of the ability to receive is broadly : What proportion of my own life and experience is occupied by my own ego, and what by others ? And there is no better or more dependable test than this : " If anyone thinks that he walks in light, and loves not his brother, the same is in darkness even until now."

3. THE GUIDE

Possibly the above remarks may have served to show that the problem of the knowledge of self can only be formulated and solved along the same lines as that of the knowledge of others ; but it is notoriously hard to see " the beam in one's own eye." Even the most honest effort may sometimes fail to discover the suspected flaw in one's own life. A man all too easily becomes disgusted with his fruitless endeavours, and in his discouragement regards himself as incompetent, rejected and wicked, or puts the blame on physical defects, incurable illness, irreparable mistakes in his upbringing, fate and the like. It is therefore important, and in many cases absolutely necessary, for the man to find someone else to hold the mirror up to him in which he is to see himself as he really is. It is deeply significant that all great ethical or religious systems have emphasized the necessity of personal guidance, declaring it to be indispensable for a man's progress and the attainment of knowledge of what he is, actually and potentially. The sacred books of the Indians of all creeds, the wisdom of China and Islam, and the mystery-religions of classical times, have all stressed the need of a guide. Teaching, precept, guidance, magical influence, prayers of the adept, were all reckoned as more or less indispensable for progress ; and we find this reflected in the various popular " secret doctrines " which are so popular to-day. The idea of personal guidance recurs even in Christianity, in a deeper and more enlightened sense. Not only is there the command to " go and teach all people," but Christ said : " Learn of me, for I am meek and lowly of heart " ; and numerous passages can be cited from Holy Scripture revealing Him as the Leader who guides His disciples, apostles and followers step by step.

As we have seen, purely naturalistic arguments lead us to the same conclusion, namely that a man requires a guide if he is to learn to know himself. The guide's task is, however, not merely that of enlightenment and direction ; the relationship between the guide and the guided is often primarily distinguished by a real communion, an association of man with man, which is independent of community of interests, family ties, the accident of living together, or sexual relationship. This association affects the very depths of the person's being, and assists in the release of fundamental moral forces and the recognition of their opposites which exist side by side.

It must not be thought that we are of the opinion that a man should remain in permanent need of a guide ; we maintain rather that a man must be brought up to be free of his upbringer, and guided towards responsibility and dependence on self. It is not the duty of the guide to relieve the man of responsibility ; and many a man who with a gesture of self-sacrifice waives his own decision, submitting in all things to the judgment of his guide, deceives himself and his guide also, because his real motive is neither sacrifice nor abnegation, but cowardice and flight.

We are not even willing to admit that a man who confidently submits to guidance is thereby relieved of his obligations in respect of his own achievements and progress. It is likely that that form of guidance will prove the most effective which allows the man to work out his own salvation as far as possible, and prepares the way to self-knowledge merely by slight indications and by encouragement. This should apply at any rate to the " healthy " ; the sick and the neurotic, enmeshed in the web of self-deception, often require more definite direction. Although, broadly speaking, the same methods and principles which apply to the psychological study of others also hold good in the study of self, it may perhaps not be without value to inquire into the special limitations and obstacles to self-knowledge and self-perfection.

4. DIFFICULTIES IN THE WAY OF SELF-PERFECTION

The mountaineer knows that there is a way to the summit, but he must not fix his gaze on the peak ; he must concentrate on the path, on the next step to be taken. If he gazes at the summit, he will trip over the stones that lie in his path. If he is always looking upwards, the summit will seem to him to be immeasurably remote, and he will not realize the distance he has already traversed. Further, if anyone imagines that he can take the steep places at a run, he will soon be out of breath. On the other hand, he may from the outset despair of achieving the summit, and, on account of his dissatisfaction with anything less than the highest achievement, not even begin the ascent. Instead of honestly admitting that the full triumph he craves for is not for him, he will seize upon every excuse in order to justify his " crying off " both to himself and to others.

It must be fully realized that a very large proportion of the difficulties encountered in life do not arise so much from an unfortunate congenital diathesis, or from the attitude of one's fellow-men, nor are they predestined ; they are the consequences of the exaggerated purposes to which men cling with every fibre of their being, and whose extravagance they cannot and will not admit to themselves. They will not, because their self-esteem depends on these purposes, and by their secret belief that they are called to higher things they are consoled for what appears to them to be the futility of their lives. They cannot, because any intelligent reflection would immediately reveal the extravagance of their aims, which could then no longer be entertained ; this would lead to the immediate collapse of all their purposes and the props that support their sense of personal value.

In many cases, therefore, it is necessary to direct " the work on one's self," not primarily on the difficulties themselves, but on the ascertainment of the motives responsible for them ; but this is a task that a man cannot usually, as we have said, discharge alone. As he does not understand his own " standpoint," he will unconsciously be influenced by it in all his efforts at self-knowledge, without ever being able to get a sight of it for himself. Even if he has acquired a thorough knowledge of all the various tricks employed by men to dupe themselves, and is accustomed to expose them both in himself and others, it will yet frequently happen that he is unable to discover the ultimate motive, and will come across material for which no explanation is forthcoming, or features that he will wrongly regard as unalterable. Only when an expert holds up the mirror to him and elucidates the questionable points is he able to realize, to his astonishment, that there are forces at work in him which he imagined already to have under control

Although the above possibility always exists and no one can assert with absolute confidence that he has definitely escaped these snares of the mind, it is possible to indicate some points, which may assist in the promotion of self-knowledge and self-training.

5. RELATION TO THE COMMUNITY

In accordance with the views consistently presented throughout this book, we see in relation to the community a valuable index even for self-judgment. In applying this index, we must take into account not only a person's inward disposition to the community, wherein we can be grossly deceived, but also and above all its practical expression. The ways in which a man can withdraw himself from the community are very various ; they all ultimately derive from fear of one's fellow-men ; that is to say, the fear of not being able to " make good " in the eyes of others, and also, to a certain extent, the fear of not being able to " get the better " of them. Apart from the forms of conduct already mentioned, such as over-sensitiveness, shyness, the belief that one is misunderstood, and so on, a great part is played by such ideas as that the person concerned has nothing to give, is of no consequence, is a bore, and whatnot, and that he is therefore bound " not to inflict his company on people." These ideas must not be confused with those which we, in common with the individual psychologists, call inferiority-experiences. The attitudes we have in mind at the moment belong to later formations of reactive origin ; they are, as it were, secondary rationalizations, defence-mechanisms against the anticipated destruction of the ego adopted by a person already deficient in self-esteem. This avoidance of one's fellows often has the same motive as the shirking of effort of every kind on the ground that the person concerned is able to accomplish so little. It would be more sensible to say that if you can accomplish so little there is all the more reason for your accomplishing that little, so that your existence may be of some use or at least in some way positive.

Similarly, in approaching the problem of one's common humanity, one must not let any possibility slip by of doing something, however small, for others. Even if one justifies one's avoidance of social contact on the grounds that such contact might cause one to degenerate, lead one into temptation, or divert one's attention from the all-important preoccupation with one's self-perfection, the genuineness of this attitude should always arouse considerable suspicion. Retiring people should always ask themselves whether they are absolutely convinced that they would still maintain their attitude, if they were definitely assured of a brilliant, or only a moderate, social success.

The flight from one's fellow-men can assume a purely religious guise. It is, of course, entirely true that, ultimately, genuine love of one's neighbour is in a certain sense only obtainable through God, and that what is lovable in one's neighbour is the image of God, God's creation, the actual or potential member of the *corpus Christi mysticum*. It is true that within each one of us there is that quality calling for the highest form of love, and that there is a possibility of recognizing and loving it, but it is doubtful whether it is possible for the average man to enjoy the experience as love. To love God in man and man in God is indeed an attitude approaching perfection, belonging to a high order of supernatural life, " modelled " upon Deity ; but it seems to me to be demanding too much of a man to expect him to make it the foundation of his rule of conduct. Consequently, when we meet people who profess such an attitude, we are not unjustified in entertaining suspicions that they are more concerned with keeping at a distance from their fellow-men than with strengthening the bonds that link them—the latter being the inevitable result of the " supernatural " kind of love of which we have spoken. It is true that a distance is also set up when this attitude is genuine ; but this

distance is of quite a different order. In the ungenuine
cases, the persons enclose themselves, as it were, in a cocoon
of glass, through which no ray of warmth can penetrate ;
but those who are genuinely capable of this mystical feat
bridge the immeasurable distance that possibly divides
them from a man who is wholly in bondage to the flesh, by
the warmth of their love, which streams throughout all
space.

Flight from mankind is not quite identical with " apart-
ness." Although there is occasional justification and necessity for solitude, it is wrong to confuse this with the self-
isolation which springs from selfishness. Justifiable solitude
is a spiritual exercise by which we oppose " distraction "
with " concentration " ; it is not on the same level as mere
shrinkage into oneself ; it can and should retain some sort
of orientation outwards. All reflex turning towards the
person or the self, to the exclusion of all else, contains the
elements of danger. All our automatic activities should also
conform to higher, impersonal—one might say super-
personal—law and order ; all personal events should be
regarded as transitional stages of correlated happenings in
the sphere of the absolute ; in other words, the whole person
must be dedicatively directed Godwards. Finally, it is
natural and inevitable that man, so far as he does not
idolize or absolutize himself, should, when reflexly turning
selfwards, find God there. " *Mène-moi dans le plus profond de
moi-même, et je Te trouverai.*" This mystical return to oneself
to find God there, in occasional solitude, but not in essential
separation from humanity, is compatible with other attitudes and mental dispositions, not only for those who have
not yet made God the centre of their lives, but also for those
who have so advanced in the spiritual life that they no
longer require such periods of withdrawal in order to fix their
minds on the ultimate. The lives of the great mystics have

repeatedly proved this. " Gladly alone, in glad communion with creation," says St. Mechtilde of Magdeburg, in discussing the " sevenfold perfections." The differential characteristic between justifiable and unjustifiable solitude is the manner in which a man accepts the interruption of his isolation ; he who is " in glad communion with creation " will even in his loneliness hear the call without resentment ; even if in the circumstances obedience to the call is painful, no inward resistance will be experienced. It should also be noticed that a man's attitude towards the community of his fellow-men is by no means a matter of indifference for his spiritual development and perfection. As St. Thomas says, [1] " In practice, love of one's neighbour comes first," although according to the scale of excellence love of God holds the first place. Therefore a proper development of love for one's neighbour is a necessary antecedent to the love given to God, and is demanded by the nature of man. Further, the garnered experience of man's spiritual life shows that our love for our fellow-men passes over into love for God. It must not be thought that love for one's neighbour must of necessity be in a temporal sense an antecedent to love for God, although this is often the case ; in any event, it can be asserted that spiritual perfection without a genuine love for mankind is absolutely inconceivable.

6. LOVE OF ONE'S NEIGHBOUR

True love for one's neighbour means " to love one's neighbour for his own sake " ; although in theory the thing that we love in him is his claim to be an image and a creation of God, his candidature for or possession of divine sonship, this need not in practice be taken into account. Now, this means that the love for one's neighbour which is practised only in obedience to the Commandment and to enable us to

[1] *Sum. Theol.*, II–II, q. 68, a. 8, *ad* 2.

acquire merit, although always praiseworthy, can hardly be called that true love which " seeketh not its own." In fact, such a disposition involves the danger that one's neighbour will thereby be degraded to a mere instrument for the " acquisition of merit," a conception in accordance with Buddhistic but hardly with Catholic sentiment. What is demanded of us is not acts of love to be performed in order to observe the Commandment, but love itself. Thus it is said, and not without justification, that love as an effect and as an emotion does not answer to our bidding. We distinguish between an effective love and an affective love ; the former performs the deeds of love in the light of cold reasoning, without being founded on or enkindling a loving and tender affection. We must add two observations with reference to this : even this cool, effective love is still of the nature of love, provided that it relates in intention to our neighbour, his joy or sorrow and not our duty or our merit being its focus ; and where loving warmth and tenderness do not exist, there is no other way that can lead to affective love than the deeds performed in response to the effective variety. It is a matter of common experience that a person we at first accepted only after overcoming a certain dislike finally becomes really dear to us. The following occurs in the *Baghavadghita* : " He who honours the gods finds them."

We may well believe that for the man who is striving for inward perfection and spiritual progress there can be no more important question than how he stands with his fellow-man. This question is not so much of importance because his disposition to the community is man's most important obligation ; it is all-decisive because this disposition provides the most delicate index of a man's inner attitude in general, and therefore of his attitude towards God.

A significant test of our relation to our fellow-men is our

attitude towards them when we are in trouble. One can observe two extremes. Some require from their fellows constant sympathy, consolation, distraction, diversion, and so forth, and, so to speak, use their misfortune as an excuse for exploiting their neighbours. Others make those round them suffer for the misfortune that has come upon themselves ; they seem to find in their trouble a warrant for giving free rein to every kind of aggression. A reaction of this kind is frequently witnessed if the person concerned is himself to blame for his misfortunes or has other grounds for self-reproach. He alone acts rightly, from a genuine sense of community and love for his neighbour, whose attitude towards his fellows undergoes no change, or only a positive change.

7. PHYSICIAN AND SPIRITUAL DIRECTOR

It is obviously impossible to deal in these final pages more fully with the problems of ethical and religious training. In many respects, the practical application to these problems of what we have either considered fully or touched upon in the preceding chapters is self-evident. Much more remains to be said which would be out of place here, being more appropriate to a system of " pastoral psychology " than to our present exposition. The purpose of our remarks on self-knowledge and self-training was mainly to demonstrate the possibility of applying the principles governing the training of " normal " character, and to a certain extent the re-education of anomalous forms, to the problems of one's own life. However, it should once more be emphasized that great difficulties are involved, and that everyone, however familiar he may be with these theories and methods, will sometimes experience the need of " consulting an expert " and confiding himself to his guidance.

If it has already been made apparent on psychological grounds that a person requires individual guidance in his efforts at self-development, it should further be evident that this guidance, so far as problems of faith and morals are involved, devolves primarily on the spiritual director, although situations do arise when, in the first instance even, others, such as parents, school-teachers, intimate friends and physicians, must take the responsibility. But all these others should recognize the limitations of their competence in these matters. The physician especially, even when he has some claim to call himself " a physician of souls," must never forget that when he provides a bridge by which the neurotic can cross from his little island of isolation into the world of humanity, he may also at the same time have to act as a *liaison* with the supernatural. The possibility of being permitted in these cases to prepare the way for grace is his highest glory and his proudest task. Therefore the statement heard on all sides that the physician, especially the psychotherapist, has nowadays taken the place of the priest, simply comes under the head of silly talk. Not only has the physician no title to speak authoritatively on religious questions, but, above all, he has not at his command the supernatural means of which the priest makes use. Recently F. Bichlmaier, S.J., has very properly pointed out that the " *ego te absolvo*," and the sacramental power in general, can never be replaced by any psychotherapeutic technique, however highly developed.

But the application of modern science to upbringing and education in general may save the priest innumerable difficulties in his duties as spiritual director. Co-operation with an *intelligent physician* may lead to more rapid success than would be possible with mere exhortation, warning, and advice without a psychological exploration of unconscious motives.

Perhaps a few words may be permitted on the *psychology of the religious life*. Even to this study modern psychology seems to be able to contribute something. It appears to us to be beyond question that intellectual doubts, hostility to religion, inability to recognize the authority of the Church, and whatever obstacles there are to the religious life, are all finally bound up with that attitude which we have described as the revolt of the creature against his place in creation, and against the finiteness of his humanity.

We are convinced that more often than not religious difficulties arise from the influences of childhood. We have previously remarked on the importance of the attitude towards the community for the attitude towards God, and therefore we need not pursue the matter further in that direction. But human life is a unity and a whole. In psycho-biology it is often misleading to assume hard and fast rules of cause and effect, for everything is interwoven. The moment that we realize that the ultimate conflict of the neurotic centres round his inability to acquiesce in his position as a human creature, we find ourselves touching upon mysteries which transcend reason and scientific method.

CONCLUSION

WE believe that we have made it quite clear that it was not our intention in this book to explain all the problems of character-formation and training with the help of recent advances in psychology, and that it cannot be maintained that the supernatural element can be excluded. On the contrary, we think that we have demonstrated *the limitations of natural means ;* and we maintain that a purely naturalistic psychology, however complete and however well founded, must eventually break down unless it be co-ordinated with religious knowledge and principles. We have seen how problems arising out of purely practical psychology and characterology immediately open up universal problems, insoluble except in terms of metaphysics, and that these problems lead us still further into the realm of revealed religion. Without being obliged in any way to involve ourselves speculatively in these ultimate problems, we are continually and inevitably being brought up against them. For example, it is impossible to establish the claims of the community idea or render it theoretically intelligible apart from religion. Community for its own sake, even in the interests of the State, the nation, civilization, or humanity itself, can never possess that compelling and triumphant force which binds man as with a spell in every circumstance. This force makes itself felt in the child who has yet to find his way to the community, and the adult who has wandered from the communal path ; it is as indispensable for individual as it is for communal development. Community regarded as a mere united front against natural forces, or as a product of purely human, natural impulses can never make that overwhelming appeal to individualized man. An individual who honestly entertained these views, when faced with the demands of community, could always retort with the unanswerable question : " Why should I become a member of the community ; why should I do anything ' useful ' ? " Only a community that enjoys transcendental sanctions can urge claims whose genuineness not even the most egocentric individual can doubt. No exhaustive exposition is required to demonstrate that this community, rooted in super-nature, and enjoying the right of imposing its demands on all mankind without exception, is and can be nothing else than the καθολική, the *una sancta catholica Ecclesia*, which bridges all the centuries, and comprises all nations, peoples, cultural systems and classes.

We believe that the characterological theory and practice advanced in this book not only do not conflict with Catholic doctrine and thought, but are based on them and require them for their completion ; and therefore we believe, and hope that we have been able to show, that a great deal of what the new psychology has taught us has long been known and only partly again forgotten.

We are, of course, well aware that we have only touched upon some fragments of the great theme of which we purposed to treat. This exposition remains fragmentary for two reasons. First, the exigencies of space compelled us to deal with some points very sketchily and to omit others altogether ; secondly, many questions are still veiled in considerable obscurity, for it must not be forgotten that educational problems, above all in their moral aspect, eventually lead to the most abstruse questions and finally to the great *Mysterium*.

We therefore repeat not only that this book is incomplete, but that the method advocated in it is not competent to cover the whole field. We do not maintain that an individual does not possess any congenital, innate peculiarities ; we have indeed assumed them. We merely maintain that these peculiarities cannot be brought to light, or hardly so, whereas the other forces which mould character—environmental influences—are not only apparent, but also susceptible of change. So far as we are at all able to understand a person's original make-up, this is possible only after the exclusion of all these exogenous factors.

In this matter we dissociate ourselves wholly from the doctrines of individual-psychology, as commonly presented. We believe that we have remained faithful to its central idea, more faithful perhaps than the majority of its unconditional supporters ; but on this point and on certain others we remain at variance. One of these other points of disagreement may be that we are unable to accept the view that man is ceaselessly characterized by the state of tension existing between the two extreme poles of power and love. Therein we see only one of the dimensions, so to speak, out of several in which human life is enacted and developed. Admittedly this dimension is immensely important, because it is the chief determinant of all man's action and conduct ; but as a man acts, so does he modify the environment which reacts on him. Now, the environment which comes primarily into consideration is, as we have seen, that of his fellow-men. Towards them, however, a man's attitude varies proportionately with the development of his will to power and his will to community. It is for that reason that these two primal tendencies, which we have carefully kept before our readers, are so decisive in the moral development of individual and social life and finally—as we explained in the previous chapter—for religious conduct.

We have been able to show, on the one hand, not only that between the views arising out of modern psychological and characterological research and the truths of religion or the educational principles derived from them there is no conflict, but also that those views actually converge on the ideals of Christianity and ecclesiastical philosophy. On the other hand, if we have succeeded in conveying the impression that upbringing, life and communal living in the Catholic sense can in many respects be the richer for the knowledge of this study, we shall hold that the purpose, not so much of the science as such, but of our brief and imperfect exposition, has been fulfilled.

Indeed, we all need guidance, because we scarcely ever have in us that love which, " seeking not its own," is more where it loves than where it dwells, and because we are lacking the certain security provided by this protective and creative quality of love. So we must continue to hobble along on the crutches of knowledge, if love will not lend us its wings. Truly knowledge cannot be a substitute for love ; but imperfect love can add to its stature by knowledge.

How this is possible we have desired to show—that and nothing more.

INDEX OF NAMES

INDEX OF SUBJECTS